Graeme Turner is Professor of Cultural Studies in the Department of English at the University of Queensland. He is author and editor of numerous titles including *National Fictions*, *Media in Australia*, *Australian Television* and *Myths of Oz*.

Other titles in the series

Australian Television
Programs, pleasure and politics
Edited by John Tulloch and Graeme Turner

Dark Side of the Dream
Australian literature and the postcolonial mind
Bob Hodge and Vijay Mishra

Fashioning the Feminine
Girls, popular culture and schooling
Pam Gilbert and Sandra Taylor

Featuring Australia
The cinema of Charles Chauvel
Stuart Cunningham

Framing Culture
Criticism and policy in Australia
Stuart Cunningham

From Nimbin to Mardi Gras
Constructing community arts
Gay Hawkins

From Pop to Punk to Postmodernism
Popular music and Australian culture from the 1960s to the 1990s
Edited by Philip Hayward

Myths of Oz
Reading Australian popular culture
John Fiske, Bob Hodge, Graeme Turner

National Fictions
Literature, film and the construction of Australian narrative
Graeme Turner

Out West
Perceptions of Sydney's western suburbs
Diane Powell

Racism, Ethnicity and the Media
Edited by Andrew Jakubowicz

Resorting to Tourism
Cultural policies for tourist development in Australia
Jennifer Craik

Stay Tuned
The Australian broadcasting reader
Edited by Albert Moran

Temptations
Sex, selling and the department store
Gail Reekie

Australian Cultural Studies
Editor: John Tulloch

Making It National

Nationalism and Australian popular culture

Graeme Turner

ALLEN & UNWIN

To my son
Jackson

© Graeme Turner 1994

This book is copyright under the Berne Convention.
No reproduction without permission. All rights reserved.

First published in 1994
Allen & Unwin Pty Ltd
9 Atchison Street, St Leonards
NSW 2065 Australia

National Library of Australia
Cataloguing-in-Publication data:

Turner, Graeme.
 Making it national: nationalism and Australian
 popular culture.

 Includes index.
 ISBN 1 86373 722 7.

 1. Nationalism—Australia. 2. Popular culture—Australia—
 20th century. 3. Australia—Civilisation—20th century.
 I. Title. (Series: Australian cultural studies.)

Set in 10/11.5 Garamond by DOCUPRO, Sydney
Printed by Chong Moh Offset Printing, Singapore

10 9 8 7 6 5 4 3 2 1

General Editor's Foreword

Nowadays the social and anthropological definition of 'culture' is probably gaining as much public currency as the aesthetic one. Particularly in Australia, politicians are liable to speak of the vital need for a domestic film industry in 'promoting our cultural identity'—and they mean by 'cultural identity' some sense of Australianness, of our nationalism as a distinct form of social organisation. Notably, though, the emphasis tends to be on Australian *film* (not popular television); and not just *any* film, but those of 'quality'. So the aesthetic definition tends to be smuggled back in—on top of the kind of cultural nationalism which assumes that 'Australia' is a unified entity with certain essential features that distinguish it from 'Britain', the 'USA' or any other national entities which threaten us with 'cultural dependency'.

This series is titled 'Australian Cultural Studies', and I should say at the outset that my understanding of 'Australian' is not as an essentially unified category; and further, that my understanding of cultural is anthropological rather than aesthetic. By 'culture' I mean the social production of meaning and understanding, whether in the inter-personal and practical organisation of daily routines or in broader institutional and ideological structures. I am *not* thinking of 'culture' as some form of universal 'excellence', based on aesthetic 'discrimination' and embodied in a pantheon of 'great works'. Rather, I take this aesthetic definition of culture itself to be part of the *social mobilisation of discourse* to differentiate a cultural 'elite' from the 'mass' of society.

Unlike the cultural nationalism of our opinion leaders, 'Cultural

v

Studies' focuses not on the essential unity of national cultures, but on the meanings attached to social difference (as in the distinction between 'elite' and 'mass' taste). It analyses the construction and mobilisation of these distinctions to maintain or challenge existing power differentials, such as those of gender, class, age, race and ethnicity. In this analysis, terms designed to socially differentiate people (like 'elite' and 'mass') become categories of discourse, communication and power. Hence our concern in this series is for an analytical understanding of the meanings attached to social difference within the *history* and *politics* of discourse.

In *Making It National*, Graeme Turner examines the ways in which the Australian nation is represented in the media and elsewhere, as well as the uses to which these representations are put. On the one hand, 'buried under the detritus of nineteenth century definitions of a masculinist national type, bombarded with tourist imagery that offers impossible dreams of an Australian lifestyle, and diverted by complacent invocations of national identity which deliberately obscure the material relations within which we all live, Australia's national imagination is looking pretty groggy'. In particular Turner challenges increasing concentration of media ownership, the ever-lengthening list of alternative news outlets that have died, the complicit relationship of journalists and politicians and the 'seamless identification of Australian national interests with those of Australian business' which helped create singular, exclusivist and traditional myths of Australianness, including the larrikin capitalist excesses of the 1980s. It is the 'lack of a dissenting voice or competing definitions' that Turner most regrets—whether in relation to the making or to the breaking of Alan Bond. On the other hand, though, Turner constantly asks the question: how can Australian cultural events like Sydney 2000 or the Bicentennial celebrations be 'turned in a more progressive direction'? Analysing significant popular texts and events—the music of Yothu Yindi, the filming of the Bicentennial's *Australia Daze*, the mainstream media's own contradictory concentration on 1788 as both 'the moment of settlement and invasion', and recent films like *Strictly Ballroom* and the *Heartbreak Kid*, Turner examines the progressive potential of the Australian mix of identities and accents. He promotes the notion of the hybrid text as part of 'a creative, resistant, cultural and political process of becoming—rather than a conservative, already completed, project of exclusion'. In this way difference and contradiction become 'actually constitutive of identity'.

Nations, Turner argues (in affirming the continuing, progressive

vi

importance of 'nation') are made necessary by the divisions, not the unity, within cultures: 'there can be no return to a unitary explanation of national identity'. Culture, as Fiske, Hodge and Turner say in *Myths of Oz*, 'has to work to *construct* any unity it has, rather than simply celebrate an achieved or natural harmony'. Australian culture is then no more than the temporary, embattled construction of 'unity' at any particular historical moment. The 'readings' in this series of 'Australian Cultural Studies' inevitably (and polemically) form part of the struggle to make and break the boundaries of meaning which, in conflict and collusion, dynamically define our culture.

JOHN TULLOCH

Contents

Acknowledgements xi

1 Introduction: making it national 1
The republic and the new nationalisms 1
In the national interest 10

2 Bond-ing: business, boats and the national character 15
The art of making money 15
Larrikin capitalism 24
Bond-ing 29
After excess 38

3 A taste of the colonial birch: the British connection 41
Making it legal: Malcolm Turnbull and the *Spycatcher* trials 41
The British connection 48
A taste of the colonial birch: media representation of the
Maralinga Royal Commission 52

4 Picnic at Ayers Rock: the Bicentenary 66
Follow the bouncing ball 67
A day of contradictions 73
Australia Daze: multiplying identity 77
Invasion Day 83
Celebrating the nation 88

5 Looking to America: the Crocodile Dundee factor 93
American Dreams 93
The American model 95
Australia World: tourism and the nation 109

6 Redefining the nation: from purity to hybridity   **119**
Caught in the act: constructing the nation   119
Against homogeneity   125

7 The media, the nation . . . and conclusion   **140**
Here we go again: Sydney 2000   140
Feeding the chooks: the independence of the news media   145
'The meanest intelligence': journalism and ethics   151
Finally . . .   156

Notes   **160**

References   **179**

Index   **184**

Acknowledgements

A number of people have assisted me in this project who deserve acknowledgement. Some may not realise that our conversation was of help to me; others have read draft sections and commented on them at some length. Those who have been of direct assistance include Tony Bennett, Frances Bonner, Patrick Buckridge, Robert Cockburn, Stuart Cunningham, John Frow, John Hartley, Chris Lawe Davies, Meaghan Morris, John Tulloch and James Walter. Others whose assistance was less direct but still greatly appreciated include Con Castan, John Fiske, Dinah Hall, Alan Lawson, Jim McKay and Helen Tiffin. I am particularly indebted to Jo Robertson, my research assistant; her enthusiasm and intellectual generosity made the beginnings of the project productive and exciting. Elizabeth Weiss at Allen & Unwin deserves my gratitude for her astute advice and criticism; she has made a substantial and a positive contribution to the final shape of the book. Finally, I would like to thank an exceptionally sharp and interested Honours class at the University of Queensland in 1992, who allowed me to try out some ideas and participated vigorously in the attempt to refine them.

For permission to reprint material published elsewhere I would like to thank the editors of *Westerly*, where part of Chapter 3 appeared; and John Frow and Meaghan Morris, the editors of *Australian Cultural Studies: A Reader*, where the rest of Chapter 3 appeared. For the use of illustrations and quotations, I wish to acknowledge the permission and assistance of the Australian Film Institute, Tony Champ, Creative Tourism Publications Ltd, Pat Fiske, Meridian Films, Mushroom Records, the Swan Brewing Co.,

Time Out, The Sunday Mail, Warner Bros. Movie World and View Films. In some cases, I have failed to trace copyright holders. For this I apologise and undertake to make any necessary corrections or additions in subsequent editions.

1

Introduction: making it national

I'm only just game enough to say it: [Australia] might be the first post-modern republic, and I mean that in the nicest possible way.

I mean a republic that exalts the nation less than the way of life. Whose principal value is tolerance rather than conformity, difference rather than uniformity. Whose outlook is unambiguously Australian, and yet is more worldly and international than republics like the United States or France or Germany or Ireland. With humanist and even some romantic traditions, but no schmaltz, false sentiment and fascism. I have this sense that the pragmatism and dogmatic gradualism which delayed the moment for so long might end up serving us brilliantly. (Historian, speechwriter and prime ministerial adviser, Don Watson)

The republic and the new nationalisms

The 1990s have produced some exciting times for Australian republicans. For many years their cause had been a minor part of political debate in Australia without ever looking like taking off. Then Paul Keating, for all these years apparently a closet republican, told the Queen in 1992 that Australia must become more 'independent'. His finger always on the pulse of public opinion, Opposition leader John Hewson couldn't wait to get out of Parliament House (where Keating's speech had been delivered) to tell the waiting press gallery

1

that the prime minister hadn't learnt 'respect' as a child. No one wanted to hear that. Not even the former Liberal premier Nick Greiner, 'dry' as any market economist, who surprised many Australians by following Keating out of the closet. Bipartisan support for a republic, it seemed, was possible.

Soon Malcolm Turnbull, the lawyer, merchant banker and republican, was touring the country to 'ascertain the views of the public' in local meetings and arguing with historian Professor Geoffrey Blainey and Senator Bronwyn Bishop on talkback radio and television. Maintaining the temperature, a burst of Pommy-bashing was led by no lesser personages than our prime minister and governor-general. Among other things, Paul Keating accused the English in general and Churchill in particular of deserting Singapore and thus Australia in World War II. Bill Hayden seemed to take his script from the third· series of *Blackadder*, describing the British High Command of World War I as a bunch of 'dolts' and the Allied commander, General Haig, as a 'knucklehead'. Topping it all off, the Australian cricketers thrashed the MCC 4–1 in the 1993 Ashes series, despite the English resorting to the humiliating strategy of selecting an Australian and a New Zealander as strike bowlers. They were heady days indeed.

The consequence of all this activity was that an idea which had seemed just a possibility took on a tinge of inevitability. To most editorial writers in 1992, and there were many on this issue, it was 'clear' that Australia would become a republic; the only question was 'when'. One can see why the possibility was so seductive at this particular time. During what is shaping up as a decade of constraints, of Australians grimly facing up to the 'hard realities' of an eroded industrial base and semi-permanent high unemployment, the idea of a republic offered white Australians their one genuine opportunity for positive change. If it was to be more than just tinkering at the edges of our constitution, the republic provided the chance for a fundamental revision of the nation. As Keating's speechwriter, Don Watson, put it in an address to an Australian Republican Movement meeting in 1993:

> The extraordinary opportunity that exists for us now—as we undertake the biggest economic changes in our history and as we learn to cope with the social problems they create, as we reorient ourselves in the world—as we do these things, unlike every other country, we still have the option to redefine ourselves.[1]

This is a romantic possibility, proffered to an electorate suffering from a shortage of *any* kind of possibilities. And it still may happen.

But, if it does happen, one would like to think that it would involve some re-evaluation of fundamental structures in Australian society— so that principles of equity and social justice could be inscribed into a new constitution reflecting Australians' contemporary views on the rights and responsibilities of all its citizens. Fundamental changes like this, however, are unlikely if the so-called 'minimalist' option (that is, the replacement of the Queen as head of state with an Australian appointee) is taken up. Even this largely symbolic option, though, is unlikely in the near future. By mid-1993, the debates around republicanism had lost their initial ecumenism as the various combatants retreated into their trenches.[2] While there is significant public support for change, it is not yet overwhelming and so it would be hard for any federal government to argue that it has a mandate for using this issue as a means of reassessing the national polity.

Whatever else it has been about, of course, the promotion of republicanism has also been about keeping the Keating government in office. Keating's newfound nationalism, of which the push for the republic is a component, is aimed at forcing the Liberal/National coalition further to the right of the political spectrum. Keating has attempted to corner the market in nationalism by calling on Australia to demonstrate its independence by cutting its last constitutional ties with Britain. To the extent that Keating maintains this progressively less controversial position, it will become increasingly easy to represent his opponents as un-Australian, Anglophile dinosaurs. Early signs of such tactics include his celebrated attack on Hewson and Howard, in which he depicted them as exhibits in the museum of Australian social history sharing their glass case with other relics of 1950s Australia: the bakelite Radiola, the Kelvinator Frigidaire and the Electrolux vacuum cleaner. Given such a political rationale, it would be naive to think of the current formation of republicanism as only a grassroots reform movement finally achieving recognition. Indeed, much of the media treatment of republican sentiment bears all the signs of a 'beat-up'.

Nevertheless, even a 'beat-up' requires some contextual support to run this long, some established ideological positions alongside which it can be aligned and through which it may establish its legitimacy. In this case, the push for the republic has been understood as the natural outcome of what is customarily seen as a decade of revived Australian nationalism.

The 1980s, as the period circulates in popular memory, might be described as beginning with the America's Cup victory in 1983

3

and concluding with the Bicentenary in 1988. Compressed in this way, 'the 1980s' is dominated by the signs of a newly confident Australian nationalism. By far the dominant sign, certainly for the mid-eighties, was the risk-taking activities of our high-flying entre-preneurs: Alan Bond, John Elliott, Rupert Murdoch, Kerry Packer, Christopher Skase, among others. The following chapter deals with this phenomenon in detail; suffice it to say here that the qualities thought to be responsible for these men's temporary or continuing successes—largely their rule-breaking, risk-taking brashness—were also held to be national characteristics. With the (often brief) ascend-ancy of such figures Australian capitalism, and the Australian business press, found its heroes.

Other, more modestly promoted, signs proliferated. Icons of traditional Australian nationalism which had been shelved through-out the seventies—the Akubra hat, Drizabone coat, R.M. Williams boots—not only reclaimed their place in everyday life but graduated to the status of high fashion. In the area of cultural policy, the nationalist influence was also apparent. Both State and federal governments began to take a serious interest in museum and heritage issues; while the federal government finally allowed the television industry access to the same kinds of funding opportunities enjoyed by film, and accepted responsibility to protect and develop the Australian popular music industry.

More immediately gratifying to many Australians were the fre-quent reports that Australia now enjoyed a new visibility overseas. 'Australia Is Flavour Of The Month' stories were themselves 'flavour of the decade' in the Australian media. Wherever one looked during the 1980s, it seemed, Australians were winning recognition overseas. British TV audiences were hooked on *Neighbours* and besotted with Kylie Minogue; Elle McPherson became the international embodi-ment of 'natural' beauty; Paul Hogan beat Hollywood at their own game, twice, with *Crocodile Dundee* and *Crocodile Dundee 2*; Robert Hughes pulled an unlikely bestseller out of the hat of Australian convict history with *The Fatal Shore*; Barry Humphries finally cracked the American market and treated us to the rare spectacle of an Australian 'woman' patronising American men on *Donahue*; Peter Carey won the Booker Prize with *Oscar and Lucinda*; Paul Keating was voted 'the world's best Treasurer' and Mel Gibson the 'sexiest man alive'; American tourists began turning up in droves to see the land of Crocodile Dundee; Alan Bond won the America's Cup and then went on to become, temporarily, the scourge of international capital; and Rupert Murdoch became the

4

nemesis of the free press on three continents as the power of News Ltd expanded beyond its critics' worst nightmares.

Australia's residual deference to Britain appeared to dissipate further over this period. As we shall see in Chapter 3, two occasions on which the British government was taken on in the Australian courts (the *Spycatcher* trials and the Maralinga Royal Commission) assumed significance as demonstrations of genuine independence. And the most exorbitantly nationalistic event of all, of course, was the Bicentenary—although, as I argue in Chapter 4, it was not without its ambiguities. The jewel in the crown of Bob Hawke's prime ministership, presided over by Australian of the Year John Farnham, the Bicentenary was nevertheless 'opened' by Australia's (then) favourite royals, Charles and Di.

The construction of the Australian national character underwriting 1980s nationalism was, of course, anything but new. The Australian it celebrated (examples we will meet later include the media constructions of Alan Bond, Malcolm Turnbull and Jim McClelland) was most often very familiar: the cheeky, resourceful larrikin who populates Henry Lawson's stories and who was enshrined as the 'national type' in the work of Russel Ward.[3] This version of the national character is prescriptive, unitary, masculinist and excluding. It is not a version of national identity that reflects the diversity of ethnicities, cultural traditions and political interests that currently exist in this postcolonial nation-state; and for this reason 1980s nationalism—pleasurable though many of its moments of excess may have turned out to be—has been criticised, even deplored. Increasingly, as we move from the 1980s through the 1990s, the orthodoxies of Australian identity associated with 'the Australian legend' have become the subject of critiques which view them as mythic inventions carrying regressive consequences for the nation that believes in them. As women insist on their inclusion within images of the national character, as indigenous Australians demand that their history be acknowledged by white Australians, as the proportion of white Anglo-Saxons in the Australian community shrinks, the disparity between the licensed batteries of national imagery and the 'realities' of national cultural experience is exposed as the consequence of longstanding discrimination, oppression and imperialism.

Therefore, while I would not regard the lively media interest in the republican issue as evidence of grassroots support for any of the specific programs of reform on offer so far, it is possible to regard such interest as evidence of a growing demand for new ways of defining or representing the nation—new ways of 'making it national'. As we turn the century, the need has become pressing to reconsider the dominant, essentially nineteenth century, images commonly employed to represent Australian identity.

It could probably go without saying, but the point of worrying about this is that the specific images employed, the established definitions of national character, prescribe what is Australian, what is normal, what is acceptable, and what is not. Such prescriptions carry both material and ideological consequences. In the introduction to their *Debutante Nation*, Susan Magarey, Sue Rowley and Susan Sheridan argue that the dominant nationalist definitions of the 1890s, those definitions which are still in operation today, supported the denigration of women in an apparently indirect but nevertheless pervasive manner: through the differentiation of Australia from an effete British culture which 'effectively coded nationalism as masculine':

> For it is masculinity that is celebrated in assertions of an Australian culture that is independent of ties to any skirts—whether those ruling the domestic hearth, or those preaching from church pulpits, or those of the mother country—an Australian culture expressed in the virility of young men assaulting the virgin bush, remote from the corrupting centres of imperial rule, drawing emotional warmth and support from a homosocial camaraderie that has undertones of misogynist and racist violence not far below the surface.[4]

In her contribution to *Debutante Nation*, Marilyn Lake traces some of the material effects of these 1890s definitions of Australian masculinity on Australian women: the evidence of wife-beating, male drunkenness and desertion in nineteenth century marriages. Contesting histories which depict Australian women of the 1890s as straitlaced 'wowsers' bent on forcing a bourgeois respectability upon their free-spirited menfolk, Lake's view is that women's attacks on masculine 'pleasures' during this period were not morally repressive but incipiently feminist. Their campaigns were 'aimed at dethroning the style of masculinity championed by the men's press—a style of masculinity that had deleterious consequences for the lives of women':

> 'Whisky, Seduction, Gambling and Cruelty'—these were the targets of the Women's Sphere. To depict women's concerns with temperance and social purity in terms of 'respectability' is to ignore the sexual politics; to describe the campaigners as Wowsers is to stigmatise them in the language of their masculinist enemies. The women's movements in Britain and the United States shared similar concerns but in

Australia, where masculinist values had been elevated to the status of national traditions, feminist activism acquired a particularly subversive, counter-cultural dimension. These women's aims were limited but they were no less threatening for that. They sought to curtail masculine privilege and those practices most injurious to women and children— notably drinking, smoking, gambling and male sexual indulgence. They did not seek a total independence for women, but to make their dependence a happier and more secure state.[5]

Lake's reading of the matter has not gone unchallenged,[6] but its explanatory power lies precisely in the kind of connections it makes between the nationalist constructions of the Australian character and women's material experience.

Debutante Nation is only the most recent example of a revision-ist history which provides us with clear evidence of the benefits to be gained from re-examining, not just the ways in which our nation is represented in the media and elsewhere, but also the uses to which these representations are put. The collection's title proposes an alternative 'reading' of the national self:

> We want it [*Debutante Nation*] to suggest that most traditional depic-tions of nation-formation are not only gendered masculine but also distinctly solemn. Our image of the nation's debut is intended to undercut this solemnity as well as to try out gendering the nation feminine: dancing rather than parliamentary processions; debutantes rather than bushranging desperadoes; a readiness to play with gender of nationhood, like some cartoons from the period which play with gender ambiguities, even cross-dressing.[7]

The need for an alternative reading (if not necessarily this one) is emphasised by the fact that the image of the debutante nation seems, in the context of the dominant traditions in the writing of Australian history, so frivolous. (In what follows, too, I am conscious that by focusing on nationalist events I almost necessarily fore-ground issues of race, ethnicity and class rather than those of gender.)

Critiques of traditional Australian nationalism[8] do not only come from feminist rewritings of history; they also come from multi-culturalism and the Aboriginal movement, and from cultural studies positions which understand nationalism itself as an oppressively consensualising ideology.[9] So wide is the field of critique within the humanities and social sciences that resistance to the orthodox definitions of Australianness has become something of a minor orthodoxy itself. Indeed, Cochrane and Goodman argue that the Bicentenary failed to produce the sense of a unified nation because

7

the very idea of 'the nation' is no longer 'secure' in the Australian popular consciousness. In particular, they suggest, the assumption that the national culture needs to be entirely homogeneous had more or less disappeared before the Bicentenary occurred.[10]

If such a diagnosis is accurate, 1980s nationalism may actually have given rise—in spite of itself—to a commitment among Australians to 'redefine' themselves. There are certainly plenty of signs within Australian popular culture that a unitary nationalism no longer goes unchallenged. The development of a sub-genre of 'multicultural' stand-up comedy, which relies on characters who express both their European ethnicity *and* their definitively suburban 'Australianness' without ever acknowledging any potential contradictions, is one such sign. The early work of Vince Sorrenti and more contemporary figures from *Wogs out of Work* or the TV series *Acropolis Now* such as Mary Coustas's 'Effie' allow audiences to recognise and endorse Australian identities which are not just tolerant of cultural differences but are actually constituted by them. Accordingly, Chapter 6 will argue that the use of discourses of multiculturalism to signify a local/Australian identity is notable in many of the films coming out of Melbourne over the last few years. In *Death in Brunswick, The Big Steal, Strictly Ballroom* or *The Heartbreak Kid*, Australian identities are not marked by their cultural purity but by their hybridity. Indeed, in these films, unlike such early 1980s films as *Breaker Morant* or *Gallipoli*, the problem of Australian identities is rarely addressed explicitly. The multiplicity of Australian identities the more recent films construct seems to render the selfconsciousness of the earlier generation of period dramas entirely unnecessary.

While this is encouraging, I would not want to claim too much for what is still only a minority trend, not a revolution. The material surveyed in this book reveals the flexibility and durability of the established discourses of Australianness. For the most part, to turn on the television, to listen to the radio, or to browse through the local bookshop's 'Australiana' shelf, is still to find the old constructions recurring—often without significant disputation. When Telecom wants to flog its frontline high-tech product (a mobile phone), what does it do? It dresses a suntanned blond male in an Akubra and a pair of shorts, pops him in a four-wheel-drive, and sends him bush with an American tourist! If 'the Australian legend' has lost most of its credibility with the critics and historians who once helped disseminate it, it still has its supporters within the wider community. Indeed, among the signs of the nationalism of the 1980s was a revival of rural-nationalist mythologies, reclaiming the experiences of those in the country towns or on the land as fundamental to our national character. The opening of the Stockman's Hall of Fame in Longreach, Queensland, during the Bicentennial year was one instance of this rural revival, and it has enjoyed considerable success in re-establishing the histories it celebrates within the nation's mythologies.

The design of the building blends the urban postmodernism of curved tubular steel with such traditional rural materials as timber and corrugated iron, creating a result that looks like a cross between the Sydney Opera House and a shearing shed. These two apparently contradictory signifiers of Australianness produce a highly contemporary form which speaks to the past and the present simultaneously. If only for this reason, the Stockman's Hall of Fame presents a dramatic challenge to those who would argue that the tradition it preserves is unable to find a position from which to stake its claim on contemporary Australian identity. The Stockman's Hall of Fame has been a success in representing its conservative constituency and in responding to many of those who want it to reflect more contemporary views on outback history. Its new 'women's wing'—dedicated to recognising women pioneers, teachers, nurses, publicans, cooks and others—is, to some extent, evidence of this. Although a 'women's wing' will not satisfy those who would rather the Hall of Fame revised its whole view of history from a thoroughly gender-sensitive perspective, it will appease some of the individual women and women's groups who have pressed for recognition of women's contribution to bush life. Its meanings are not progressive, but the Hall of Fame does demonstrate that even what some might regard as tired or irrelevant definitions of the nation maintain the capacity to revive and resituate themselves within a changing Australian identity.

The most popular example of the rural revival, though, is ABC Radio's Sunday morning talkback show, *Australia All Over*—promoted as 'Australia's most-listened-to radio program'. (Its audience is national, therefore it has an advantage even over networked commercial programs, but the claim is still staggering.) *Australia All Over* has reconstituted the 1890s *Bulletin* and put it to air. It offers us a trip back to a time when Australians saw their culture as fundamentally rural, when the Digger was the archetypal hero and war the defining masculine/adult experience, and when the Lawson–Furphy blend of the bizarre and the sentimental provided the core source material and the appropriate mode for shared

9

reminiscences. Talkback callers confide easily in 'Macca' (Ian McNamara, the host), whose doggedly amateurish delivery legitimises his as a genuinely populist voice. Tirelessly empathic, Macca operates like a veteran bartender: he expertly elicits stories, opinions and personal details without ever needing to offer any of his own. The music chosen to break up the parade of calls, letters, bush poems and sentimental reminiscences is a mixture of Australianised country and western and traditional bush music, with the odd novelty tune thrown in. The success of this combination has led to spinoffs, the *Australia All Over* books and albums marketed through ABC shops around the country. Whatever one ultimately thinks of *Australia All Over* (it feels like a time warp to me) it is in such cultural products that the power and continuity of the old nationalism, as well as the sweep of differences which will have to be accommodated by its successors, is manifest.

In the national interest

National cultures are not simple repositories of shared symbols to which the entire population stands in identical relation. Rather, they are to be approached as sites of contestation in which competition over definitions takes place.
(Philip Schlesinger)

The problem for the old nationalism—and I believe it is a problem that must ultimately be fatal to its continued survival—is that it still addresses a single national character and depends upon a singular version of history. It is incapable of incorporating, and is therefore implicitly hostile to, the multiplicity of identities and histories currently competing for representation within the discourses of nationality. Nevertheless, at the moment, the dominant discourses used in representing Australian identity are still those which derive from the old nationalism. It is not easy for competing constructions to break into the circuit and 'denaturalise' the established imagery— of the land, of the bushman, of rural communities and so on.

Once established, discourses of nationality are notoriously hard to dislodge or deconstruct. The history of the 'uses' of nationalism in Australia over the last decade highlights, not these discourses' monolithic predictability, but their canny flexibility, their readiness for continual appropriation and deployment as they participate in the construction of a national culture. This is because these discursive formations are 'modular'.[11] That is, the discourses conventionally used to represent the nation come to 'mean' the nation almost irrespective of their context of use. Established discourses of 'the national' can be wheeled into place on a wide range of social terrain and put to work for a wide variety of political or ideological interests—even competing or contradictory interests—at any one time. (The 'national interests' served by Alan Bond's America's Cup boat *Australia II*, for example, were not the same as the 'national interests' served by his entrepreneurial activities; but the discourses used to represent them were, as Chapter 2 demonstrates, precisely the same.) While the 'natural' authority of nationalist discourses is guaranteed in advance of their particular deployment—and this makes them especially powerful influences upon their readers—the specific meanings generated through specific representations of the nation, seductive as they usually are, cannot be guaranteed: they are still the subject of interpretation by those 'reading' the text. At times—and the material dealt with in Chapters 3 and 5 gives instances of this—it is quite difficult to tell what meanings are likely to be produced by most readers from these nationalist representations, or what ideological interests the possible meanings might serve.

Nevertheless, the generally consistent effectiveness of the established discourses of nationalism means that they are worth appropriating. A political party attempts to position itself as the one which speaks for the nation, by aligning itself with dominant groups or constituencies: the middle class, business or 'the family', for instance. Similarly, other, less formally constituted, groups of interests also make their bids for temporary identification with the discursive category 'the nation'. Beer companies define their product as the 'Australian' one; petrol companies mask their foreign ownership with ad campaigns which attempt to naturalise their enclosure within the nation. What is won is the capacity to speak on behalf of the nation.

There is no reason why such pairings of interests should be accepted as legitimate. When the union movement and employers' groups both offer their plans for dealing with the recession, both claim to be speaking on behalf of the nation. However, for most members of the public, only one claim will be convincing; the other will be seen as pleading for 'special interests'—presumably those of the members of that particular group. The objective of both groups is to successfully represent their own interests and those of the nation as identical; so the actual performance of the representation aimed at accomplishing this identification is critical. It is these

11

performances which this book examines: how 'the national interest', broadly conceived, gets appropriated to more narrow objectives through specific representational tactics employed in the media or in other domains of popular culture.

The analyses which follow concentrate on these media representations. The modern nation-state, it has been argued, is itself a product of the spread of mass communication systems—in particular, the press.[12] As Benedict Anderson points out, in modern national communities none of us will ever meet most of our fellow citizens and so our common identity has to be 'imagined' rather than directly experienced.[13] That being the case, the print and electronic media (although neither radio nor television figure in Anderson's account) are crucial mechanisms through which the national consciousness can be constructed.[14] This is something new nations such as Australia have recognised for many years. While Australian governments have gradually relinquished their interest in managing the development of the nation's print media—even losing interest in principles of local ownership—they have made assiduous use of 'state-funded image production'[15] as a deliberate strategy of nation formation at home and promotion abroad. The film industry is the most obvious instance of this. Australia also has a history of some sensitivity about the kinds of representations to which it has been subject. The uproar over the ABC-TV series *Sylvania Waters* is one instance of a deep concern about how our identity is represented to overseas audiences, but there are others.[16] In Chapter 5, I deal with concerns about the national image projected through tourism promotions.

This book is not a comprehensive survey of the uses of nationalism in Australian popular culture. I have selected my sites of analysis, and the analysis itself deals with representations rather than with broad social or economic movements. The events and relationships I have selected, though, are significant and rich: the hero-worship of the Australian entrepreneurs and the 'nationalising' of the figure of Alan Bond; the relationship between Australia and Britain approached through two legal disputes (over the Maralinga atomic tests and the *Spycatcher* memoirs); the Bicentenary, particularly the Aboriginal countercelebrations; the ambiguities in the Australia/America relationship, as viewed through the theme park Movie World, *Crocodile Dundee* and tourism advertising; and finally the crucial role played by the news media in the process of nation formation. This book does not offer a critique of nationalism per se but rather of the uses to which it is put. Accordingly, the sixth chapter will develop a more positive argument for a hybrid national identity as an alternative to the 'cultural purity model' through discussion of some recent Australian films and the work of the multiracial band, Yothu Yindi.

There are some continuing themes. The often mischievous, often sycophantic, often plain ill-informed activities of the Australian news media—particularly print journalists—pepper these analyses. The dangerous unanimity of print reporting in Australia—the provision of alternative sources of news and comment is actually getting poorer, not richer—is particularly evident in my account of the business press but is a serious problem elsewhere, too. Among the consequences of the narrow range of perspectives available to Australian newspaper readers is the way in which critical consideration of Australian society in the mainstream media has been dominated by analysis of the economy. The idealisation of 'the market' as the pre-eminent social regulatory mechanism has not gone away just because 'economic rationalism' is now being discredited. It survives in prevailing assumptions about how the media assess the nature and development of Australian society. Business has maintained its position in centre stage as the interests of industry and the interests of the nation are represented as if they were almost indistinguishable, most of the time.

One of the things that provoked my writing this book was the frequent experience of witnessing businessmen (and it *is* usually men) making public statements which, though patently self-serving, were made in the name of the 'national interest'. Many industry leaders talk about the state of the nation as if their prosperity and the nation's prosperity were synonymous. The right of business to make a profit seems to have acquired the same kind of social justice status as the right of all citizens to free speech, shelter and the protection of their government. When business fails, it asks for government assistance. When it succeeds, it pockets the profits. Increasingly, business leaders have acquired the roles of community leaders: roles once more variously played by civic officials, clerics, artists, intellectuals or scientists. Representatives of business have actively sought the opportunity to speak to the nation at large as disinterested, authoritative voices. Far too often, these voices have uttered antidemocratic, discriminatory, even racist, opinions. In the debates over Mabo—the High Court case that opened the way to selective restoration of native title to land in Australia—the alliance between big business and some sections of the press has fuelled existing racial prejudices in a manner that has been little short of sinister. Consistently over the last few years, business has deflected

13

the blame for the recession—a recession at least deepened, it might be argued, by Australian business's failure to adapt positively to the restructuring of international capitalism—onto other, less powerful and less privileged, groups. Among those blamed in recent times are migrants (for taking 'our' jobs), women (for taking 'our' jobs), Aboriginals (for claiming 'our' land), and environmentalists (for opposing 'our' developments). Yet it is to·the business community that the media encourage us to look for leadership, for self-sacrifice, for nation formation. Sadly, the history of Australian business over the last decade has not been dominated by self-sacrificing, nation-building entrepreneurs.[17]

So that is my starting point; it is to provide more substance to such observations that the arguments of the following chapter are developed. That business has the right to speak for all Australians has rather been taken for granted—certainly by the mainstream media. There has been too little examination of how this identification with the national interest has been constructed and maintained. In Chapter 2, I address the issue through a discussion of the media's representation of business, the economy and the 'nationalised' figure of Alan Bond.

2

Bond-ing: business, boats and the national character

In the 1980s, political debate in Australia collapsed almost entirely into a discourse of economic management: not only did the difference between the parties reduce, for a time, to one of management styles, but activists on issues once considered 'social' and intrinsically important (from racism, the status of women and human rights to public education and the arts) had to reconstruct their objects and their practices in order to prove them 'not uneconomic'. A social-factory thematics became ubiquitous, like the dream of controlling time: by 1990, 'productivity' was a value to be extracted in any activity from manufacturing to aerobics to writing poetry. (Meaghan Morris, *Ecstasy and Economics*)

There's no trick to making money—if that's all you want to do. (*Citizen Kane*)

The art of making money

There was a time when a suspicion of capitalism and a lack of respect for business seemed to be a permanent feature of representations of Australian life. When one goes back through the *Bulletin*'s early decades the hated figure of the 'fat capitalist' crops up at every point, from the cartoons to the leaders. During the Depression, the figure of the 'foreign banker' is similarly pilloried in the popular press—usually in terms we would now recognise as anti-Semitic—

15

reinforcing popular explanations for the severity of the Depression which blamed the influence of overseas bankers on the domestic economy. There seemed to be little question then that the interests of international business and those of Australia were fundamentally opposed.

Such attitudes to the businessman were not merely motivated by a bourgeois fastidiousness about the 'vulgarity' of trade or commerce. The principles of solidarity fundamental to Australian laborism—that central plank in Australian social politics—militated against a great enthusiasm for gung-ho capitalists. Anyone whose life was dominated by the making of money had to be doing so at someone else's expense and therefore could not be trusted. If this is a valid characterisation of the dominant pattern of representation of Australian attitudes in the past, it is hard to explain the sudden change in the Australian representations of and attitudes to business which peaked in the 1980s but remains fully installed in the 1990s.

As with most shifts in the way in which everyday life is represented to us—through the media, through conversation, through the accepted discourses of a particular historical conjuncture—this shift appears to have completed itself before anyone noticed that it was under way. Consequently, it seems unremarkable now that, in media and other representations, 'the state of the economy has become, quite literally, the state of the nation'.[1] Of course, this is not a *natural* connection. There are many alternative ways of conceiving of the state of the nation, most of which would relegate 'the economy' to a secondary role: as an effect of, for instance, socio-political decisions about social justice or cultural identity. As Michael Pusey has put it in his critique of economic rationalism, 'society' itself is now often talked about as if it were an 'opponent' of the economy—rather than, as in some earlier understandings, the primary subject of politics around which 'the economy' should be structured.[2]

This is not to be a discussion of economic rationalism, however, although it does play a role in what follows. What interests me here is how business comes to play such a conspicuous and significant role in popular representations of Australian life during the eighties and, still, in the nineties. During the first half of the eighties, in particular, the businessman—improbably—emerged as a media celebrity, a 'star'. The exploits of John Elliott, John Spalvins, Alan Bond and Robert Holmes à Court received the kind of front page treatment previously given to politicians and sports stars. Around each of these figures a personality was constructed and a mini-

16

narrative formed, endowing their behaviours with complex motivations and cultural resonance. Accordingly, Bond was the determined immigrant who made good in 'the Lucky Country'; Elliott (notwithstanding his blueblooded patronage and affiliation with the Liberal Party) was the larrikin with the MBA from Harvard; Holmes à Court was the aristocratic 'throwback' to a British mercantile past.[3] These constructions helped to legitimise the 'greed is good' mentality that appeared to fuel their individual careers; each of these star businessmen was represented as working against tradition in one location or another and thus operated as a sign of a new, aggressively Australian, version of capitalism.

Significantly, this was not regarded as a parochial formation. Australia's star businessmen were represented as the vanguard of a new international capitalism—competitive, pragmatic, unfettered and exciting. Australians were leading the world, taking on the establishment here and overseas with a brash vigour that took the market's breath away. Their behaviour suggested a new way of thinking about business—as a domain of action, derring-do, even of style:

> Greed may be a bad thing, but to all but a few malcontents it sure beat socialism, at least in the 1980s. Someday the world may pay dearly for the economic excesses of this decade, but if there was any saving grace to what was occurring now it was the fact that the eighties had a sense of style.[4]

What was being naturalised by this 'sense of style' was rapacious, socially destructive activities, but they didn't necessarily appear that way at the time. That they didn't is due to two parallel but quite contradictory strategies used to represent the new Australian capitalism.

One strategy, still with us today, was to depict the new capitalists as the 'hard men', the ones who draw their knowledge from the 'real world' in order to make the 'tough decisions' that would affect 'every Australian's life'. Business acquired a hard pragmatic edge, a privileged insight into the *realpolitik* of the Australian future. As a consequence, 'the market' became the place where we found the 'real world'; indeed, 'the market' was talked about as if it were not the theoretical abstraction it is—as if one could actually *go* there any time. The alternatives to market forces—'social planning' or, worse, 'social engineering'—were talked about as if they were a little like 'family planning' or 'genetic engineering': as, respectively, dated and moralistic or perjoratively academic interventions into the natural order of things.

The second strategy works in the opposite direction. To use Helen Grace's formulation, it moves away from logic and towards aesthetics.[5] Grace has described how business acquired both a visual and a narrative style through its representation in the business press during the late 1980s. Despite the invisibility of 'the real action' of business, and its frequent failure to actually produce anything material at the end of its deals, the media turned business into a spectacle:

> On the surface, there is nothing to see in the business world. Deals are done in secret. The telephone is used a lot, and people talking on the telephone do not represent an exciting spectacle. Columns of stock prices are less interesting to read than the telephone book and the intricacy of deals remains hidden behind dense legalistic language. On the whole, then, no spectacle is immediately observable. So it has to be produced by emphasising, as a site of action, one particular aspect of its operation. The site chosen for this emphasis is the floor of the stock exchange. Here the constraints manifest at every other level of the business world are suspended in a frenzy of activity giving the appearance of complete chaos. The spectacle is such that visitors' galleries, where spectators as well as speculators can observe the action, are provided as part of the architecture of these sites of the arbitrariness of capital's value creation.[6]

The spectacle takes place within an entirely fictionalised world, says Grace, where, far from being among the pragmatic and the material, we are dealing always with abstractions:

> Let us then consider that realm of absolute reality—the world of economic reality. But we find that, in reality—if there is such a place—we are dealing with fictional entities: futures trading (commodities that do not yet exist); junk bonds (which symbolise the only logic which operates in this field of danger—the greater the risk, the greater the return, *if* there is a return at all); something which is called credit, but which is in fact, debt. . .[7]

Produced from among these abstractions, the economic life of the nation is a 'daily soap opera, full of the most extreme occurrences'. The heroes and villains of this soap opera are the star performers of the moment.

Performance is the crucial issue here. During the 1980s, the business press became connoisseurs of the stylish, the slick, the outrageous (read underfinanced) deal.[8] Just at the point when the *rest* of society's activities were redefined in terms of productivity (as Morris points out in the epigraph to this section), the productivity of *business* ceased to matter. Instead, business was

18

breathtaking, brilliant, beautiful, formally expressive. Hard-nosed business journalists wrote like *aficionados*, abandoning critical distance as they described the deals in language more conventionally applied to an artistic or, perhaps more appropriately, a sporting spectacle:

> Murdoch with a billion or two in his hands is like watching Maradona with a soccer ball. The performance is that dazzling. John Elliott is equally as exciting, though he is more of a thug on the field. Put both into a sports stadium in the right circumstances and 80 000 fans would go wild.[9]

Just as art critics talk of artistic movements, of 'schools' defined by their representational techniques or thematic concerns, the Australian business media talked of a new breed of capitalist defined by a personal style, by an aesthetics of the deal. McManamy's book on the stockmarket crash of 1987 sees both the Australians and the New Zealanders as such a breed, coming from a particularly 'hard' and 'pragmatic' apprenticeship:

> The new money Kiwis who managed to succeed against the odds without question were the slickest dealers in the world, inventors of the most intricate corporate structures found anywhere, pioneers of creative accounting and finding new ways to milk markets, and clear leaders in flouting normally accepted business conventions.

Postmodern capitalists, raiding the past, outraging stuffy traditionalists and unashamedly reclaiming the primacy of the individual: their careers are documented with undisguised relish in McManamy's book. It would be wrong to put McManamy's enthusiasm down to personal pathology;[10] he is reasonably representative of most day-to-day business reporting of the time. When Bond was about to be destroyed by his contest with Tiny Rowland over control of the Lonrho group in 1988, *Business Review Weekly* (which one might have imagined was the most informed journal on Bond's affairs and the risks involved) began its otherwise rather dull and sober assessment with an enthusiastic appreciation of good ol' Bondy's audacity:

> It is vintage Bond. At a time when his share price is under heavy attack, Alan Bond is planning another big takeover. It is to be the biggest yet and is intended to pave the way for even greater glories on the corporate battlefield.[11]

Of course, they couldn't have been more wrong. As we shall see later on, 1988 had produced ample signs—although not many

19

had so far surfaced in the business press—that there were few glories left for Alan Bond on the corporate battlefield or anywhere else.

Something happened to the representation of business and the economy over the eighties which was essential to what are now complacently referred to as 'the excesses of the eighties'. One thing that happened was an expansion of the business media. Television reveals a modest increase in business news but the development of the newspaper and magazine market was substantial: during the decade it included *Business Review Weekly, Australian Business, Australian Investment, Investment Planning* and the short-lived *Business Daily.* The large metropolitan dailies expanded their business coverage, separating it from the rest of the paper—in most cases—into its own section. Business journalism became more specialised, giving free rein to its particular characteristics. The sources for business reporting are narrow, overwhelmingly from within business itself. Journalists' structural dependence upon and personal familiarity with their limited sources increases the likelihood that they become 'advocates for their sources', 'spokesmen . . . rather than dispassionate observers'. Such an identification is reinforced by the role of business reporting within the paper; because business journalism is not required to attract a large readership, it tends to cater to its own constituency more than is healthy.[12] Consequently, says Rodney Tiffen, 'business reporting— writing for a business audience while relying on business sources—is potentially prone to sycophancy, and there is considerable stroking of the business ego'.[13] Tiffen's research reveals that business and economics writers are much more openly opinionated and prescriptive in their work, and admit to the desire to influence policy and debate.[14] As Tiffen goes on to say, this is a dangerous propensity when the opinions and prescriptions may well turn out to be those of their sources.

The business media developed just such a complicit relationship with the highest flying sections of Australian business during the eighties. Eventually, and with pleasing symmetry, the decline of the entrepreneurs was paralleled by the failure of the business magazines: *Australian Business, Australian Investment, Investment Planning* and *Business Daily* have now abandoned the field to the *Australian Financial Review, Business Review Weekly* and the variously expanded business sections in the metropolitan dailies. Nevertheless, despite the closure of some media outlets sympathetic to the excesses of the eighties, what seems to have been the overarching enabling condition—the ideological centrality accorded to business within Australian culture through the extraordinary consistency of the discourses used to represent it—does not seem to have changed much at all. It deserves closer scrutiny than it has so far received.

Of course, it would be wrong to argue that this situation is peculiar to Australia. The emergence of the economy as the primary definer of the state of the nation is a common feature of western democracies.[15] Mike Emmison's research suggests that the historical moment at which the term 'the economy' starts to be used in its contemporary sense is roughly the same across all western cultures: while the meaning had been available for about two hundred years, the contemporary usage is fully installed during the 1930s. The term's origin in the earlier *oeconomy* (which referred to the government of the family in a much wider sense than the financial) is lost as 'the economy' breaks out of the generalised notion of the state's (or family's) welfare and becomes visible as a specific institutional structure with its own specific interests. This transition occurs in partnership with the growth of capitalism.

As capitalism develops, the idea of the economy provides an increasingly powerful device for legitimising preferences for the regulatory mechanisms of the market over those of the state. Economics naturalises the 'laws' (significantly, not the 'behaviour') of the market, thereby justifying their effects and their prominence in commonsense understandings of the welfare of the nation.[16] There are, of course, numerous theoretical traditions in economics, recommending radically different ways of relating specific economic decisions to specific social ends within any particular historical context. This necessarily makes the understanding and management of the economy a political activity, but that is usually masked by the way the economy is talked about. Emmison agrees with Voloshinov, that 'the ruling class' always try to make the needs of the economy seem 'eternal'—as above the concerns of politics.[17] In this way, unpopular political decisions can be taken and policies can be justified while avoiding the charge of class or sectional self-interest. When working most actively at naturalising specific political and social choices as the irresistible effects of the inexorable workings of 'the market', the nation's economy becomes 'more important than its citizens'.[18]

Such an account is unsympathetic to the emergence of the economy in public discourse and to the discipline of economics itself. Emmison is keen to defend what has been displaced by

21

economics' fetishisation of the market: social justice; the equitable distribution of wealth; culture. Such a critique is increasingly widespread[19] throughout the western world as capitalism restructures itself towards a globalised market and as it invents new ways of explaining, justifying and administering this restructuring. Everywhere it is possible to see examples of the broad trend I am describing: it comprises the media's complicit representation of business, the emergence of 'the economy' as a metonym both for the nation-state and for the globalised market seen to be its successor, and the administrative successes of economic rationalism in many western societies.

There are particular aspects of this cultural and political movement in Australia which concern me here. I should emphasise how radical has been the inversion of Australian political and cultural values signified by the embracing of business, economics, and the administrative agenda of economic rationalism. The principles of Australian laborism,[20] a broadly observed social contract expressing a genuine commitment to the redistribution of wealth (albeit, as Morris points out, among white men[21]), would not seem to provide particularly fertile ground for the fetishisation of wealth acquisition (as distinct from wealth creation), or for a wholly cynical admiration of sharp business practices as a mode of performance. Nevertheless, despite such an apparently hostile ideological and ethical context, these new versions of competitive capitalism have flourished in Australia. Furthermore, they received crucial political support from the most unlikely of sources: the alliance between business and Labor governments at the State and federal level since 1983 is probably unprecedented in Australian history.

In the second epigraph to this section, I quote a remark from Orson Welles' classic, *Citizen Kane*. Anyone can make money, *Citizen Kane* suggests, if they are prepared to sacrifice their friends, family and supporters along the way. The small shareholders in Quintex, Bond Corp, Tricontinental and Rothwells—among others— might suggest that this is a lesson that got lost in Australia during the 1980s. However, there are still limits to the extent to which the lesson is remembered today; its importance will continue to be missed as long as newspapers describe what entrepreneurs like Christopher Skase did to make money as 'business'.

Over the last decade, high profile entrepreneurs were proffered as role models for the whole society despite their questionable business practices, their flouting of Australian taxation obligations, and the speculative nature of their enterprises. How did this seamless identification between these Australian businessmen and the Australian nation construct and maintain itself? Given the evidence, how could Australians have believed that big business was working in their interests? This was a period when capital investment in Australia hit new lows, to the extent that some critics on the Left talked convincingly about a 'capital strike'.[22] It was a period in which, despite or perhaps even because of the Accord between the federal government and the union movement, we saw a massive shift in the distribution of the national wealth away from wages and towards profits.[23] It was a period of almost unprecedented industrial peace and union docility accompanied by an extraordinary abuse of corporate responsibility—ranging from Skase-like directors' fees and asset-shifting to giant executive salaries. At a time when business seems to have least understood its own social responsibilities, representatives of business proliferated on the boards of virtually every public and semi-public institution. Advisory committees in universities, charities, government instrumentalities of all kinds spent half the decade explaining what their organisations actually *did* to business representatives on their boards, who then told them they could solve all their problems just by being more 'market-driven'. As the deregulated banks responded to competition by lending almost indiscriminately to business, individual Australians languished under the burden of high interest rates aimed at reducing their capacity to borrow. Foreign debt accumulated at an alarming rate, primarily in the hands of the private sector and then in a limited number of companies, but Australians were told that this was a debt we all had to service. When the economy floundered, business was routinely asked to nominate the causes; just as routinely, their nominees were unquestioningly accepted by the media as those responsible for the social and economic disasters befalling us. Thus, at a time when Australia faced disasters 'created by big business, banks, Keating's use of monetary policy, global trade wars and some strangely hot dry weather', intelligent and successful businessmen were happy to blame 'environmentalists, unions and Aboriginal people' for 'irrationally impeding development'.[24]

In the following section, I want to examine one aspect of this complex phenomenon in order to suggest how the alignment between representations of the interests of business and those of the nation was established. Then I will outline a more detailed example of this 'discursive nationalisation' of business and the complicity of the media in this process, by reviewing the media construction of the figure of Alan Bond.

Larrikin capitalism

Entrepreneurs have never been high on the list of Australian heroes. We reserve our applause for marathon runners, tennis and swimming pool champions, TV and film stars and the occasional scientist for their individual pursuit of excellence and the effort they put into achieving their goals.

Even the corporate sector itself, smitten with the virtues of scale and forgetful of the fact that today's industrial giants were but entrepreneurs' dreams of 50 or 100 years ago, has until recently overlooked the importance of entrepreneurial vigor in wealth creation.

But now the established patterns of power and privilege are being broken up as rapid changes in technology place a premium on the alertness and fast reaction times that entrepreneurs possess. The more democratic style of our times has encouraged people to chase their own ambitions, to do their own thing. (Peter Stirling, *Business Review Weekly*, 11.1.1985)

At the beginning of Ben Elton's comic novel, *Stark*, we meet an entrepreneur from Western Australia, Sylvester (Sly) Moorcock. Sly got his start in business by capitalising on personal knowledge about a close friend's family firm; it was a pie company whose share price was temporarily in trouble because of a failed attempt to 'ponce up' the humble meat pie (they had introduced a ham and cheese variety). Once installed as his friend's family's boss, Sly was on his way:

> Now a lesser maverick than Sly might have stopped there, content to be the new head of a successful bakery . . . but Sly was destined to be more than a baker, he wanted to be a bastard. So he smashed the company up, flogging the Cream-Horn machine to one rival, the Viennese Twirl twirler to another. Before long, there was nothing left of his friend's family firm.[25]

Sly learns that successful companies, 'going concerns that make things and create jobs', are vulnerable to takeover, from time to time, and also that the assets of these companies, if sold off separately, 'can add up to a considerably greater value than the sum total of the share value quoted on the index'. Sly becomes an asset-stripper, an exponent of 'scorched-earth capitalism': 'you buy something, smash it up, flog the bits and move on'.

The curious consequence of this behaviour surprises and ultimately irritates Sly:

> Sly found himself lauded and held up as a role model to other young Australians. Far from being seen as a vandal whose job was destroying other people's jobs purely for personal gain, he was presented as someone who created work, bringing money into the state and helping to keep the wheels of commerce turning.[26]

Ben Elton's sketch is immediately recognisable as an attack on the Australian media's treatment of their businessmen heroes and the excesses of the eighties.

On radio and television during the 1980s, the premier voice of Australian business reporting was Robert Gottliebsen. His breathless, gee-whiz delivery alerted us to high drama in the way parents reading story books to children tend to do (this in itself suggests something of business's relation to the ordinary Australian). As Ernie Dingo's TV caricature of Gottliebsen on *Fast Forward* suggests, this was ridiculous to most Australians—and, as Dingo's parody emphasises, it must have seemed to come from another planet to black Australians. But Gottliebsen's delivery style accurately reflected the media's sense that these were heady days for Australian business. To watch Max Walsh—in the days of 'CarWash', the Carleton–Walsh Report on ABC-TV—interviewing a high-flying Australian businessman was to watch someone very excitable indeed. Often, one felt, Walsh could hardly contain his pleasure at being so close to someone who had been so close to turning the international business community on its head.

What was common to Elliott, Skase, Bond, and before them Murdoch and Packer, is that they were seen as ruthless, unorthodox but successful, outsiders in the world of international business. While they were loathed and despised by the British in particular, this in no way inhibited their cultural and financial success. Often aggressively 'Australian', always resolutely practical and unsentimental, they were the front-row forwards of postcolonial capitalism, acting out the Antipodean fantasy of occupying the central institutions of the colonial power. With ultimate, ludicrous logicality, Bond and Elliott claimed their destiny by becoming beer barons to the world.

In personal style, Bond and Elliott were the clearest examples of the successful ocker. The satirical ABC television show, *Rubbery Figures*, portrayed Elliott by way of a rubber puppet with an enormous red nose and a can of Fosters in its hand, continually braying and haw-hawing like a drunk at a GPS rugby reunion.

25

Bond's puppet was round and shiny, his America's Cup T-shirt grounding him in the Australian character. Both men were known 'stirrers', both pursued their most popular successes overseas against our old rivals—the British, the Americans—and both seemed to have come to their successes 'the hard way'. They were unequivocally new-money (although Bond's art acquisitions and the university he founded suggested some discomfort with that); and they were self-confessed rule-breakers, cheerfully serving as the scourge of the bastions of traditional capital. They were larrikin capitalists.

As John McManamy has said, there could be no better symbol for the arrival of the larrikin capitalists than the America's Cup.[27] When Bond's boat won the cup, the connection between the national character and the Aussie entrepreneurs was completed. Here was a vindication of the risk-taker; an exemplar of the way ahead for the Australian economy. The *Sydney Morning Herald* of 28 September 1983 saw all kinds of omens in the win. Its editorial was headlined 'A spinnaker-led recovery'. 'Australian technology, ingenuity, seamanship, brawn, bravado, and courage have matched the best the United States can offer', it said. 'What we can do in yachting we can do elsewhere as well.' The *Age* started out by comparing the virtues of Australia in 1983 with those of America in 1851 (when the first America's Cup was sailed). In both cultures, the *Age* suggested, the 'entrepreneur, the new-money capitalist' and the 'buccaneer' bore the 'hallmarks' of 'determination, incurable optimism, crassness, impatience, disrespect for authority, and a dogged refusal to accept that established things cannot be changed'. The *Age*, though, was not entirely overwhelmed; it moved from this somewhat populist mode into high seriousness:

> It may be argued that Mr Bond is the embodiment of a narrow range of virtues; that an Australia populated by Alan Bonds would be an unhappily competitive place; that the aggressive brand of capitalism he represents is not an unequivocal good. But if in this remarkable victory, the culmination of a sustained and courageous campaign over many years, we have seen not the whole truth, we have still seen a truth. It is that teams led by vigorous entrepreneurs can achieve much.[28]

From then on, the Australian entrepreneur was not just the front-row forward, he was the whole team. The business magazine *Rydges*, predictably, complained that the natural abilities so triumphant in the America's Cup win were in danger of being smothered by too much government regulation. Government agencies seemed suspicious of 'any display of entrepreneurial verve', thus preventing the 'unleashing of whatever entrepreneurial skills we possess'.[29] *Business Review Weekly* spoke unashamedly as an advocate for the larrikin capitalists: *'BRW* itself has given a special place to entrepreneurs since it began more than four years ago, in recognition of the vigor and vitality that are the hallmark of the entrepreneur, and to encourage and inspire others to follow their example'.[30] *Rydges*, not to be outdone, offered parents a guide to how they might 'create the entrepreneurial spirit' in their children, passing on the comforting information that most successful businessmen had not been particularly bright at school because of their impatience with 'incidentals' and their preference for seeing 'the whole picture'.[31] And in case anyone thought there was something residually un-Australian about all of this, *BRW* published an extraordinary piece by Max Hartwell, offering us a new history of Australia's development in the nineteenth century as the product of entrepreneurial individualism.[32]

The mythology spread. *Time* magazine eventually caught on, headlining its story 'First It Was Australia, Now It's the World'.[33] In this treatment of the 'new breed of players' winning respect in 'global boardrooms', *Time* foregrounded the freshness of Bond, Elliott and the others—noting that their opportunistic style came from learning their trade 'the hard way'. Their success and ingenuity were undisputed; indeed, the article noted that Bond had even pulled off the feat of marketing non-alcoholic beer in the 'predominantly Muslim Middle East'.

Amongst all this, two mildly resisting voices—from opposite sides of the ideological fence. In 1985, the *Far Eastern Economic Review* story 'Sailing Close to the Wind', while otherwise a classically mythologising study of Bond's corporate career, did report the following warning from the chairman of the National Companies and Securities Commission, Henry Bosch:

> 'Some of those who instigate or take a frequent role in the takeover process have been elevated to folk heroes. The acceptance has been far too uncritical.'
> The chief market regulator went on: 'Success in the field of manipulating the stockmarket and the takeover rules, success as a paper entrepreneur, is no guarantee of the ability to run anything. The process of making capital gains through the stockmarket is not the same as the process of generating real wealth'.[34]

Stern, but forlorn. The business media ignored such warnings; it is almost impossible to find substantive articles bent on taking them seriously until after the October 1987 crash—and even then interest only built gradually.

Predictably, perhaps, the more thorough criticism came from the Left. David Uren in *Australian Left Review* attacked the takeover merchants, queried the principles upon which banks were currently lending to business, and suggested that the activities of the new entrepreneurs and their supporting bankers threatened the stability of the Australian economy:

> The new entrepreneurs are being carried to their positions of wealth and power by forces which tend to destabilise the capital base of the corporate sector. Institutional shareholders no longer have a longterm commitment to the companies they own. . . . [I]t does not augur well for the future of Australian business—or the rest of Australia—that its ultimate owners, the banks and financial institutions, have so little commitment to it.[35]

Events have proved the wisdom of these concerns, although even Uren did not maintain them consistently. He was later to write much more gung-ho material for *Business Review Weekly*.

It might be said that Australian business has enclosed itself within the mythologies of 'Australianness' before now. That is certainly true. Paul James has traced the 'new nationalism' in Australian corporate advertising back to, at least, the 1960s and such campaigns as Esso's 'Energy for Australia'.[36] The use of the available discourses of nationalism by BP, Utah and other multinational companies probably require little explication. The Australian Association of National Advertisers ran a seminar for the industry on the value of nationalism in corporate advertising in 1981, reinforcing my hunch that the last decade has exploited this tactic to an unprecedented degree.[37] James also notes that there have been occasions when business and government have cooperated in joint programs of nation formation to effect economic change: the Advance Australia campaign of the Project Australia committee in 1979 is one example.

The enclosure of the corporate sector within discourses of the nation, then, is not new. What *is* new in this case is the comprehensiveness of the discursive regime within which the meaning of the larrikin capitalists was constructed (it went way beyond corporate advertising, for instance, as it became the common sense of a wide range of media representations), and the nature of the discourses selected: the chauvinistic larrikinism of these entrepreneurs, their *lack* of responsibility, were the very things used to recommend them to the population as familiar and appropriate cultural icons.[38]

Reviewing the media's performance as it constructed this homology between an aggressive entrepreneurial business ethic and conventional definitions of the Australian character, one has to be struck by the lack of any dissenting voice or competing definitions. Of course, it almost goes without saying that the world view of the large, highly diversified media institutions and that of big business are sufficiently equivalent that it is pointless to accuse the media of bias towards business; they *are* business. Nevertheless, one is also struck by the apparent arbitrariness of this national campaign of hero-worship, an arbitrariness which is exposed when we see how easily the media jumped off the bandwagon when it finally ran off the road. As the effects of the stockmarket crash of 1987 began to bite, and as individual entrepreneurs were held to account by public instrumentalities such as the Australian Broadcasting Tribunal or one of the rash of royal commissions, the same scribes who salivated over risk-taking entrepreneurialism now surreptitiously wiped their chins in the name of corporate responsibility. The media were entirely complicit in the excesses of the eighties, as everything they needed to say about Bond and the others—but didn't—was there for them to say right from the beginning. In the next section, I want to develop this theme by following the way in which Alan Bond was built up and then knocked down by media representations—none of them true, perhaps, and maybe none of them entirely wrong, either, but all of them serving interests other than those of the nation.

Bond-ing

The biggest thing since peace in 1945: triumph unites nation.
(Headline in the *Sydney Morning Herald*, 28 September 1983, on the winning of the America's Cup)

They said you'd never make it
We've seen you guys before
No-one's ever goin' to take it
It stays bolted to the floor
They said you'd never make it
But you dreamed of other things
You were sailing for Australia
With a boat that sails on wings
They said you'd never make it
But you finally came through

For all of you who've made it
This Swan's made for you
(Swan beer commercial, 1986)

Donald Horne once observed that the America's Cup has a lot to answer for. I think I know what he means. The Cup licensed more than its share of misguided rhetoric which legitimised the larrikin capitalists and protected business and the banks from closer scrutiny, thus making the 1980s worse than they might otherwise have been for Australia. That said, it is possible still to feel pleasure at the memory of the win; the series exploited its dramatic potential to the hilt by having the result hinge on the final race. It was especially easy to be wholeheartedly nationalistic in this instance because the old fogies from the New York Yacht Club did everything in their power to represent themselves as mean-spirited guardians of Old World traditions barely able to control their distaste for the uncouth upstarts from Down Under. Given the participatory glow experienced by many Australians, it is easy to see how we might have failed to notice how orgiastic the media treatment of the Cup was at the time. To go back over the press reports as the Cup campaign reached its business end (not an inappropriate metaphor in this case) is to discover how vigorously and explicitly the contest was promoted as a national enterprise.

It is hard to think of a sporting contest which has been as obsessively dealt with by the Australian media (although Sydney 2000 looks set to outdo it). Even before the finals series began, the story had moved from the sports to the news pages. The *Australian* provided a liftout supplement to preview the races, and announced its support in a front page headline on 14 September: 'We're all with you, Australia II'. The finals were the subject of news reports, detailed coverage in the sports pages, feature articles, cartoons, letters and numerous editorials. The *Australian*, in particular, seems to have decided that this was one sporting event it could get fully behind: yachting's old money elitism and longstanding connection with business made the sport more consonant with the paper's market demographics than was, say, the Australian Rugby League team. By the time the finals got under way, the paper was running a flash on the front page beneath its masthead announcing 'The *Australian*: Proudly Sponsoring Australia II'. The *Australian* was also notable for the extent to which it made the race a major concern for its editorial writers: they devoted an editorial to the contest immediately before the final series began, three during the series, and two after the win. To the suggestion that this might have

30

been a touch excessive—a suggestion which did turn up from time to time in the letters pages—the editorial of 26 September had this response:

> For a few it has become tediously trendy to deny interest in the America's Cup. 'Just millionaire's [sic] playing with their toys' is in most cases followed by other cliches from a pseudo-socialist philosophy. Such people seem to have lost their common touch. A taxi-driver, as good a yardstick as any to measure public interest, hopes Australia II wins the America's Cup.

It went on to quote this taxi-driver's opinions *verbatim*. The *Age*, obviously in the hands of pseudo-socialists lacking the common touch, ran a cartoon which depicted a couple watching the race on TV and sympathising with the underdog while behind them a jackboot steps on East Timor, but such countervailing representations were few in the lead-up to the Australian victory.

When the victory occurred (28 September 1983), the newspapers went completely gaga. The *Australian* ran its famous headline 'Yes, we can do anything if we try'—a little unfair in its implication that previous challengers hadn't really been trying—and placed the roman numeral II beside its masthead's map of Australia. The victory occupied the whole front page, four further news pages inside, and an eight page 'souvenir' liftout. The *Sydney Morning Herald* used the headline 'The Cup Comes Down Under' for its front page, reserving the most hyperbolic headline of the day for inside: 'The biggest thing since peace in 1945: triumph unites nation'. The *SMH* also provided a souvenir liftout, and covered the story with an editorial, news reports and business reports. The *Age* finally climbed on board with 'How We Won the Cup' as its headline, several pages of news stories, a Bond retrospective, a business report and an editorial. The *Age's* editorial was perhaps the most explicit in its depiction of this sporting achievement as the culmination of 'a courageous, innovative and well-organised industrial campaign'.

There is a remarkable consistency in the discourses used to construct the meaning of the America's Cup victory in the national press. Routinely and syllogistically, Bond becomes a metaphor for the typical Australian so that the win might be hailed as a vindication of essential Australian virtues, and these virtues are located uniformly in the new Australian entrepreneurs. (Of course, these typical Australian virtues and these Australian entrepreneurs are all male; the discourses of national character in play here routinely and unashamedly privilege the masculine.) Despite the invocation of

31

typicality, however, Alan Bond himself is represented in relatively complicated ways. There is no attempt to hide his pugnacious, driven style. Indeed, this is seen as contributing to his success: 'this aggressive, 45 year old self-made millionaire prides himself on being able to succeed where others have failed'.[39] His business history is given the most positive gloss:

> 'We're the "Mission Impossible" people' Bond said recently of his business. 'I am a specialist at regenerating a company. We buy companies that are run down. We put management in and fix them. We take on difficult problems'.[40]

No need to guess where Ben Elton got his idea for *Stark*. Bond's 'masterminding' of the whole 'industrial campaign' is variously 'Churchillian' and 'Napoleonic'.[41] Bond's individualism and egoism, however, are the more macho aspects of a figure who in most other respects is seen to be an ordinary, entirely patriotic, Australian man.

Bond is seamlessly stitched into the national character, his 'Australianness' discovered in his larrikinism, his egalitarianism and his humble social origins. The *Australia II* designer Ben Lexcen admired Bond's deliberate goading of the old fogies from the NYYC: 'Bond is like a kid running a stick along a wire fence with a bunch of mad dogs behind it. He really knows how to stir these guys'.[42] In a widely quoted instance, Bond refused to accept gifts of Rolex watches offered to his crew members unless everyone in the whole team—even his 'lonely sailmaker'—received one. When Bond refuses to be disheartened at the loss of the first two races, the Anzac spirit is invoked and, in the process, history undergoes a major revision. 'Australians are known for fighting with their backs to the wall at Gallipoli', he said. 'We won that one, so don't count us out yet'.[43] Even this liberty with history is forgiven, as 'merely the symptom of Bond's boundless optimism, bred by the spaces and riches of WA'.[44] As to his humble origins, typical is the *Australian's* 26 September editorial during the finals series—headlined 'America's Cup: Australia's bond'—which celebrated the national unity forged through the heroic efforts of 'two people, Alan Bond and Ben Lexcen . . . [the] former apprentice signwriter from Perth [and former] railways boilermaker . . . from the backblocks of NSW'. Finally, any inconsistencies in the press portraits were used to signify Bond's creativity and unconventionality—thus identifying him with a whole range of creative and unconventional developments in sport and business over the eighties, from the winged keel to Australian accounting.

The conflation of sporting and business success we see in the *Age* editorial is evident in all the editorials of 28 September 1983. The connection was so unquestioned, it would seem, that even the *Financial Review* had the story on its front page and dealt with it in the editorial. There is very little difference between the *Financial Review*'s treatment of the meaning of the event and that of the mainstream press. While the editorial admitted that yachting was a rich man's sport, there was something in this for all Australians. It was the 'risk-taking capitalist buccaneers like Bond who generated employment for Australians on the dole. If other entrepreneurs were as bold as Bond then the economy would work to the benefit of every Australian'.[45]

There is, of course, no reason why Alan Bond or anybody else connected with *Australia II* should have been seen as essentially 'Australian' characters. That they were constructed as such, however, changed the meaning of the race from being 'millionaires playing with their toys' to an event of national significance. One needs to ask in whose interest this meaning worked; there is no doubt that it was of great assistance to Alan Bond in his business dealings, for instance, and it was widely exploited by Bond Corp after the event. Indeed, it is impossible not to be impressed by the comprehensive success of Bond's 'nationalisation'. The mythic connection between Bond, *Australia II* and the national character was so culturally embedded within a year or two of the victory that *Australia II* had become a staple component of the image bank for nationalistic advertisements. When arguments about a new Australian flag came up for their periodic airing in the mid-1980s, the boat's boxing kangaroo emblem was mentioned as a candidate. Indeed, so widespread was the appropriation of the boxing kangaroo as an Australian icon, that Bond Corp had to bear down hard on its copyright and merchandising rights.

The media construction was not just mythic, it was also narrative. The story of Bond and the America's Cup, as told and retold throughout the eighties, is that of the self-made Australian armed with determination and ingenuity taking on the world and winning. The prize is not just the Cup, but the achievement of continuous upward mobility[46]—the reward for persisting and overcoming the pessimism of the 'knockers'. This narrative structures Bond's Swan Lager advertisements: the 'They said you'd never make it' promotions. Here the mythic linkage between business and the Australian character is constructed with a shameless literalness in order to sell more of Bond's beer.[47]

Alan Bond in heroic
mode with Webber's
portrait of Captain
Cook.

We have only to look at what has happened to the image of
Alan Bond since the late 1980s to see how bogus all of this was.
Far from being a paragon of Australian virtues, Bond is now
routinely disowned; his 'meanings' are now articulated by way of
an explicit disconnection between what he is and what Australians
are. (Significantly, Bruce Stannard's last-ditch attempt to redefine
Bond in a positive way was titled, 'The Big Aussie Battler'.[48]) From
being merely a 'tottering tycoon' or the 'wheeler and dealer who
could not stop'[49] he came to be seen as a threat to the freedom of
the press, an unfit person to hold a media licence and finally
someone whose withdrawal from public and corporate life was
applauded by key writers within the financial press. Bond's and
Australia's interests were no longer synonymous. Tom O'Regan has
pointed out that, in 1988, 10 per cent of the national external debt
was due to the borrowings of this one man; while Jim McKay claims
that Bond Corp owes Australian banks more than $15 billion, or the
equivalent of $700 for every Australian.[50] It took the business press
a long time to accept such judgements, but eventually the full cast

of Bond's admirers had to publicly dissociate themselves from him. The reaction to Paul Barry's 1993 *Four Corners* report on Bond's evasion of the constraints of bankruptcy suggests that many Australians are outraged that Bond has not been punished in some way for his exploits.

This reversal did not happen overnight. Even during 1987, when Bond's movement into television, the acquisition of an interest in Chile's telephone industry, the extraordinary ignorance of the public interest obligations of electronic media proprietors revealed in a Jana Wendt interview about alleged payments to Sir Joh Bjelke-Petersen, and finally the stock market crash, all invited commentators to take a more circumspect look at Bond Corp, he survived media scrutiny. In their review of the effects of the crash of 1987, Bond's committed fans at *Business Review Weekly* made an extraordinary misjudgement in suggesting that Bond would survive the crash better than most.[51] The starstruck admiration for the successful businessman so endemic in the business press continued to support Bond throughout this period.[52]

Tony Champ's cartoon accompanied a newspaper article on Bond's bankruptcy. (courtesy the *Sunday Mail* and Tony Champ)

In 1988, however, the tide finally began to turn. This was the year of the Australian Broadcasting Tribunal (ABT) inquiry which eventually found that Bond was not a 'fit and proper' person to hold a television licence. While the business press generally still supported him for most of this year, the *Australian* and *Times on Sunday* ran particularly tough pieces on Bond's business holdings, his disregard for the proceedings of the ABT and his lack of interest in the human rights record of his business connections in Chile. Daily newspapers of the time are peppered with bad news for Alan Bond. The ABT hearings and the debacle over Bond's takeover of Castlemaine XXXX, which eventually destroyed that company's Queensland monopoly and opened the way for the product of a new company (Powers) to emerge as the local beer, revealed Bond as a bullying figure, contemptuous of his public responsibilities. Even at the *Business Review Weekly* we hear some rumblings,[53] the first sounds of a role model being dismantled.

I am not going to map the decline of Bond's fortunes much further here; Paul Barry's *The Rise and Fall of Alan Bond*[54] has done that in far more detail than I need for my argument. Suffice it to say that, as the tide of revisionism gathered, the ABT hearings seem to provide the impetus for Bond's final discrediting. Bond recognised this, and fought the tribunal and its findings with great determination, meanwhile giving interviews to old supporters like Bruce Stannard as a means of publicising his concern at the way the media were treating him. One can understand his surprise at the categoric collapse of his standing with the media. It is hard to explain their abandonment of Bond simply in terms of their having finally learnt the 'truth' about him and the instability of his business empire; 'the truth' had always been there and it had never influenced the media's judgement before.

My suspicion is that Bond begins to receive a different kind of media attention once he becomes a major media proprietor with the purchase of Kerry Packer's Channel 9. As Bond stops being a media creature and threatens to become a media player of a particularly ruthless mould the media turn on him, partly in self-defence. Editorials in the *Australian* and the *Sydney Morning Herald* attack Bond for abusing his public responsibility as a TV licensee, for his 'contempt for the wishes of the Australian community'.[55] *BRW* has to be dragged kicking and screaming (its list of the top businessmen in 1988 includes Bond and still talks of him as a 'role model'), but eventually it too sings along with a hard-edged critique of the structure of Bond Corp.[56] The month of

April 1989 is a shocker for Bond. The *Bulletin* attacks Bond on three fronts in three consecutive weeks,[57] the *Four Corners* story on Bond's tax shelters goes to air, the ABT finally tables its report, and the battle with Tiny Rowlands gets even tougher. More is to come, of course, with WA Inc around the corner.

By this time, there was no turning back and the columnists and editorial writers raced to disconnect themselves from Bond. Paul Barry published his account of Bond's 'love affair with other people's money', *The Rise and Fall of Alan Bond*, in 1990; and by 1991 even Channel 9's *Sixty Minutes* was sure enough of its brief to denounce its former boss. Probably the most interesting example, and certainly the most complete demolition, came in Frank Robson's piece in the *Weekend Australian*.[58] Here the meaning of Bond is mercilessly pried loose from all that represents Australianness. Interviews with old school friends and former business associates reveal the kind of details which are humbling by their very banality: Robson even tracks down someone who was reputed to have defeated Bond in a school fight! Bond emerges as a boaster and a dobber (and a poor fighter) at school; as a fledgeling entrepreneur, we are told, his lust for the deal could get out of control, causing him to 'dribble with enthusiasm'; he is accused of disloyalty to his mates and of cheating on his wife;[59] some say the America's Cup was primarily a strategy for breaking into business's big league . . . and on it goes. By the end there is little left of Alan Bond, role model for Australia.

It should be said that without the hero-worship in the first place the reputation of Alan Bond would not have needed to be destroyed like this. It is hard not to be contemptuous of the hypocrisy generating the high moral tone adopted by many journalists when they finally decided to attack Bond. For Bond, who admittedly seems to have been happy to see himself as the model of the new Australia just seven years earlier, it must have been hard to stomach such attacks; for example:

> It needs to be said upfront and without the slightest qualification, that the collapse and consequent removal of Alan Bond from public and corporate life in Australia is entirely appropriate, and indeed desirable. . . Bond Corp is . . . exactly the sort of enterprise we do not . . . want in our society.[60]

This was written in 1990, by which time Bond was simply one among many 'tottering tycoons'. With the revelations of the operations of WA Inc and the collapse of state banking enterprises in Victoria and South Australia, and with the exploits of high-flying entrepreneurs such as Skase and Connell looking more criminal than courageous, the whole fantasy of larrikin capitalism had started to unwind. Those same editorial writers who had jumped on the bandwagon at the beginning of the 1980s were quick to point the moral finger—although even at this juncture the real lessons about the limits of capitalism's social conscience appear not to have been learned:

> The fall of high-fliers is not necessarily a sign of bad times for the economy. . . The roaring pre-crash market for a brief time created the illusion that there was a free lunch, that is, vast profits at little risk. The illusion has been shattered, and that ultimately is likely to be good for the economy.[61]

Once again, anything that is good for the economy can't be all bad!

After excess

The streets these days are full of cockroaches and most of them are human. Every man has a right to protect his family, himself and his possessions. To live in peace and safety. Sanctuary Cove is an island of civilisation in a violent world, and we have taken steps to ensure it remains so. (Advertisement for the exclusive residential estate, Sanctuary Cove, 1987)

Larrikin capitalism was indeed, in Ben Elton's phrase, 'scorched earth capitalism'. Manufacturing industries were destroyed by asset stripping, the media industries were run so far into debt that the prospects of their remaining in Australian hands were drastically reduced, foreign debt in the private sector ballooned out without achieving any significant productive investment outcomes, and the shareholders of Bond Corp, Bell, Quintex, Westpac and many others must still rue the day they put their trust in their company directors. While all of this worked against the interests of the vast majority of Australians, that small group with direct access to business profits or who benefited from the explosion in executive salaries did rather better. Rather than an heroic enterprise in the national interest, larrikin capitalism was elitist, viciously individualist, uncomplicatedly avaricious.

At its most naked, larrikin capitalism was proud of such an ethic. In the advertisement quoted at the head of this section,

Queensland property developer Mike Gore founded his pitch on the premise that those who had money would now want to avoid having anything to do with those who didn't. Sanctuary Cove was the ultimate enclave for successful Australian capitalists, fittingly decked out as a sportsperson's heaven with its Yacht Squadron, golf courses and tennis courts, and boasting the one acquisition no Australian entrepreneur could be without, its own brewery! Sanctuary Cove went so far as to set itself up as an alternative location to the nation; its advertising had Mike Gore as a latter day Captain Cook sailing in to take possession. Gore threw his own Bicentennial bash—the 'Ultimate Event' consisting of the Ultimate Golf tournament, the Ultimate Tennis tournament, the Ultimate Bowls(!) tournament, the Ultimate Airshow, all capped off by the Ultimate Concert starring Ol' Blue Eyes himself. While it was not the Ultimate Success, it was an event made for the media and thus an effective means of advertising Mike Gore's 'vision'. Not everyone was blind to its contradictions, however; John McManamy found the experience of taking part in the Ultimate Event distinctly uncomfortable: 'Here we were in a so-called egalitarian society', he said, 'celebrating privilege'.[62]

Also contradictory was the media construction of the persona of Mike Gore. Despite the nature of his enterprise, Gore—like Bond and so many others—was represented as if he were the typical egalitarian Australian man. Roughly spoken, beer-gutted and white-shoed, Gore looked like most other Gold Coast real estate wheeler dealers and thus passed for an ordinary 'self-made' Australian with the national press. Reporters overlooked the boofheaded redneckery of his 'vision' in order to install him as the latest in a long line of adventurous Australian enterpreneurs leading the rest of the world. Of course, there is little that is mythically or discursively 'Australian' about Sanctuary Cove, modelled as it is on the walled estates of the rich in the United States which rely on the power of money to protect their occupants from a predatory society, and looking as it does like a set for *Miami Vice*. Gore, though, certainly sounded Australian and that was good enough. Fortunately, and in a rare sign of the limits of the property market's flexibility, Mike Gore did overestimate Australians' elitism and eventually went broke; properties at Sanctuary Cove now sell for much less than the original price.

Among the more fundamental contradictions of larrikin capitalism—given the importance that discourses of nationalism assumed in its legitimation—was its anti-statism. It vigorously resisted the principle of government control of the economy in general (except for industry assistance, of course) and corporate affairs regulations in particular; national boundaries became irritating impediments to the free play of the market. As Australian business becomes less distinguishable from transnational business in an increasingly globalised market, its interests and those of the nation-state must come increasingly into conflict. The crucial fact about the excesses of the eighties is that this progressively more tenuous relationship between the interests of big business and those of the Australian people was comprehensively masked. It was masked precisely by the bonding I have been describing—a bonding between the individual entrepreneur and the discourses of national character which established at the level of representation a commonality of interests that existed at no other level.

The consequences have not just been temporary. There has been a radical redistribution of wealth in Australia over the last ten years and, despite all the public recanting, business has made real gains in extricating itself from state control. As Pusey points out, notwithstanding the censorious rhetoric that has accompanied the recognition of the mistakes of the eighties, 'the state now has a much reduced capacity to control Australian business or to compensate and protect its population from further predatory attacks'.[63] And among the reasons for this is the way nationalism was used against the national interest by an alliance of the media and the larrikin capitalists.

3

A taste of the colonial birch: the British connection

Our choice of lawyer Malcolm Turnbull for the 1987 Business Award may seem a little obscure, but of course it isn't. (Business Review Weekly, 11.12.1987)

Making it legal: Malcolm Turnbull and the *Spycatcher* trials

Business is not the only domain in which the national character was invoked for personal gain in the 1980s. This first section of the chapter takes as its starting point the rise to prominence of Sydney lawyer Malcolm Turnbull during his conduct of author Peter Wright's defence in the *Spycatcher* trials. I see this as an illuminating moment of convergence—where the meanings of business, the law and the national character merge into each other. What follows is initially an extension of the case developed in Chapter 2, in that it demonstrates how the media representations of these trials and Turnbull's celebrity were framed overwhelmingly in nationalist terms. Further, it demonstrates how these nationalist representations routinely defined 'the Australian' in opposition to 'the British'. I will focus on this binary relationship in the second and third sections of this chapter in discussing another legal contest between representatives of Britain and Australia—the Royal Commission into the Maralinga atomic weapons tests.

First, to business, the law and *Spycatcher*. In late 1993, as I write this, with Alan Bond having already been in and out of gaol, Laurie Connell facing trial on race-fixing charges, the National Crime

Authority allegedly in hot pursuit of John Elliott, and newspaper editorial writers now sounding like models of commercial probity, one might think that the law is cleaning up the mess created by business and the banks during the 1980s. It should be remembered, though, that this mess was at least partly due to the inadequacies of Australian company law—and to the shrewdness with which some members of the legal profession exploited these inadequacies to benefit their clients, while regularly modifying their own practices to head off criminal investigation. The activities of some of Australia's corporate lawyers over the last decade have been just as dodgy as the activities of some of Australia's accountants. It now seems that when foreign bankers were characterised by the Australian business media as fuddy-duddy traditionalists who had failed to keep up with the times because 'they didn't understand our accounting systems', this was incorrect; foreign bankers' failure to understand our accounting was occasioned not by their bewilderment at its complexity but by their astonishment that it could be considered within the law. Similarly, foreign regulatory agencies' failure to prevent asset-stripping takeovers by Australian entrepreneurs was often taken as evidence of their old-fashioned legalism, as giving the iconoclastic Australians a competitive edge. Far from being seen as necessary constraints upon the excesses of larrikin capitalism, the remaining legal impediments to the free play of the market were, as we saw in the previous chapter, blamed for Australia's failure to respond to the challenges of an internationalised economy.[1]

Larrikin capitalism should not be cut adrift from its crucial relationship with the law and lawyers: it was enabled by legal advice which ignored the law's public (in favour of its commercial) responsibilities and by legal structures which were not up to the task of protecting the public interest. If there is one overriding feeling that most of us experience as we witness the ritual trials now dealing with 'failed businessmen', it is frustration with a legal system that can so easily protect the rights of those who exploited their shareholders and their fellow taxpayers while it so categorically fails to protect the rights of their victims. In my view, this frustration is further fuelled by evidence that no longer is the law a set of limits on business, and thus still relatively autonomous. The law has now become almost encapsulated *within* the domain of business: as if our legal system and its functionaries are themselves yet another *effect*—like the health and education systems—of a rationalistically conceived economy. In this context, then, and as the legal aid system haemorrhages to death, the law has become yet another domain appropriated from and then denied to the vast majority of the population who are the subjects of this ever-narrowing circle of capital and power.

In the washup to the 1980s, the contradiction that arises between the law's public responsibility to protect the national interest and its specific responsibility to serve clients who were no longer intent on acting in the national interest has not so far been highlighted—except perhaps in relation to the WA Inc Royal Commission. The very technicality of the law as a professional practice has protected it, I suspect, from the close scrutiny directed towards its clients—although this should change if the proposed introduction of fully commercial competition occurs. I also suspect that the legal profession has so far managed to maintain its identification with the national interest, despite its implication in the excesses of the 1980s, more successfully than its clients have managed to do. While the cracks might be there,[2] the authority of the law—even corporate law—does not seem to have sustained any significant damage. In what follows I want to deal with one instance in which we can see how the law's cultural meaning, in this instance and at this time, was constructed. With the *Spycatcher* case, the profession of the law—or more correctly one of its members—had available to it the Bond route: it was offered some territory upon which it could represent itself in the image of the national character.

The mid-1980s trials over ex–MI5 agent Peter Wright's memoirs, *Spycatcher*, started out as a pretty forlorn effort by the publishers, Heinemann, to head off the British government's curiously bloody-minded attempt to prohibit publication in Australia as well as in Britain. The strategy adopted by Peter Wright's Australian defence was twofold: one, to maintain that the book contained no information that had not already been published in other spy memoirs; and, two, that the British government had no right to prevent the publication of a book in Australia. This latter argument, ultimately about the British government's failure to acknowledge Australian sovereignty, was the one most eagerly taken up in the media and provided the dominant flavour for the goings-on in court.

These ended up as high farce, in which Wright's Australian lawyer, the young Malcolm Turnbull, baited and tormented a string of Sir Humphrey–like British Civil Service types. The hearings increasingly acquired the atmosphere of an Ashes series between the two nations, and was described through the media in ways that placed the Australian/Peter Wright/*Spycatcher* team on the side of truth, democracy, humour and fair play while placing the British government/anti-*Spycatcher* team on the side of secrecy, privilege and stuffy meanness of spirit. It was 'Bodyline' all over again. Even Mr Justice Powell, on the bench, seemed to see the trial in these terms, ironically referring to his status as 'a lowly colonial judge' sitting in judgement on Her Majesty's government. Once it became clear that there was a populist and anti-British spin to be put on the whole affair, the editorial writers got involved:

> It would appear that in Britain there has been too much secrecy for too long. From the 1930s, Britain's security services were devastatingly penetrated by a group of Cambridge-educated homosexual Marxists who rendered invaluable service to the Soviets. This compromise of British intelligence also compromised the intelligence of Britain's allies.[3]

This editorial from the *Australian* ended up asking if British government secrecy provisions only operated effectively when suppressing information about the failure of secrecy provisions.

In Britain, the coverage of the trials took on a very high profile. Dramatisations of the trial were telecast daily, playing out the colonial melodrama to the full. The British were treated to a selection of the 'funniest, wittiest, and most ironic one-liners to emerge from the transcripts' (this is how the *Australian* put it), within the unique spectacle of an Australian court's 'casual modernity'—a modernity which included female court officials![4] The villain in this melodrama, 'portrayed as a cheeky hotshot with a nasty glint in his eye', was Turnbull. Turnbull was depicted in a similar manner in the Australian print media—we were denied the television dramatisation—and not surprisingly hit a responsive chord. He became something of a local hero, the irreverent and witty champion of Australian interests against those of the British government.

The Australian media's treatment of Turnbull over the course of the trial and again upon the subsequent publication of his book, *The Spycatcher Trial* (Heinemann, 1988), was shamelessly mythologising. Interviewed after Justice Powell had found in his favour, Turnbull showed admirable modesty—'you win some and you lose some'—but the *Sydney Morning Herald* was not to be put off. Turnbull's impeccable credentials as an Australian nationalist were wheeled out: 'his ancestors came to Australia as free settlers in 1802, building the first Presbyterian church in the country'. And a personal history of resistance to British stuffiness emerged from the story about Turnbull's response to the English vicar who had refused to perform the marriage ceremony for Turnbull and his wife-to-be, Lucy Hughes:

> Mr Turnbull said the Anglican vicar wondered why he should marry a non-practising Presbyterian (Turnbull) and a non-practising Catholic (Hughes). Mr Turnbull explained that it was the vicar's duty, as the agent of the State Church, to discourage and, if possible, to prevent fornication outside marriage.[5]

This story was widely used across the media, as were a number of exchanges between Turnbull and Sir Robert Armstrong, universally regarded as the decent but hapless fall guy for the Thatcher government. Turnbull's apparent lack of deference to the British officials and their counsel was read as a sign of nationalist independence:

> [W]hen faced with an attitude from some members of the opposition of, 'he's only a young man from the colonies, don't worry about him', Turnbull proved them wrong. He treated them with an almost healthy disrespect and also proved that the Australian system is no longer dependent on the mother country'.[6]

Clearly, Turnbull must have supported this image by feeding stories to the press. It should be said, though, that the press needed little assistance to produce their own characteristic hyperbole. 'Who, then', asked the *Weekend Australian*, 'is this most accomplished of younger Australians?':

> Who is this Jack to the Thatcher giant, this previously little-known Sydney lawyer who humiliated Whitehall's most powerful mandarin, Sir Robert Armstrong, and who has been described by some British commentators as a potential future prime minister of Australia?[7]

As the cultural cringe of that last clause suggests, in Turnbull we had found yet another example—like Alan Bond a few years earlier—of an Australian who could show 'them' (Britain, America, the world) that we were not to be underestimated. As with the larrikin capitalists, Turnbull was quickly claimed as a champion of Australianness because he made the rest of the world sit up and take notice.[8] Turnbull's cheek, his apparently cheery refusal to take his battle with Armstrong personally, his history of 'audacious challenges to authority' (as one account of the vicar story described it) and the depth of his ancestors' roots in Australian history all characterised the lawyer as the classic Australian male hero— shrewd, witty, egalitarian and world-class.

The highpoint in Turnbull's popular celebrity coincided with his receipt of the *Business Review Weekly's* award for Businessman of the Year. As the magazine's editorial of 11 December 1987 acknowledged, however, the relations between law and business were not entirely explicit; to some, the editorial suggested, the choice of a lawyer may have seemed 'a little obscure'. But the award provided an occasion for a clarification of the relationship. While the legal profession should be considered as part of 'the services sector', the editorial went on, there were deeper reasons for establishing the connection that Turnbull's award proposed:

> We are accustomed to seeing the parades of QCs, junior counsels and teams of solicitors at important cases of corporate litigation. On page 55 we explain how Turnbull and his wife Lucy went about beating the Thatcher Government in the *Spycatcher* book litigation. Turnbull told the audience [at his presentation] on Monday evening that in this case his opponents were overmanned, with him battling between eight and 16 expensive lawyers at different times. There are inefficiencies in all areas of business, and Turnbull singled out the legal profession as one where business could cut its costs.

The editorial's account of Turnbull's speech continued to develop this analogy between the efficiency of legal businesses and Australian business in general. Turnbull's success at law exemplified how Australian business might become more competitive and efficient in the era following the stockmarket crash of 1987. And in case the reader still felt that there were principles of law which were not entirely consonant with those at work in business, Turnbull's closing aphorism was recommended to us: 'just as freedom of speech is important (for the press), the ability to think laterally and challenge ideas is important to business. Freedom is the companion to efficiency'.

It is tempting to reveal how constructed this local hero image was by referring back to Turnbull's relatively patrician past. However, one only needs to move forward a few years to a point when Turnbull's reputation is more closely bound up with that of the corporate world—he went on to set up a merchant bank with Nicholas Whitlam, among other ventures, and continued his association with Kerry Packer—to see another set of representations applied. In the *Good Weekend* published with the *Age* and the *Sydney Morning Herald* on 13 April 1991 we again find Turnbull as the subject of a major story—the cover story, in fact. Times, however, have changed: by 1991 the business practices of the eighties have become discredited, Turnbull himself is seen to have profited from those practices, and his local hero status is fast fading from memory. The story now is a very different one for the press and as a result the meanings given to Malcolm Turnbull are radically different too.

The cover photo is intimidating: Turnbull leaning aggressively over a desk, unsmiling and threatening. The headline: 'Malcolm Turnbull—Humility Is For Saints'. Inside, it is Turnbull's complexity, volatility and personal power that form the subject:

> Suddenly. He can turn. The charmer becomes the menacer, the defender of freedom of speech its most sophisticated challenger. He laughs, and disarms, but always be on guard. Malcolm Turnbull, at 36, is one of the most powerful lawyers in Australia, and inspires a wide range of feelings among those who know him.
>
> 'He's a prick', says ex-business partner Nicholas Whitlam, who says he is being restrained in what he says so as not to fuel an ongoing feud.
>
> 'He's wonderful, kind, generous and warm and friendly', says actor Kate Fitzpatrick, a longtime friend.
>
> 'He's a turd', says former Labor senator Jim McClelland. 'He's easy to loathe, he's a shit, he'd devour anyone for breakfast, he's on the make, he's cynical, he's offensively smug. He's a good exploiter of publicity, although I applauded the way he ran *Spycatcher* against Margaret Thatcher.' [9]

No longer is Turnbull the simply explicable local hero, with the history of resisting British authority, who championed Peter Wright on behalf of all Australians—a symbol of national independence. In this article, he is complex and frightening: a symbol of the combination of law and commercial power that I have suggested is one of the legacies of the eighties.

Of course, there is no reason to see this portrait as any more 'accurate' than those which preceded or have followed it. Nevertheless, the Malcolm Turnbull we encounter in the media these days is a much more contradictory—and thus more plausible—character than the one we met during the *Spycatcher* hearings. On the one hand, for instance, Turnbull turns up as an eloquent and committed spokesperson for the republican movement; here, clearly, his *Spycatcher* credentials have paid off. On the other hand, in 1992, when two local representatives were 'encouraged to resign' from the board of Bond University in order to make room for representatives of the Japanese owners, EIE, it was widely alleged that Turnbull convinced the locals to depart. One thing is clear, however: with the temporary exception of his work on Keating's Republican Advisory Committee, Turnbull's activities now are more easily understood as being within the sphere of business, rather than the law. The transition has been completed.

The media-constructed persona of Malcolm Turnbull operated as a site at which a whole range of interests and discourses converged: those of commercial law, the public good, the entrepreneurial spirit of Australian business, the larrikin•essence of the masculine national character. This convergence interests me because, at particular moments, it elevated those placed within its protective circle above criticism. Turnbull himself is probably only interesting inasmuch as his public career shows how effortlessly media constructions can temporarily produce this kind of mythological status; more symptomatically, however, he remains a supremely clear example of what has become a worrying but largely unchallenged partnership between law and business.

The British connection

It is self-evident now, in Britain and in Australia, that Australian courts are better than English courts. British courts on this matter were sycophantic. They yielded to the executive. The same applies to the British press. Whatever we say about our courts and our newspapers, there can be no doubt when it comes to political subjects that Australian courts and newspapers are freer than English courts and newspapers. (Gough Whitlam, launching Malcolm Turnbull's *The Spycatcher Trial*)

In the *Spycatcher* case, Australia's national interest was defined primarily in opposition to that of Britain. Just as interest is generated for an Ashes series by the promoters' exaggeration of 'traditional rivalries', or just as Australian narratives routinely pit an Australian working class hero against a British aristocratic system to produce a nationalist response (think of the films *Gallipoli*, *Breaker Morant*, and TV's *Bodyline*), the public notoriety of this legal battle was a direct result of its representation as a nationalist contest against the British. The opposition also structured the contest's meaning in the United Kingdom. Just as Turnbull's aggressive challenging of British authority assured his heroic status in the Australian press, the stoic behaviour of his British adversary, Sir Robert Armstrong, won admirers in Britain. When Sir Robert Armstrong returned home after being forced to admit to an Australian court that he had been a little 'economical with the truth' (but not exactly whom his economy had been protecting), the British *Mail on Sunday* hailed him as a hero:

It should be an occasion for national celebration that Sir Robert Armstrong is back with us again—alive and well. Though it's far from clear whom he was protecting and why, the fact is that he stepped ashore upon a foreign field to fight the good fight on behalf of us all. Viciously assailed by native tribesmen, he held up high, however tattered it eventually became, the flag of this country.

Sir Robert is indeed the stuff upon which the Empire was made— Gordon of Khartoum, Clive of India, Lawrence of Arabia—what mighty names and what mighty deeds they commemorate. Welcome to this pantheon of heroes, Armstrong of Sydney.[10]

It would be easy to regard Turnbull's temporary celebrity as the natural expression of an Australian nation irritated by the arrogance of the former colonial power overlooking the small matter of Australian sovereignty. Certainly the Australian media's interest in the whole affair was related to its potential to develop into a full-blown postcolonial battle along the lines of the uproar that occurred when Bob Hawke put his hand on the Queen's back, when Paul Keating did the same, or when Keating took the republican case to the Queen at Balmoral in 1993. There is, though, nothing natural about the expression of nationalism; it served particular interests at the time and was exploited skilfully by Turnbull himself as a means of winning his case and setting up his future career. Nevertheless, as fewer Australians have British ancestry now than ever before, and as the issue of Australian republicanism continues to grab headlines here and in Britain, it is worth pausing to consider the extent to which the British/Australian relation continues to be a defining force, an important discursive field within Australian popular culture.

In their analysis of Australian multiculturalism, *Mistaken Identity*, Castles, Cope, Kalantzis and Morrissey chart what they call the 'demise of nationalism in Australia'.[11] What multiculturalism has done, they argue, is to banish that 'traditional', unitary definition of the Australian national character which we would identify with Russel Ward's *Australian Legend* and which comes from a particularly narrow conception of an Australian way of life—Anglocentric, masculine, suburban–rural and so on. What assurances there might have been in a singular and representative 'Australian identity' before 1945 were swept aside in the waves of immigration after the war, and by the changing policy orientations of successive governments which have integrated the effects of these waves of

49

immigration into an officially pluralistic national identity. Within the consequent 'ambiguity and complexity', the authors suggest, the old nationalism is unsustainable.

The signification of a national identity is no longer a simple matter, *Mistaken Identity* argues—'the homely simplifications needed to make nationalism work are no longer plausible'. Admittedly, 'residual symbols and images are there, but they are overlaid by other inescapable realities'.[12] As the points I made in my opening chapter would indicate, I don't believe the evidence supports this. While much of *Mistaken Identity*'s general argument persuades me, this suggestion, coupled as it is with the naive view that because images and symbols stand for something else they are therefore not 'real', does not. As we shall see, it is *precisely* this simplifying procedure that is enacted in the media's representation of the events I have so far dealt with, and in the events I am about to take up.

Up to a point, of course, Castles et al. are right. Among the reasons why the old Anglo mythologies might be losing their purchase on the Australian imagination is the changing demography of the population who are the subject of that imagination. In 1945, Australia was an 'unusually homogeneous society', in which 90 per cent of the population were Australian-born and English-speaking.[13] Today, 40 per cent of Australians are immigrants or children of immigrants and half of these are of non-British origins.[14] And although these non-British immigrants still find that they must swear allegiance to the Queen of England when they take out their Australian citizenship, this is widely regarded as a ridiculous anomaly. Little wonder that a strategy aimed at defining Australian difference through comparison with the imperial power seems anachronistic to many non-Anglo Australians.

Cultural criticism which overstates the importance of the British influence on Australian popular culture today is likely to be seen as a hangover from the 1960s; and a generation that has grown up without even the memory of bonfires on Empire Day[15] is bound to view the British legacy differently from the way its elders do. Nevertheless, I find it impossible not to insist that certain events over the last decade have been overwhelmingly framed through nationalist representations and that prominent among the discursive strategies used in these representations has been the defining of 'Australianness' in opposition to 'Britishness'.

While Castles, Cope, Kalantzis and Morrissey generally question the contemporary importance of such traditional nation-defining tactics, they do admit their implication in current debates about

50

republicanism. Indeed, these authors' scepticism about the intellectual or political substance of the drive towards a republic derives exactly from their sense of its connection to arguments about the relations between Australia and Britain:

> [T]he justification for casting off the monarchy and the old flag is not separateness but the need to affirm that our future lies in another, non-British arena; not the assertion of primordially separate ethnicity, but the contrary assertion of an increasing ethnic pluralism which has created a distinct, non-British, national identity.[16]

Mistaken Identity is scathing about the limits of 'Keating republicanism'—'it involves no more than asking Mum to go and live in the national granny flat'[17]—but I think the authors are correct in placing the old colonialist relation at the centre of the matter. Doing this, however, does contradict the book's general position because it implicitly concedes the power of those anachronistic 'images and symbols' which elsewhere the book holds to be less important than other kinds of 'realities'. It is wise not to underestimate the power of images, of the way in which the meaning of everyday life is constructed through representation. While it seems undeniable that the influence of British values on most Australians' everyday lives has become ever more ghostly over the last thirty years, in media discourse the Australia/Britain opposition nevertheless continues to be wheeled in and operated as a means of making sense of Australian events, characters and stories.

That both these things may be true (that is, that the British connection is going but not yet gone) does not bother me here; I am happy to concede that culture is the product of its divisions and its contradictions. However, in the case I am about to outline, the consequences of specific instances of this method of representing the nation do bother me. As the present book repeatedly demonstrates, nationalist discourses do not necessarily serve the nation's interests. In the remainder of this chapter, I want to show how the meaning of the Maralinga Royal Commission was constructed through a set of 'homely simplifications'. These simplifications may not have exploited nationalist sympathies for personal gain—as was the case with Alan Bond and Malcolm Turnbull—but they actively, perhaps even deliberately, obscured the clarity with which the national interest, broadly conceived, could be understood and pursued.

A taste of the colonial birch: media representation of the Maralinga Royal Commission

> *[T]he aftermath of the tests, at one time a symbol of Anglo-Australian cooperation, has been to drive another nail into the coffin of Anglo-Australian friendship. The long tradition of Australian resentment at the seemingly superior and knowing attitude of the British, leading simple and trusting Australian manhood into danger, has been reinforced. Just as Gallipoli and the Bodyline controversy built up a deep feeling of righteous anger against the pom, so the nuclear tests today appear the epitome of cynical and arrogant British botching.* (Denys Blakeway and Sue Lloyd-Roberts, *Fields of Thunder: Testing Britain's Bomb*)

> *Could it happen again? Could an Australian government in the future ever be so grovelling before a 'great and powerful friend' as to risk damage to our land and our people in the insouciant way which came naturally to Menzies whenever the interests of the United Kingdom were concerned?* (Jim McClelland, *Stirring the Possum*)

At the end of June 1993, the Australian federal government accepted the British government's offer of $45 million towards the clean-up of the Maralinga and Emu nuclear test sites in South Australia. This was less than half the estimated $101 million cost of 'rehabilitating' the area, and contained no provision for compensation to Aboriginals or other victims of the long-term effects of the testing. (Aboriginal groups alone had claimed $45 million in compensation for the loss of their land.) The British government stressed that its contribution to the clean-up did not imply liability, nor readiness to consider claims for any further compensation. The *ex gratia* payment was accepted by the Australian government as a 'full and final settlement' of all Australian claims, but in a joint statement the Australian ministers involved insisted that the agreement implicitly endorsed Australia's view that the British government was morally and legally liable for the rehabilitation of the irradiated land.[18]

On the face of it, this could be regarded as implementation of recommendations of the report from the Royal Commission into the Maralinga tests. Britain was finally being made to pay. A number of factors refuse such a reading of the matter. Firstly, the payment is well short of the cost of the most minimal rehabilitation and stands in place of an acceptance of liability. Secondly, it comes after a long period of obstruction or, at best, inaction from our government on this issue—not a sustained and committed pursuit of justice. Thus one has to consider carefully whether the agreement might be intended to repair existing or control future damage. And thirdly, the figure chosen would seem to indicate that the financial liability for the clean-up was to be shared more or less equally between Australia and Britain. If this constitutes the final achievement of the Royal Commission there is little reason to celebrate. The 1993 settlement, though, is just the most recent footnote to the matters dealt with in the remainder of this chapter—although its implications will be considerably amplified by what follows. In the following discussion, I examine how the Australian media gave the work of the Maralinga Royal Commission its dominant meaning: that of a process through which the Empire struck back to expose the devastating material effects of colonial domination. This meaning has also structured reports of the 1993 settlement. It requires challenge and critique, not only because of its singularity but also because of the effects its dominance has produced.

Between 1952 and 1957, Britain conducted twelve full-scale nuclear weapons tests on Australian soil. The first test, at the Monte Bello islands off north-western Australia in 1952, was followed by two at Emu Field in South Australia in 1953. A further two devices were exploded at Monte Bello in 1956 before testing was transferred to the permanent site at Maralinga, where it continued until 1958. As well as test explosions of atomic bombs, there was also a series of 'minor trials' in which the effects of nuclear accidents on military installations and equipment were inspected. These minor trials, we now know, spread plutonium over a vast area, making a more insidious contribution to the irradiation of the land than the bombs themselves. All of this occurred with the acquiescence if not the full knowledge of the Australian government of the time.

It is hard to tell what the 'Australian public' thought of the tests at the time; if one is to deduce their opinions from press reports of the tests, they would seem to have been wholeheartedly in favour of the exercise. However, although these press reports are our major category of primary evidence, to see them as a direct or 'accurate' reflection of popular opinion is extremely risky—in theory and in practice. Researchers have found traces of greater opposition than was acknowledged in the contemporary news media. We know, for instance, that 'Ban the bomb' demonstrations occurred, that the Labor Party pressed energetically but unsuccessfully for an inquiry into the safety precautions for the second Monte Bello bomb, that the letters pages in the newspapers were dominated by protests, and that a Gallup poll showed that 60 per cent of Australians opposed the tests.[19] Little of this surfaced in contemporary press reports. In Adelaide, the *Advertiser* rarely mentioned the likelihood of any safety problems resulting from the exercise despite its taking place so close to home. Indeed, as the tests were repeatedly postponed because of unfavourable weather conditions, the *Advertiser's* reporters began to represent the safety precautions as excessively bureaucratic, even silly. Inevitably, Chapman Pincher, the British science and defence writer, was covering the event for the paper and he likened the wait for the momentous event to the experience of an expectant father waiting for a baby that never arrived. Quick to take the hint, Oliphant produced a cartoon which depicted a chain-smoking father pacing outside the Maralinga Maternity Ward. The day after the test did occur, there was the sequel: the father shouting joyfully, 'It's a bomb'.[20]

Tame and Robotham describe the Australian press response to the tests in the following way:

[T]he Melbourne *Argus* of 27 September 1956 captured the mood best with its coverage of the Maralinga test of the same date.'Bombs Away!' trumpeted the paper's front-page headline, followed by the immortal first paragraph: 'Maralinga Thursday: the atom bomb's gone up at last'. Worse was to follow. 'Minutes after the explosion, Government members cheered and Labor MPs shouted 'Thank goodness' and 'At last, at last' as Mr Beale, Supply Minister, announced in the House of Representatives the test had been successful.' Still later in the story the euphoria and hysteria increased: 'As the [radioactive] cloud faded, convoys of trucks and jeeps brought back the servicemen who'd faced the blast at close range. AND EVERY FACE WORE A SMILE [sic].. . . They could have been coming back from a picnic'.[21]

If it is hard to tell who might be speaking through the discourses used to construct such reports, the Minister of Supply Howard Beale's description of the tests might help; to him, they were 'a striking example of inter-Commonwealth cooperation on the grand scale. . . England has the bomb and the know-how, we have the open spaces and the willingness to help the motherland. Between us, we shall help to build the defences of the free world'.[22]

Noel Sanders describes a similarly contradictory brew of discourses—of nationalism and Empire, of destiny and modernity—in his discussion of the exploration for and marketing of Australian uranium in the fifties.[23] The Australian government seized on uranium and the atom bomb as signs of a transformed modernity, a chance to leap from an agricultural past to a technologised future in the new role of supplier to the major powers. Sanders notes the *Sun-Herald*s inevitable claim that the 1953 test had, like so many other events before and since, 'put Australia on the map', as well as the opinion of W.C. Wentworth, MP who saw it as the most important material event in history, second only to that more spiritual event—the birth of Christ.[24] The *frisson* of playing a part in the geopolitics of the Cold War, of assisting Britain's attempt to remain a world power (by finessing what amounted to a technical breach of its non-proliferation agreements with the United States and Canada), is discernible in government rhetoric of the time. In Australian government pronouncements, a scenario emerged: from a position in the front row of the imperial chorus, Australia would stand on the world stage not quite in partnership with, but certainly in some relation to, the major atomic powers—in any case, a long way from riding on the sheep's back. A sea change in Australia's sense of itself was at hand. In such a climate, Sir Ernest Titterton's extraordinary remarks seem entirely appropriate: he saw it as 'axiomatic' that, as a consequence of our implication in nuclear politics, 'one or more of our capital cities will be destroyed in the next 50 to 100 years'.[25] Such a probability merely underlined the national aggrandisement sure to follow.

Plausibly constructed though it was, this euphoria could not last long. Even the Menzies government soon realised how little care had been taken in the testing and how it had encouraged the British to act like unruly house guests; once it became clear that the host would give them the run of the house they started to put their feet on the furniture and drop ash on the rug. The first scientific reports to question British claims about the limits of the fallout were completed and suppressed in 1957; they detected fallout as far from Maralinga as Townsville in northern Queensland, and constructed an entirely pessimistic map of its dispersal.[26] I need not elaborate the details here but over the next 25 years there was a steady stream of claims, accusations, scientific research and attempts to contain the damage. Britain was called back for a limited clean-up in 1967 (Operation Brumby), but this merely involved ploughing the scattered plutonium and bomb debris into the ground. A further operation in 1979 removed some of the contaminated soil but still left the majority of the site untouched.[27]

As the years went by, and as the dangers of radiation became more generally understood, survivors of the tests started to question the extent to which they had been informed of these dangers. Pilots had been instructed to fly through the nuclear cloud to collect dust particles; ships had been instructed to sail into the drop zone off the Monte Bello islands; soldiers had been sent into 'ground zero' within minutes to commence cleaning up—mostly without any kind of protective clothing ('just a slouch hat and shorts', as one survivor put it on the TV program *Hinch* in 1991).[28] As white Australia began to acknowledge the importance of the land within Aboriginal culture, the forced evacuation and irradiation of the Maralinga people's country assumed the dimensions of an outrage. The inadequacy of the attempts to evacuate all Aboriginals from the area also came under scrutiny; warning signs in English and the patrols of a solitary officer were the sum total of these attempts. Finally, as the environmental dangers of nuclear energy and the dumping of toxic waste became of general concern, the enormity of what had occurred at Maralinga began to sink in.

By the late seventies, the trickle of reports had become a flood of accusations about the inadequacy of the clean-up methods, the plight of the surviving service personnel, the callous incompetence of those in charge of safety during the tests, the silencing of scientists who had evidence of widespread nuclear contamination, the dispossession of the Aboriginals from their land, and the long-term effects on the site area itself. With the change in government in 1983 and the gathering of more evidence about the condition of the test site, and with the Labor government needing to restore some of its environmental credentials after overturning Labor Party policy on uranium mining, the Royal Commission was set up in 1984. The primary issues to be dealt with are usefully laid out in a series of articles in the *Canberra Times* published the month before the Commission commenced.[29] The articles highlighted the relationship between Britain and Australia in the administration of the tests; what they called 'the modern-day massacre' and de-tribalisation of Aboriginals in the test area; the management of safety by the British and in particular the role of the Australian nominee, Sir Ernest Titterton, on the Safety Committee which was meant to safeguard Australians' interests; and the question of whether or not we were told the truth about the size of the bombs exploded or the hazards they presented to Australians.

On Anzac Day, 1992, Paul Keating delivered a speech at a memorial on the Kokoda Trail in Papua New Guinea which established him for the first time as a nationalist. The speech revised some of the standard components of Australian mythology in order to write Kokoda in and Gallipoli out, and it renewed the licence for some other components—roughly, that the British used us in World War I and lied to us in World War II—which helped stitch this new mythology back into the old one. Keating's interpretation of World War II history—'Churchill sold us out'—raised something of a storm here and in Britain; whatever its virtues as history, its political acumen lay in its successful exploitation of many Australians' apparent (Oedipal) readiness to view the British–Australian relation as a treacherous one. The Australian news media's treatment of the Maralinga Royal Commission was similarly exploitative. While the Commission was still in Australia, reporting was often factual, issues-oriented and low key. The full range of issues raised in the *Canberra Times* articles did seem likely to be addressed. This changed when the hearings moved to London. Once there, the range of issues raised and meanings generated contracted as the story slotted itself into a popular history of British–Australian colonial relations that has us as the resistant victims of British hegemony. The story took on a higher profile and became, consequently, more sensational: the coverage was increasingly personalised and opinionated as it acquired bigger headlines and moved closer to the front page.

The President of the Commission, 'Diamond Jim' McClelland, has admitted deliberately provoking Her Majesty's Government with some strategic pommy-bashing on the opening day of the London hearings.[30] In order to speed up the British provision of files and witnesses, and to puncture any illusions that the Commission could be fobbed off by a bunch of Sir Humphreys, McClelland issued a statement attacking the lack of cooperation and preparedness he had encountered. It had the desired result, both in the increased media attention and in the fact that the Commission received more rapid and thorough cooperation from the British, in the end, than from the Australian Public Service.[31] In the British press, it must be said, McClelland's outspokenness won him a great deal of support; he was applauded for cutting the red tape that was, after all, also restricting British service men and women from gaining access to information that would assist their own claims against their government.[32] It should also be noted that the Commission took place in a slightly different context for the British press; it became part of a series of 1980s investigations into Britain's political management of its official secrets—a later episode of which was played out in the *Spycatcher* trials.

In the Australian press, evidence of the British support for the Commission's work was buried. From the first day, the hearings were constructed as a juicy opportunity for an avenging Australian nationalism to punish a complacent and undifferentiated British Establishment. In a piece headlined 'Her Majesty's Govt gets a taste of the colonial birch', Evan Whitton gushed like a fashion reporter: McClelland, he found, was as 'handsome as ever', an 'impeccable dresser' presenting 'a delightful study in pink and grey'. For the British counsel Robert Auld, Whitton could only manage 'a plump

JUDGE'S DREAD

Time Out's report of the Maralinga Royal Commission's London hearings wears its opinion on its graphics. (text courtesy of *Time Out*, illustrator unknown)

Eleven weeks ago Justice James McClelland made headlines by pilloring Whitehall in public for withholding vital documents from the Royal Commission on British nuclear tests in Australia, which he had travelled to London to head. Before returning down-under this week, 'Diamond Jim' spoke to *Paul Charman* of his largely critical impressions of the Old Country, including the miners' strike, Ponting, telephone tapping, our apparently insuperable class system and, above all, his utter distaste for 'that silly woman' Mrs Thatcher.

man with thinning hair'. Nevertheless, throwing disinterest to the winds, Whitton did muse that 'it must have been quite a treat for Mr Auld to hear a colonial judge giving his client, Her Majesty's Govt, such a thorough birching but it has to be said that his client has made a quite remarkable ass of itself'.[33]

Robert Milliken, in his book *No Conceivable Injury*, has suggested that the real entity on trial in these hearings was science itself; if so, it was a particularly Anglo formation of science. Even Milliken ends up describing the hearings as 'total war' between the British and Australian counsel.[34] And although McClelland's initial outburst may have fanned the flames, the situation does seem to have been ripe for a colonial battle before he said a word:

> The first hearing was marked by chaos, confusion, threats of violence and strident Australian nationalism, as Fleet Street reporters jostled for space in the overcrowded conference room with Australian television crews. One Australian cameraman demanded to know if a stenographer was English or Australian and, on learning she was English, set about haranguing the hapless woman for walking in front of his camera—'deliberately'. . . and preventing Australian audiences from getting the full picture.[35]

From such a start, it is no surprise that within two weeks the London sittings had become, in the *National Times*' words, 'one of the most bitter wrangles between Australia and Britain for many years'.[36] Of course, it wasn't any kind of wrangle between 'Australia' and 'Britain' at all; at best, it was a wrangle between a group of Australian lawyers with unprecedented access to the British and Australian media, their British counterparts, and some sections of Whitehall.[37]

Once given the 'McGuffin', however, the media continued to develop the narrative. Much was made of Australian attempts to extract information from the British—both during the hearings and back in the fifties. The late Sir Robert Menzies emerged from the hearings as a hopeless Anglophile, but even he had been reduced to sending a frantic telegram to Britain after fallout from the second Monte Bello (Mosaic) test in 1956 was detected drifting over the mainland. 'What the bloody hell is going on!', his telegram read (possibly the most Australian sentence Menzies ever uttered!). The phrase was widely taken up in headlines as a metonym for the whole set of colonial relations.[38] The effect was to construct, inferentially, an homology between Menzies' predicament, the predicament of the Royal Commission itself, and ultimately the predicament of the Australian people. As secret after secret was uncovered, the headlines were less and less restrained in their accusations about British 'lies'.[39] One of the tests in 1956 turned out to be twice the magnitude the Australians had originally been informed it was—a bomb, the headlines told us, with five times the destructive power of the one which wiped out Hiroshima. It seemed entirely plausible that commentators should conclude that the revelations would 'further strain Australia–UK relations already fragile since hearings in Australia indicated 27 years of British duplicity over the tests'.

For most Australians reading these press reports, such fragility bothered us not a jot. Even though my interest here is in challenging these media representations, it would be hypocritical to deny how exciting it was to read the daily revelations from a position of absolute moral superiority. The spectacle of an instrument of the Australian government bullying the British establishment into hurt submission was a deeply satisfying one. Coupled, as it was, to a genuine attempt to defend the rights of citizens against a callous and incompetent bureaucracy (leaving aside for the moment the question of *whose* bureaucracy), it was a heady mixture. The effectiveness of nationalist discourses lies in the fact that their seductiveness is assured in advance; in this case, as in so many others, they offered us pleasures that were irresistible.

McClelland, like Turnbull a few years later, became something of a national hero; his impeccable nationalist credentials included an Irish-Australian background and service in the Whitlam government. His abrasiveness in London and his 'fuck you' attitude to British officialdom[40] endeared him to both the British and the Australian public for much the same reasons: he was the perfect stereotype of the Australian male in Britain *and* he was on the side of the angels. According to the position one can construct from the press reports, particularly those in the *Sydney Morning Herald*, his Anglophobia was far from being a disqualification; rather it was a perfectly appropriate attribute which could only bring him credit since his Commission daily produced justification for his condition. McClelland's outspokenness, like Turnbull's disrespect, was legitimised by his nationalist principles; interviewed on TV's *Sixty Minutes* when he returned from London (but, significantly, before the Commission had completed its hearings), McClelland accused Menzies of being a 'lickspittle to the British' and defended his own actions in London as the only way 'a colonial' was going to get any results.

The nationalism which provides the major discursive frame for the reporting of the Maralinga Royal Commission dramatically narrowed the meanings of the inquiry. Progressively displaced from the foreground were the effects upon Aboriginal people, their land and their communities; the extent of the contamination of Australian land is still unknown and was not vigorously pursued by the Commission at all. Even the plight of the British and Australian veterans depending upon the findings of the Commission as support for their own claims for compensation gradually gave way to this narrative of postcolonial politics, this melodrama of duplicity and betrayal—of British lies, British stooges, British bastardry. The story settled into the genre of the political thriller rather than the historical mini-series, the climax occurring with the naming of the guilty, the uncovering of the plot. Issues such as who would pay, who *should* pay, what needed to be done and who would do it, were all left to the report itself and thus would always risk being ignored.

The discourses of nationalism served at least two further functions in this case. Firstly, as I have suggested, they unequivocally defined the Royal Commission's activities as in the national interest, effectively conflating the interests of the government which set the Commission up with those fractions of its people who were its subjects—the Maralinga Aboriginals, armed services veterans. This, despite (for instance) the Australian government's long and uninterrupted history of obstructing veterans' claims for compensation on the basis of sickness produced by their exposure to radiation at Maralinga. One could see how the government's interests might be served by this representation, however implausible, of its role as champion of its citizens' rights. Better still, once established, the nationalist narrative made it clear that the British were to blame.

It should go without saying that this was a gross misrepresentation of, at least, the Australian government's degree of culpability. On the issue of the evacuation of the Aboriginals, for example, while McClelland took some delight in exposing British ignorance of Aboriginal culture, the white Australians involved were no better. Among the reasons why the evacuation was so difficult is that Aboriginals were not even included in the Australian census during the 1950s. White Australians were responsible for the traumatic treatment of two Aboriginal families found in the drop zones after tests began; one family was sent off on foot to a destination 650 kilometres away—three of its members are said to have died on the journey. Insensitivity to the effect of dispossession and evacuation on the Aboriginal communities is not solely attributable to British ignorance. As Kingsley Palmer puts it, 'it suited the British and

Australian governments in the 1950s to believe that the land was of no importance to desert Aborigines, and that the area, which was the ideal place to perform the tests, was more or less empty'.[41] The expertise of Australian anthropologist A.P. Elkin was sought in order to see that the Aborigines' 'well-being was not interfered with in any way'. However, Elkin's advice was entirely consonant with the objectives of the British and Australian governments; it was complicit in the eventual dispossession of the very people whose 'well-being' he was supposed to protect. Palmer wrote:

> [T]he potential effect of the bomb tests on the sacred sites and on the socio-religious life of Aborigines was ignored [by Elkin] because it was considered irrelevant. According to Elkin, in time Aborigines would leave their traditional ways and lifestyle behind, and all of its associations, and would develop into 'modern' men and women. . . .[42]

In relation to this issue, as with many others, evidence of Australian culpability was submerged under the weight of another story.

The second function served by the discourses of nationalism in this case was, however, even more destructive. The clarity of the position that McClelland took against the British allowed the Commission's report, when tabled, to be seen as irredeemably tainted by McClelland's Anglophobia. Alexander Downer—currently shadow Treasurer in the Australian parliament—launched one of several attacks on the report as politically biased ('antagonistic to the tests'), and on McClelland himself ('that embittered, gaudy relic of the Whitlam Government'). Itself a vigorous political document, Downer's *Quadrant* article reversed all of McClelland's orthodoxies, defending Menzies, Titterton, the lot.[43] Some editorial writers had also taken this line. The *Age* confined itself to ticking off the Commission for its lack of diplomacy, while accepting the arguments it presented.[44] But the *Sydney Morning Herald* (whose news reports, it should be noted, had been among the most rabidly nationalist), attacked the 'standing of the Commission' itself. The Commission's credibility was damaged by the 'Pom-bashing antics of its chairman', and was thus in need of renovation if its recommendations were to have any hope of implementation.[45] With the pomposity of a newspaper intent on slaying the monster it had largely been responsible for creating, the *Sydney Morning Herald* agreed that the Commission's case was proven but saw it as unlikely to be of any use to a government stuck with the 'embarrassing dilemma' of asking the British to shell out. For the rest of the press, the story was a dead duck almost as soon as the report came out;

the government, whatever it might have pretended at the time, must have felt the same.

As I say, this is not surprising, given the meanings attributed to the event. For many Australians, the report of the Maralinga Royal Commission consigned its subject to the past; it represented the completion of a ritual of separation which had to be performed if Australia was finally to be its own place. The *Age* editorial on the report said as much, smugly suggesting that 'what happened in Australia in the 1950s would not happen today'. Historian Stephen Alomes, writing in 1987, also felt confident that the Royal Commission had 'put the last nail in the coffin of Australia's colonial relations with Britain':

> An Australian commission exposed British deceptions and Menzies' colonial servitude through hearings held in part on British soil. Furthermore, Jim McClelland savaged contemporary English inefficiency. The colony was no longer deferential and obedient.[46]

Here the press's chosen narrative is delivered unalloyed, raw mythology offered as history. But neither the *Age* nor Alomes should go uncontested.

For a start, it *could* happen again. In 1987, Kim Beazley approached the Maralinga community to allow NASA to use the Woomera range for rocket tests. Beazley's letter sought community agreement but it did contain the threat that the government 'reserves the right to make use of the Prohibited Area [the irradiated area of the test sites, which borders on inhabited Aboriginal land] for rocket launchings if that becomes necessary or expedient in the interests of the Commonwealth'. By May 1989, Beazley had expanded the plan to that of a 'military mega-range', testing 'rockets, missiles and other war material' over Aboriginal land. He faxed the Maralinga community asking for their permission to use their land for this weapons research on a more or less permanent basis.[47] The request presumably depended on the assumption, once again, that as the Aboriginals were not making use of this land they would not mind if it were used by the government. There is a Defence Department plan to turn the area into an international 'war games park', although its current status is not known.[48] There have been reports suggesting that the area has been offered to the United States as a replacement for its Philippine bases, and there is also evidence of French interest.[49] It *could* happen again.

From a second angle of attack, the media narrative of British guilt and Australian innocence started to break down into its constitutive fictions. Between 1989 and 1991, the British journalist Robert Cockburn published a series of reports—largely in the London *Times*—of further scientific evidence from Maralinga being covered up by the Australian government.[50] Cockburn produced two television documentaries—one for the Australian program *Dateline* on SBS (screened on 17 August 1991) and one for the BBC's *Nature* series (screened in Britain on 28 October 1991). Both drew on a report by the Australian Radiation Laboratory which had been hushed up by the Department of Primary Industries and Energy, and which revealed that contamination of the test sites and surrounding areas was even more extensive than previously thought. Some of the areas thus surveyed included those to which Aboriginals had been allowed to return under the misapprehension that the land was safe. The *Dateline* story was about an Australian cover-up in the interests of the British. It accused the Australian government of having no intention of pursuing the British to implement the Royal Commission recommendations but rather aiding and abetting them in their attempts to avoid public scrutiny. Indeed, the story presented the interests of the Australian and British governments as largely identical, and thus antithetical to those of the Aboriginals. The deal eventually struck on the clean-up would tend to support such an account.

A chilling moment occurred in the *Dateline* program when Jim McClelland was taken into the studio and shown the footage the viewers had themselves just seen. He was devastated: 'It's news to me', he said, painfully aware of how futile this made his own best (and hitherto apparently successful) efforts appear. The 'British bastardry' thesis got more complicated as we watched: 'the colonial cringe is alive and well', he finally admitted as the complicity of a succession of Australian governments (including the Hawke government) in a series of cover-ups stood revealed.

The *Dateline* story produced a burst of media interest which threatened to undermine conclusively the Royal Commission mythology. *Hinch* presented a story on the survivors, the soldiers who had participated in the tests and were now dying of cancer. The Australian government's obstruction and callousness formed the key theme of that story. The Aboriginal delegations' visits to London also caught the attention of newscasts, although none that I saw drew the inference that this direct approach indicated a loss of faith in the good will and intentions of their own government. There has been no sustained revision of the narrative I have presented, however; since mid-1991 Cockburn has found it very difficult to get his articles published in Australia and has largely given up trying. There are still many further questions to be asked, and there has been no class (as distinct from individual) compensation for any of the groups claiming it. None of this has been changed by the British government's payout. If anything, the settlement will make it even more unlikely that new information will be published.

My initial interest in the Maralinga Royal Commission was related to the apparently programmatic way in which the media's use of the discourses of nationalism revved up for the Bicentenary. As I said in Chapter 1, the 1980s is regarded as a period of an exceptionally brash and confident nationalism, and it is possible to see the reporting of the Maralinga Royal Commission as homologous with this cultural movement (as in Alomes's account, for instance). And yet my research suggests that it might also be explicable as the product of, for example, strategies adopted by the Australian press to make the Commission into a story, of the government's defence of its own interests in deflecting blame and discouraging closer scrutiny of its own files, or of the royal commissioner's own weakness for self-promotion.

Whatever we might agree on as the appropriate constellation of contributing sources for these discourses, I want to close by saying what were in my view their consequences. The effect of the dominance of these discourses in this case was to make it seem as if a victory had been won; closure was complete even before the Commission's report was written. As we have seen, however, the victory was only at the level of media representation; while part of the clean-up bill has been met, material compensation is yet to eventuate. Instead, veterans have continued to die before their claims come to court, the life expectancy among those Maralinga people displaced from their lands has dropped to thirty years, and a section of Australia the size of the United Kingdom in one estimate, five times its size in another, has been rendered uninhabitable for 240 000 years—whether it is 'rehabilitated' or not. That our government should, first of all, oversee such a series of events, then attempt to ameliorate their effects, achieve so little, and still appear to be serving the national interest is due, at least in part, to the power of those discursive strategies used during the reporting of the Commission which told the Australian public it was all fixed when Jim McClelland was rude to Whitehall and Evan Whitton called Her Majesty's Government a remarkable ass.

4

Picnic at Ayers Rock: the Bicentenary

So far, we have looked at instances of the unofficial, relatively implicit, uses of nationalism: where nationalism is deployed in order to advance particular, rather than national, interests and where those interests are actually masked by the use of nationalist discourses. I want to move on to a case where the nationalism is more explicit, to an official program of nation formation which announced and defended its intentions of serving the interests of all Australians.

The 1988 Bicentenary has been widely criticised for the often crude chauvinism of its claims on the national interest, and for the entrepreneurialism of the events which took place under its aegis. The Coca-Cola sign covering the sail of the lead ship in the re-enactment of the First Fleet, while not part of the official program (and thus with no other option than commercial sponsorship), has nevertheless become a symbol of the commercialisation of the national ritual and thus of the diminution of its cultural significance. The merchandising of Bicentenary products and souvenirs, and the gravy train of grants and endorsements associated with the Australian Bicentenary Authority's (ABA) activities, have given the whole affair a thoroughly capitalist meaning. Rather than joining what has become a well-rehearsed chorus about these aspects of the Bicentenary, in this chapter I want to suggest that the event enabled us to observe a decline in traditional nationalisms; implicated in its imputed failure as a national festival are signs that a redefinition of Australian versions of nationalism is on its way.

There are a number of provocations for such a suggestion. Firstly, I would not be alone in seeing the black protests during the

66

Bicentenary as turning points in Aboriginal attempts to place land rights on the social issues agenda in Australia. Secondly, there are one or two analyses of the Bicentenary which have talked about its effects, not in terms of the success or failure of individual events, but in terms of processes set in train which may turn out, in the long run, to be positive. Patrick Buckridge's discussion of the relations between Australian literature and the Bicentenary is one such account. Buckridge first reminds readers of some of the controversies surrounding the literary establishment in that year—controversies which questioned Australian writers' right to claim the status of the 'literary' on the one hand (Greg Sheridan's attack on a 'boring' Patrick White), and the legitimacy of the decisions made by various arts funding bodies on the other (Ken Methold's notorious 'Letter from Mount Isa'). Buckridge then suggests that 'despite all the consensual rhetoric generated by the Bicentenary, and perhaps because of it, the institution of Australian literature may actually in the course of the year have become more sharply aware of its internal conflicts and hierarchies'.[1] Buckridge goes on to see this as a positive development, allowing a 'serious and continuing analysis of the Australian literary system as a whole'.

I think it is time someone argued that the Bicentenary—admittedly somewhat in spite of itself—played a significant part in provoking a 'serious and continuing analysis' of the way in which we think of Australian nationhood. What follows then is an occasionally ambivalent assessment of the Bicentenary's contribution to a revised nationalism.

Follow the bouncing ball

I dunno, I reckon the government'll bugger it up.
(Talkback radio caller, early on 26 January 1988)

Most Australians will recall the incremental waves of promotion which led up to the bicentennial year, 1988. In the most frequently repeated television advertisement, a large cast of Australian celebrities were collected in front of Ayers Rock/Uluru waving flags, punching their fists in the air, and singing 'Celebration of a Nation'. Their dress and demeanour were that of participants in a bush picnic. The song itself was too histrionic for some tastes, and the collection of famous faces too transparently heterogeneous, but there was an affability about the ad which enhanced its appeal. The celebrities' performances were not entirely convincing; one could detect a touch of selfconsciousness, an embarrassed awareness that such full-tilt nationalism was probably a little excessive for the average Australian. Indeed, the 'Celebration of a Nation' campaign (like other elements of the official promotion) appears to have been designed precisely to deal with the very real possibility that Australians would not spontaneously respond to the Bicentenary celebrations with anything like sufficient enthusiasm.

In comparison with that of some other settler societies, everyday life in Australia is not especially full of the signs of patriotism when there are no major sporting contests going on. Despite the popular conception of Australians as fiercely nationalistic, there are few 'Australia—love it or leave it' bumper-stickers to parallel the American variety. The spectacle of the national flag flying over private homes is much less common in Australia than in the States, and the widespread use of the Canadian flag (or at least the maple leaf symbol) by private citizens in Canada—on bumper-stickers, earrings, badges and so on—is not replicated here. As a rule, white Anglo-Australians are slightly awkward about expressing a generalised patriotism, preferring to localise it around a specific event—typically, a sporting event. Perhaps as a consequence of this, there are still relatively few formal occasions on which Australians are expected to ritually express their patriotism.[2]

Peter Spearritt has noted that European Australians have been uncertain about, and slow to develop, 'indigenous' national rituals.[3] Where we *have* developed such rituals, they tend to be marked— perhaps even made possible—by their contradictory nature. It is as if the existence of some ambiguity is a precondition so that the ritual may be observed without undue embarrassment. The celebration of Anzac Day is framed by discourses of triumph and survival although it commemorates a defeat. The Australian celebration of Christmas is still dominated by rituals inherited from the northern hemisphere; they demonstrate their impracticality in the southern hemisphere annually, thus building into the celebration a forced quality, a secondhand phoniness. Australia Day, putatively the most important national holiday, falls well behind Anzac Day in terms of its actual significance in most Australians' minds and is probably equivalent in observance to its ideological antithesis, the Queen's Birthday. Granted all this, to ensure that Australia Day 1988 was celebrated with the enthusiasm appropriate to the bicentenary of a proud and patriotic nation was always going to require a great deal of work.

As I said at the beginning of this chapter, there has been much general comment about the commercialised hoopla, the proliferation of advertising and merchandising tie-ins accompanying the Bicentenary, but I think we can be quite specific about what the official promotion's purposes were. To my mind the promotional campaign emanating from the Australian Bicentenary Authority had an almost pedagogic objective: Australians were being *taught* their bicentennial behaviours. 'Celebration of a Nation' was not just a method of raising the emotional temperature of the nation in readiness for 1988. It was also a practical demonstration of what was expected of Australians celebrating the bicentennial year. It probably worked. The picnic at Ayers Rock, supplemented by what one reveller interviewed in Pat Fiske's documentary, *Australia Daze*, referred to as 'a traditional Australian sausage sizzle', was repeated all over the nation on 26 January 1988.

For those who might consider national identity to be natural or inherent, being *taught* how to celebrate one's nationality may seem more than a little contradictory. One of the obstacles which settler nations have to overcome is an Old World view that regards their 'nationality' as inauthentic. *All* nationalities, of course, are invented[4] and all relatively recently—despite the often lengthy mythic histories upon which they draw for their legitimation—but the process of nation formation is especially explicit in settler societies. Since the 1960s, Australia has been particularly deliberate in its official projects of nation formation. From that time on, the official construction of cultural identity has been progressively required to confirm but not exclusively delimit the available definitions of our national character. As Australian cultural policy has ever so gradually renounced the late nineteenth century definitions of the national character referred to in earlier chapters, it has taken on the obligation of constructing alternative definitions, of incorporating the networks of cultural differences and similarities which mark postwar Australian society as distinctive. The Bicentenary was a site at which this obligation was particularly explicit, visible in the teacherly ways through which the Bicentenary publicity addressed its audience. One TV ad, which taught us a 'bicentennial song', even had us following the bouncing ball as we learnt the words. Predictably perhaps, for a nation in which few people can sing all the words of the national anthem, most of us now would have trouble recalling a single line of the bicentennial song.

Earlier versions of nationalism, which define the nation through its unity rather than through its managing of networks of differences, are more easily operated through such large national promotions as the Bicentenary. In 1988, we should be pleased to acknowledge, the ABA had no real possibility of invoking such a model of nationalism. The Bicentenary theme, 'Living Together', promoted a multicultural Australia through its emphasis on cultural difference and variety. The ABA's contradictory attempt to simultaneously signify cultural difference and national unity, and the multiculturalist agenda seen as the motivation for such an attempt, met with resentment from (among others) the Anglo Right, who regarded the whole thematic project as an abandonment of Australia's predominantly British heritage (indeed, nationhood) in favour of non-British 'minority interest groups'. From this so-called Anglo perspective,[5] the celebrations might have been much simpler than they turned out to be—perhaps along the lines of 1938's sesquicentenary. Up to a point, the reactions were understandable: to celebrate a nation which is united but diverse, on a day which is the moment of both settlement and invasion, through rhetoric which foregrounds difference and reconciliation over uniformity and assimilation, was not a simple public relations exercise.

To further complicate the context within which the official Bicentenary program was planned and executed, there is a strong tradition amongst Australian cultural critics and historians which is healthily sceptical about this style of event. Nationalism itself, as we have already seen, is a vigorously debated ideology within the academic community and any event unequivocally devoted to its advancement would have little prospect of support from many of our foremost cultural commentators. Critiques of the commercialisation of public rituals, of the anti-democratic nature of such mass celebrations, of the tactlessness of celebrating white settlement at all, of the Philistinism inherent in a popular rather than a more highbrow calendar of events, of the predictability and regressiveness of the dominant discourses used to represent Australian nationalism—all provided potentially powerful angles of analysis, no matter what form the Bicentenary ultimately took.

Given such a context, it is a wonder that the ABA[6] program had any success at all; there is no doubt, however, that there were some successes in 1988. Some of the Bicentenary projects—the Powerhouse Museum, the Bicentennial Histories, for two—have already proven the value of their contribution to contemporary Australian life. The TV program which launched the Bicentenary, *Australia Live*, was screened on both commercial and government networks to enormous ratings. An estimated one and half million people took part enthusiastically in the nation's biggest ever picnic to welcome the replicas of the First Fleet to Sydney Harbour on 26 January 1988. There is overwhelming evidence from the press, television, film and radio talkback that Australians participated in large numbers in Australia Day 1988 and experienced that participation as a source of deep national pride and exhilaration. It would be wrong to assume that such experiences were just a well-taught 'following the bouncing ball'; for many Australians the Bicentenary produced a moving spectacle, moments of genuine pride and in some cases even gestures toward a reconciliation of the great contradiction at the heart of our nationhood. In a telling paradox, Sydney's march of protest at two hundred years of white domination was the largest gathering of black Australians since white settlement and in the long term may well prove to have been the most significant Bicentenary event.

At the time, many intellectuals and commentators rightly felt that the complacency of the Bicentenary rhetoric and the con-sensualising rhythms it set up needed to be vigorously challenged. (The kind of complacent rhetoric I have in mind would include what became quite routine claims that Australia is 'the best country in the world', that everyone 'gets a fair go', and that there is no class system restricting individual opportunities. Bob Hawke, for instance, made all of these claims during the TV program *Good Morning Australia* on Australia Day, 1988.) Such an objective was, presumably, behind the public criticism of the project made by Sylvia Lawson, Meaghan Morris, Peter Spearritt, Donald Horne, Patrick White and many others. The specific politics motivating these writers' critiques at the time have faded from later accounts, however, so that Australian intellectuals have become rather too glib in dismissing the Bicentenary as little more than a meaningless burst of Americanised hype. To characterise the Bicentenary *only* in this way is to ignore the weight of evidence to the contrary. The further we move away from 1988, the less convincing are those descriptions which do not account for the pleasure of the millions of Australians who found their participation in the Bicentenary to be satisfying and worthwhile. In some of the most recent critiques, such pleasures are only acknowledged in order to be denigrated—as if the only ones who found meaning in the Bicentenary were the dupes of a marketing machine.[7] This is far too crude an understanding of the public participation in the Bicentenary and of the Bicentenary's contribution to the meanings of nationalism within Australian popular culture.

Patrick Buckridge suggests that it is a mistake to see the

Bicentenary as only 'a series of completed projects'. Rather, he says, we should take a longer view, and think about it as a set of influences pressing upon, and perhaps working towards change within, 'existing cultural institutions and discourses'.[8] Such a view returns the Bicentenary to its historical context, so that we might see it as a series of occasions on which already constituted debates over national identity become unusually public and explicit. What is particularly refreshing in Buckridge's approach to the Bicentenary is his rejection of suggestions that its success depended upon the sense of national unity its celebrations engendered. Buckridge is far from convinced that such an outcome was either necessary or desirable. Viewed from his perspective what some have called the 'failure' of the Bicentenary—that is, its failure to deliver to us a newly unified nation—may turn out to be its achievement.

The Bicentenary might be thought of as a set of sites and processes where we can witness the official production of nationalism in Australia for once reaching its limits. These sites and processes are not well defined and their temporal boundaries are probably still to be reached. But the limitations the Bicentenary revealed do seem to be centrally implicated—now, I would suggest, even more than at the time—in many Australians' recognition of the plurality of Australian identities and their confidence in the validity of these identities. For this reason the Bicentenary continues to be of interest and to demand analysis and critique as the most exorbitant and the most contested program of nation formation in Australia's postwar history.

The task confronted by this program was obviously complicated by the fact that while many of the identities which had sustained us in the past were suddenly looking strikingly threadbare, in need of repair or disposal, there were no obvious or widely accepted replacements. Australians faced (then and now) the complex necessity of sorting through competing versions of Australian identity in order to decide which ones might work—and for whom. In what follows I want to suggest that it is this very complexity, indeed the contradictoriness of any two things one would want to say about the Bicentenary, which may be the Bicentenary's most significant contribution to the formation of the 'national' in Australian popular culture.

A day of contradictions

What did most to make Australia Day so triumphant was the dignity of most Aboriginal protests and the patriotism of the huge crowds that poured into Sydney and lined the Harbour—patriotism the original planners had tried to push aside. . . . [T]he most moving event was the one the high officials had not really wanted, the arrival at the narrow throat of the Sydney Heads of the First Fleet Reenactment after crossing the world as homage to the voyage undertaken in 1788. (Geoffrey Blainey)

You can't get serious problems solved by a circus. (Patrick White)

Just a day like any other. (Man in the street, *Australia Daze*)

I have never in my whole life felt such a sense of national pride. (Talkback radio caller)

Reviewing the press and television coverage of Australia Day 1988 for this book, I have been struck by certain aspects of the treatment of the Aboriginal protests. While the media's initial treatment of the Aboriginal cause was less than exemplary (as we shall see a little later on), they proved surprisingly ready to respectfully acknowledge its moral force on 'the big day'. What the media coverage of the Aboriginal protests disclosed was a degree of recognition that the national celebrations would inevitably, even while proposing national unity, expose the inequities and divisions within the nation. For the *Sydney Morning Herald*'s 'Bicentennial Special', Australia Day was a 'Day of Contradictions' which was as marked by expressions of difference as of unity: 'Inhabitants of two very different Australias ended a day of widely differing significances—a day which looked back on an often inglorious past, yet gave renewed hope for a glorious future'.[9]

It is true, as Tony Bennett has pointed out, that the 1988 celebrations were more nationalist than their precursors—that is, the allegiance to a nation-state independent of Britain was more explicit in 1988 than in 1938.[10] It was not, however, an unambiguous or univocal nationalism. Indeed, as I noted in Chapter 1, the nationalism of 1988 was marked by its historic location in a time when the idea of the nation-state was itself under challenge and when its Australian variant was seen increasingly to be inadequate to the needs of all Australians. Peter Cochrane and David Goodman make

73

the point that the declining authority of earlier versions of nationalism added to the difficulties faced by the Bicentenary Authority:

> The Bicentenary would have been far less trying had it come at a high point in the Menzies era: then we would have had a solid statement of good government, cultural homogeneity and consensus. The idea of 'nation', then, was ontologically secure.[11]

As a result, the ABA had to continually negotiate competing claims for cultural centrality: from histories which alternatively described '200 years of nation building and 200 years of territorial occupation'; from versions of the national character which moved between the bush legend and modern urban culture or between the British tradition and ethnic diversity; and from projections of our economic future which exposed the incompatibilities between nationalism and internationalism.[12]

Cochrane and Goodman go on to place such tensions within the context of the decline of western nationalism, generally, in the face of a newly globalised capitalism. I am less interested in this here (although it will play a part in the argument of Chapter 6). While conflict between the global, the national and the local is not irrelevant, in postcolonial settler societies like Australia the most pressing conflict is that which structures the relations between the settlers and the indigenous inhabitants. Certainly it is *this* contradiction—between those who celebrated the Bicentenary as marking a moment of foundation and those who mourned it as marking the launching of an invasion—which is the most pronounced in representations of the Australian Bicentenary; and I will deal with it in more detail in a subsequent section of this chapter.

Histories of the Bicentenary must, inevitably, record the numerous contradictions inherent in the project and visible in its enactment. The deference of the 'colonial' competed with the independence of the 'postcolonial' in all the media representations of the visiting royal couple, the Prince and Princess of Wales. Talkback radio was riddled with opposing views: some were appalled that royalty should be participating in the occasion, while others were flattered by Princess Di's choice of a green outfit for Australia Day ('we've decided to call it Bicentennial green', gushed Kerri-Anne Kennerley on Channel 10's *Good Morning Australia*). Rivalry between Sydney and Melbourne bedevilled the ABA's planning throughout and surfaced again on 26 January. Peter Spearritt records that the Melbourne *Herald* followed its report of the fireworks in Sydney with the 'dour' headline: 'Meanwhile it's Ham and Eggs in

74

Melbourne', referring to a breakfast for three thousand people at the Myer Music Bowl sponsored by Heinz (the first, and probably the most substantial, official celebration in Melbourne to mark Australia Day). Spearritt goes on to suggest that the day was not celebrated widely outside Sydney at all—a claim that would be hard to sustain against the evidence of the film *Australia Daze* (evidence not available to Spearritt at the time he wrote his analysis)—and concludes in classic Melbourne style that Australia Day 1988 was merely a 'glorified celebration of Sydney Harbour'.[13]

It should go without saying, of course, that individual Australians experienced the Bicentenary differently. Even an event as placeless and as highly mediated as *Australia Live* produced major variations in response. As much a performance of television as of nationality, *Australia Live* was a four-hour program incorporating more than seventy live satellite link-ups which went to air on the evening of 1 January 1988. Meaghan Morris has said what needs to be said about the program's panoramic form,[14] but the newspaper reviews are interesting. The *Age* called it 'a triumph', a 'dizzying' 'carpet ride' to ever more spectacular and colourful locations, performed without a hitch.[15] Phillip Adams, who also featured in the program itself, was 'quite impressed'.[16] But there were many dissenting voices, notably that of Michael Morton-Evans in the *Australian*. For him, the technical ingenuity of the program was 'ruined by its banality', its propagation of 'one vast Australian cliche':

> It's bad enough that most of the world already identifies the average Australian with Mick Dundee without our television industry having to reinforce this erroneous image.
>
> Where were our writers, our painters, our designers? Where were Australia's great thinkers? With the exception of Manning Clark, all were disappointingly absent. It was almost as if we were ashamed to admit that we were capable of serious and meaningful introspection at this important time in our country's evolution.[17]

A familiar critique, across a wide range of Australian cultural production from the films of Paul Hogan to the designs of Ken Done, this laments an opportunity lost—that of redressing international misconceptions of Australian culture.

According to Meaghan Morris, such a response misunderstands what *Australia Live* was: '*Australia Live* was not a failed portrait of a national identity, nor a poor dramatisation of an Australian social text. It was a four-hour tourist brochure for international, including Australian, consumption'.[18] Accordingly, 'a certain dullness was thus a generic feature, and not an aesthetic flaw':

:lentlessly repetitive aerial shots and domestic close-ups produced a ...k-alike effect, an echoing sameness linking places and personalities in a consistent indistinction, which was perfectly appropriate to the project of the show. Airline inflight magazines and travel advertisements are 'dull' in precisely this way.[19]

For the editors of *Broadcast Engineering News*, however, *Australia Live* was anything but dull. In a four-page feature, complete with diagrams of the satellite link-ups and a blow by blow discussion of the development of the production, the program was described as a 'major television event'. It had also served a unique function in becoming the site at which Australia's regional rivalries could be resolved. The TV program enabled the ABA to avoid the political embarrassment of situating a 'gala' opening event in one of the capital cities, a decision 'which would alienate the rest of the country and leave the organisers open to attack'.[20] Television had solved a political problem through technical ingenuity and became the space where the nation could be at its most 'national'.

Nations are made necessary by the divisions, not the unity, within cultures. In its 'implausible' drive to articulate the private to the public, to reconcile the interests of the individual with those of the state, the nation is definitively 'Janus-faced'.[21] As for nationalism, Homi Bhabha reminds us that it too is 'by nature ambivalent'.[22] This is doubly the case in postcolonial societies where indigenous populations have been dispossessed and where successive waves of immigration multiply the complexities of tradition and ethnicity which have to be negotiated.[23] As I suggested in Chapter 1, what has changed in the way Australian nationalism has lately articulated itself, and what I regard as the hopeful development which became especially apparent during the Bicentenary, is that this complexity is now relatively widely acknowledged. Consequently, it is also relatively widely acknowledged that any future constructions of the Australian 'national character' have to be plural, and that the 'national character' cannot be thought of as a naturally emergent phenomenon. Rather, it is something that we must ourselves culturally, collaboratively, produce—no matter how 'troublesome' such a process may be.[24]

Once it stops being natural, national identity becomes overtly political and plastic: something we can (should) intervene in and influence. For countries such as Australia, with multiple ethnic and cultural traditions, there can be no return to a unitary explanation of national identity. Rather, Australians need to explore ways in which we can make best use of the multiplicity of our possible identities. Kevin Robins, writing from a European context in which the empire has begun to strike back through reverse migration, offers some clues as to how we might do this:

It is in the experience of *diaspora* that we may begin to understand the way beyond empire. In the experience of migration, difference is confronted: boundaries are crossed; cultures are mingled; identities become blurred. The diaspora experience, Stuart Hall argues, is about 'unsettling, recombination, hybridization and "cut-and-mix" and carries with it a transformed relation to Tradition, one in which 'there can be no simple "return" or "recovery" of the ancestral past which is not re-experienced through the categories of the present'. The experience of diaspora, and also of exile, as Edward Said has powerfully argued, allows us to understand relations between cultures in new ways. The crossing of boundaries brings about a complexity of vision and also a sense of the permeability and contingency of cultures. It allows us 'to see others not as ontologically given but as historically constructed' and can thereby 'erode the exclusivist biases we so often ascribe to cultures, to our own not least'.[25]

My view is that the Bicentenary did deposit a residual sense of the 'contingency of cultures'. The survival of contradictions, of cracks in the official discourses of nation, is the encouraging sign of other possibilities, other explanations, successfully competing for representation. One of the locations where this competition is recorded in some detail, and where a sense of multiple possibilities is made palpable, is Pat Fiske's film about Australia Day 1988, *Australia Daze*.

Australia Daze: multiplying identity

This is what for me is being an Australian. This makes more sense to me than all that stuff that's happening on the harbour. (White marcher at the Aboriginal protest in Belmore Park)

If it wasn't for wogs, Australia wouldn't be Australia. (Italian-Australian youth, Mornington Peninsula)

We're the oldest living culture in the world, and we're proud of it. (Aboriginal spokesperson)

Australia Daze documents the Australia Day celebrations in a particularly comprehensive fashion. Filming from midnight to midnight with 24 camera crews, the production must have collected a vast amount of data. This was further supplemented by TV news footage, live TV coverage of the event, and recordings from radio (including talkback calls). There were film crews on a farm near Mount Isa in Queensland, on the pier at Victoria's Mornington Peninsula, in the Triple J studio with H.G. Nelson and 'Rampaging' Roy Slaven for their 'call' of the celebrations, in country towns in every State, in Sydney itself. Significantly, there were six crews at the Aboriginal march in Sydney. The pun in the documentary's title reflects the objectives of the project: to capture the multiplicity of ways in which Australia Day 1988 was celebrated throughout the nation.

The result is a rich and resonant film which presents us with the variety of Australias being celebrated and at the same time highlights key social divisions within the nation. Early in the film, for instance, we move from footage of excited crowds arriving in central Sydney to shots from the Matthew Talbot Hostel for men; the contrast is justified by the voiceover of a talkback radio caller who accuses the Bicentenary of diverting us from the real problems facing the country—the gap between the rich and the poor, for one. Such juxtapositions recur throughout the film without ever being facile; in virtually every case divergent opinions are given their due, allowed to present themselves within a context that resists an easy response—either of acceptance or of dismissal. *Australia Daze* is a remarkably generous documentary which manages to be that way without entirely sacrificing its political point—that a significant number of Australians, albeit a minority, had little to celebrate in 1988.

The multiple locations provide access to a broad range of characters and understandings of the meaning of the day. In Cairns, we meet a woman who is celebrating the coming of Christ's teaching to Australia; a little later we meet a man who, when he offers his view on the Aboriginals, proves that Christ still has some work to do in Cairns: 'they're overpaid, underworked, and ninety per cent of them are useless'. Such a view is not allowed to stand uncontested. A group of teenage girls at the same luncheon tentatively explain to the interviewer that blacks are disadvantaged because people are 'racial' about them. The generational contrast, at least, is a hopeful one.

In rural Tarnagallan, Victoria, a middle-aged woman is interviewed while standing on her roof attaching a homemade land rights flag and a banner offering a 'tribute' to the Aboriginal people of Australia. It provides a striking counterpoint to the preparations for the march in colonial dress through the main street, the highlight of the day.

Interviews with migrant Australians challenge the stereotype of grateful assimilation. At a large gathering in a park on the Mornington Peninsula, a middle-aged Greek man explains how migrants have made Australia a better country. An Italian-Australian youth on the pier claims, to the general agreement of his Anglo-Australian friends, that without 'wogs' Australia would be 'down the hole'. 'How many Australians do you see working in a factory?', his girlfriend asks—a point implicitly taken up by a stockman from Mount Isa who suggests Australians are so workshy that we have had to bring in a lot of 'imports to run the joint'. Signs of multiculturalism are found throughout the film: Chinese dragons, Greek dancing and bagpipes playing Waltzing Matilda are all incorporated into Australia Day marches.

Australia Daze, like *Australia Live*, is panoramic, a spectacle marked by its broad sweep rather than its precise differentiations. It features a full cast of street parties, parades, barbies in the park, booze-ups in the town pub, birthday cakes in the shape of Australia with 200 candles (in Parapardoo, they thoughtfully found a cupcake to represent Tasmania), wet T-shirt competitions, beer-drinking competitions, a quick tour of a Kings Cross sex club by a fat English spruiker (they had a Bicentenary special offer on), and one celebrated long shot of a couple making love on the cliffs of Sydney's North Head. Throughout this mix of individual Australians and their varied cultural practices, one repeatedly encounters an explicit acceptance of cultural diversity and confidence in the tenure of that diversity within the nation. Consequently, there are few occasions when doubts are expressed about any individual's entitlement to the nationality being confirmed through the Bicentenary rituals. There is one highly significant exception to this: a couple of stockmen at Mount Isa.

The film crew follows these men as they herd and break horses, occasionally pausing for a yarn or a smoko with them in the shade of their ute. The stockmen are the most classically iconic representations of a 'traditional' Australia in *Australia Daze*. Framed by establishing shots which foreground the landscape, the weathered faces and slow delivery of these men are the raw material for all those commercials from BHP, Fourex, Fosters and the numerous other companies which have attempted to 'nationalise' their image by drawing from the reservoir of bush iconography. What the two men say, however, explicitly disconnects them from the national celebrations. 'I'm not interested in that kind of thing', says one, and later reveals that the only reason he might be tempted to go to Sydney would be to see 'Lady Di'. The Bicentenary leaves them cold, partly because the way of life which *they* identify as Australian is on its way out. Men are leaving the bush, going to the cities or the mines, and life on the land is becoming increasingly solitary and unproductive. Multiculturalism has only made it worse. As more and more 'imports' arrive, the number of nationalities even in country towns multiplies. The result is a dilution of the bloodline: 'it must end up getting bred out—the Australian', one of them says. Their view of the future is sceptical; one even suggests that the white man's time in Australia is already running out: 'the white man, where he'll wipe himself out, the Aboriginal could live here for another 14 million years. The white man, he won't last long. If he goes for another 200 years, he'd be lucky'. Rather than seeing themselves as living at the heart of Australia, these men talk of their way of life as if it has already gone. Notwithstanding their mythic and visual resonance, they seem to the viewer, and one imagines to themselves, anachronistic. Given the fact that these figures are still current signifiers of Australian life, their deployment in the film reinforces Cochrane and Goodman's claim that Australians have reached a point where we need a 'new paradigm of national representation'.[26]

Significantly, the real core of *Australia Daze* is not located in this contrast between the old and new versions of white Australia. Rather it is in the contrast between white and black Australia. This contrast is localised so that, largely, it is not the mass of 'typical' white Australia which is directly implicated; instead, the opposition is structured around a comparison between the celebrations on Sydney Harbour, as experienced by a thirty-something millionaire from the eastern suburbs, and the gathering of black and white Australians at Redfern Oval and Belmore Park.

We accompany the thirty-something millionaire on his morning bicycle ride with friends and his coffee break in Kings Cross; we join his family and friends on the harbour in what is clearly a most expensive boat; and then attend the party in his harbourside home after the big day. This is the kind of lifestyle most Australians would normally envy, the Great Australian Dream, but the film makes it difficult to envy this man. Rather than representing his lifestyle as an unquestioned ideal, *Australia Daze* depicts him as the epitome of the conscienceless wealth and privilege I identified with the excessive eighties in Chapter 2.[27] At one point his boat takes on a

The First Fleet re-enactment, *Australia Daze.* (courtesy of Pat Fiske and AFI Distribution)

second wave of passengers—members of the Young Presidents Organisation. 'A lot of fun' apparently, these people are from a club of millionaires aged under forty who employ at least 50 people. Thirty-something tells the interviewer this with evident pride in the club's exclusivity, unembarrassed by its glorifying of material wealth.[28]

Australia Daze frequently cuts from shots of Aboriginals protesting at their dispossession to shots which construct this successful white man as a sign of excessive possession. He becomes a register—not of what they must become, but of what they must overcome. While there are aspects of his representation which are serendipitous—for example, he, like everyone else on the boat, is clad in white, further enhancing the visual and thematic contrast with the black, red and yellow of the marchers—other aspects seem very deliberate. The millionaire's face is on screen more than any other in the film, always shot from slightly below as it looks coolly, chin uplifted, into the distance. His air of composure and confidence is exaggerated by the ubiquitous sunglasses, the handsome and well-tended face made into an icon of success to the point where his whole representation becomes ironic. His behaviour both on board and at home bespeaks an assurance of power that is increasingly offensive. At one point in the evening party, he stands with an arm around two women whose sunglasses he has removed so he can see their eyes. His own glasses stay on, his liberty with theirs the *droit de seigneur* of the rich and fashionable.

The spectacle on Sydney harbour is most often presented to us from the vantage point of this man's boat and, to the extent that this is so, its meanings are compromised or at least complicated. For the film, the tactic helps to correct the visual asymmetry that might otherwise exist between the spectacle on the harbour and the March for Freedom, Justice and Hope from Redfern Oval to Belmore Park. The two events seem commensurate as we watch this film, and the historical signficance of the march grows as the film continues. The sequences shot at Redfern Oval are particularly sympathetic, close-ups with moving cameras producing a rich sense of community. The camera follows individual members of the crowd as they greet acquaintances with smiles and handclasps. Where the power of the harbour spectacle is represented through helicopter shots of the epic scale of the event as a whole, in the Aboriginal march scenes the emphasis is upon the nature of the involvement of each individual. The pride and exhilaration on the faces of the participants make it impossible to doubt the significance of this ritual of affirmation. A white woman connected with the 'Migrants for Aboriginal Rights' group is entirely convincing as she says, 'This is what for me is being an Australian; this makes more sense to me than all that stuff that's happening on the harbour'. When this remark is followed by a cut to the yuppies on their boat, notwithstanding the visual force of all 'that's happening on the harbour', it is hard for the film's viewers not to sympathise with her.

Not only does *Australia Daze* offer a gentle critique of the divisions existing within Australian society, it also provides us with evidence that we might be further along the way towards a hybrid national identity than the ABA ever imagined. The film's panorama of Australian identities is politically inclusive without being sentimentally indiscriminate. As a result, *Australia Daze* documents the Bicentenary's success for many Australians, even for some whose dispossession the event had failed to understand or remedy. Crucially, however, it is in the black protest that we find *Australia Daze*'s most positive and sustained images of the power and durability of a collective identity, and an insistence on the necessity of reconciliation.

Invasion Day

Well I heard it on the radio
And I saw it on the television
Back in 1988
All them politicians
Words are easy, words are cheap
Much cheaper than our priceless land
But promises can disappear
Just like writing in the sand
('Treaty', Yothu Yindi)

In a personal and perceptive account of Australia Day, Sylvia Lawson outlined her opposition to the official celebrations and her astonishment at 'how difficult it had been made for most Australians to exclude themselves from the bicentennial embrace'.[29] For Lawson, the most meaningful event was the Aboriginal protest:

> [The march] was the biggest gathering of Aboriginal people in their 50,000 year history. For once white supporters, also gathered for the first time in tens of thousands, stood back as the traditional leaders from Northern Australia wove their way into the park.
>
> The emotional impact of this moving and dignified statement of survival will not be easily forgotten by those present.[30]

Lawson goes on to express great disappointment at the way in which this was ignored by the Australian media, and describes her own frustrated attempts to publish a 'qualitative' account of the march in a newspaper.

One would probably have predicted that the Australian media might play down the Invasion Day protest, given the contradiction it exposed and the protest's potential to compromise the official celebrations. Certainly, the days leading up to 26 January provide ample evidence of a media beat-up, suggesting that the black march would erupt in violence and spoil the nation's birthday. The *Bulletin* had disingenuously lamented the difficulties in ascertaining what blacks might want from white Australia, on the one hand, while darkly hinting at the cost of misjudging the seriousness of their intentions, on the other hand.[31] In the *Sydney Morning Herald*, a feature headlined 'Black Rage' did a lively job of scaremongering: it reported on black groups' intentions to embarrass the government and disrupt official functions—even raising the hoary old spectre of financial aid from Libya. However, it also appreciated the political opportunity 1988 presented to the Aboriginal movement through their unprecedented access to the international media. The importance of international coverage was admitted to be an effective means of increasing the external pressure on the federal government.[32] In two short accompanying articles,[33] the paper implicitly endorsed black activists' reading of the situation; the international media were quoted as nominating the Aboriginal rights issue as the only really interesting angle they had on the Bicentenary.

As Australia Day approached, a series of news stories raised the possibility that the Aboriginal demonstrations might turn violent. A *Sydney Morning Herald* editorial warned Aboriginals that their effectiveness would depend on their 'discipline' and restraint.[34] In numerous reports, the organising of buses to move blacks from around Australia to Sydney for the day of mourning was described by way of military metaphors: the buses were a 'convoy', for instance, displaying the Aboriginals' 'battle colours'. Some treatments were openly inflammatory:

> The blacks have arrived. In dirt-splattered, flag-waving vans they rode into a city that has been waiting uneasily for them to come. Like outlaws in a western movie, they were watched with anxious disquiet as they rumbled in at dawn.
>
> Just before daybreak, the buses from Brisbane had pulled over at a truck-stop about an hour out of Sydney.

The March for Freedom, Justice and Hope, *Australia Daze*. (courtesy of Pat Fiske and AFI Distribution)

The young men and women on board almost instinctively began to don their battle colours.[35]

As the expectations produced by such reports built up, the police responded soberly: 'Go-easy on blacks—order police' was the headline in the *Sun-Herald* on 24 January, confirming that 'trouble' was definitely expected.

Significantly, the black leaders, while issuing routine denials, offered little in the way of a response which might further feed the flames. The day before the event, accordingly, the press took another tack; as the projected 'racial' violence now seemed unlikely to occur, another handy stereotype was wheeled in. 'Hitches in Aboriginal plan for united protest' (the *Australian*, 25.1.1988), 'Black leaders row over Redfern protest march (*Sydney Morning Herald*, 26.1.88) and 'Bickering disrupts black protest' (the *Australian*, 26.1.1988) said the headlines. Among the tactics customarily used to legitimise white disregard for black demands is the construction of black groups as politically divided, childishly diverted by trivial internal disputes, and thus simply not up to the 'big-picture' politics of white Australia. We have seen these discourses more recently in newspaper treatments of the Mabo debate and of the negotiations leading to the framing of the federal legislation. They were certainly deployed with some consistency to play down the significance of the March for Freedom, Justice and Hope on Australia Day.

Of course, none of these media-generated expectations was justified. The march was an extraordinary demonstration of black unity—and, for that matter, of the potential for black *and* white to unite behind a common cause. There was no drunkenness, there was no 'trouble', and police were not required to 'go easy on the blacks' to avoid souring the taste of the day. None of this should have been surprising. As Sylvia Lawson says, in subsequent reports 'a lot of emphasis was put on the fact that the march was peaceful' but it had only been 'the media which had ever suggested that it would not be so'.[36]

Given such distorted treatment of the prospect of the black march, the reports after the event are in fact surprisingly positive. Reviewing the press and television news coverage of the day, it is difficult to support Sylvia Lawson's claim that the march was ignored. It was the second story on most TV bulletins (yielding first place to the celebrations on the harbour), and featured prominently in newspaper coverage. While Lawson writes that the live television coverage of the day ignored the group of protesters at Lady Macquarie's Chair on the harbourside, this was not true of television news reports later on. Additionally, several newspapers devoted specific reports to the protesters there—with pictures. The extent of the coverage was less notable, though, than its manner.

The obvious success of the march allowed media reports to emphasise its joyfulness, thus, I suppose, limiting the extent to which it compromised the official celebrations. Thus, for Ken Brass in the *Australian*, 'it began as the most solemn day in a year of mourning' but ended with 'undisguised rejoicing at the coming together' of the Aboriginal nation. With some relief, perhaps, he reports that the 'Aborigine's day of protest' had become, 'like the rest of Australia's, a day of celebration'. Nevertheless, Brass does not forget what it is that the Aboriginals are celebrating or their difference from 'the rest of Australia':

> Mr Foley went on: 'Let's hope Bob Hawke and his Government gets the message loud and clear'.
> He looked out at what Mr Galarrwuy Yunipingu, the chairman of the Northern Lands Council, was to call 'the biggest crowd I've ever seen to mourn the injustice of the past'.
> Presumably sensing the unity and perverse cheerfulness of the black and white mourners, he added: 'This is what Australia could be like'.[37]

The *Sydney Morning Herald* feature directly focused on the contradiction between black and white Australia and respectfully foregrounded the views of 'the other Australia—that part of the country that rejoices not in the events of 1788, but sees them rather as the beginnings of subjugation and degradation'.[38]

The level of respect evident in these reports is uncommon, generally, in the Australian press's treatment of Aboriginal issues. In a piece which continued to mobilise military metaphors but with an important shift in alignment—from seeing the Aboriginals as outlaws to seeing them as 'veterans'—the *Age* was in no doubt of the significance of the event:

> The march made a slow but peaceful progress, even stopping to allow a car to drive past. But as it edged closer to the city and as white Australians stood on the footpath to cheer them on, the atmosphere became electric.
> Soon after the thousands of white supporters had joined the march at Sydney's Belmore Park, one white woman sat down and wept. Black and white. Australians hugged each other and others cheered and whistled . . .[39]

From such a report we do receive a 'qualitative' view, one which gives credit to the black and white Australians involved: 'these were veterans of a 200 year old war, as one banner read, and the pride was more than obvious'.[40] While perhaps not yet exemplary, this is light years away from the coverage of Aboriginal issues we are accustomed to reading in our newspapers. It would be pleasant to believe that the shift occurred in response to the dignity and justice of the black cause as expressed in this march—that others responded in the way Sylvia Lawson did. If such a response occurred, however, it did not last; its influence was sadly missing from the newspaper coverage of the Mabo debate in 1993. Nevertheless, that it might seem to be present in the coverage of 26 January 1988 suggests that something important *did* begin to happen during the Bicentenary.

I would not be the first to suggest that the most important 'unintended consequence' of the Bicentenary was the elevation of Aboriginal rights in the national consciousness of social policy imperatives.[41] As Meaghan Morris has intimated, the continual presence of the Aboriginal protest also had an effect beyond the boundaries of that issue; it challenged and interrogated the current ideas of nation by forcing people to accept that 'the very nature' of the nation is ambiguous, contradictory, contested:

> The 1988 protest showed that precedents . . . can be destroyed as well as revised. Aborigines had already changed the Re-enactment's significance by proclaiming a year of Mourning—and by making a Landing impossible. So proceedings began in open admission that the ceremony was not a 'factual' mimicry of the past, but a political event in the present. Once the basic premise had been altered, the ceremonial 'present' became, for the official script of the day, a field of suspense and evasion. Speech after speech from the dais skipped hastily from 'the mistakes of the past' to expressions of faith 'in the future'. The *significant* present was elsewhere: with people lying in the sun, having picnics, watching boats and milling about, but above all with the insistent critical accompaniment of the Aboriginal protest. Audible and visible in most telecasts on the day, extending later into media commentary, news items, current affairs shows, and the television archive of future Aboriginal images—that protest effectively historicised, on Aboriginal terms, an entrepreneurial 'national' event.[42]

Against all expectations then, the experience Meaghan Morris describes suggests that the Bicentenary may have usefully articulated itself to processes through which all Australians could begin to become more comfortable with an ambiguous, contested, mutable but honourable, formation of national identity.

Celebrating the nation

> *While they don't exist as spaces and assemblies, the public*
> *realm and the public are still to be found, large as life, in*
> *media. Television, popular magazines and photography, the*
> *popular media of the modern period, are the public*
> *domain, the place where and the means by which the*
> *public is created and has its being. The clue to its where-*
> *abouts is not to look for citizens in the city centre . . , but*
> *to look for the public in publicity.* (John Hartley, *The Politics*
> *of Pictures*)

The positive note just struck in the preceding section, and the
generally positive line taken throughout this analysis, runs against
the grain of most critical accounts of the Bicentenary. Fundamental
to many accounts is the representation of 1988 as a year of lost
opportunities for 'analysis, appraisal and reform'.[43] While I wouldn't
stop there, I don't disagree with such a judgement. There is another
kind of appraisal, however, with which I do want to take issue here
because its elitist resistance to, ultimately, *any* kind of mass-mediated national event causes it to misconstrue how a national 'public'
is actually formed.

Several of the contributions to Bennett et al.'s *Celebrating the*
Nation: A critical study of Australia's Bicentenary are written from
this kind of position. Its operation is signified, firstly, by an acknowledged discomfort with popular representations of cultural
nationalism and, secondly, by an often unacknowledged discomfort
with the kind of publicity which enables such representations to
occur. Reading Jennifer Craik's account of Expo 88, for instance,
one can't help but feel that the exhibition could never have found
a form of publicity, a medium of representation or performance,
which would enable it to be successful for its target audience *and*
for this critic.

Craik's critique is interesting in that it employs 'ambivalence' as
its central theme,[44] describing an exhibition which justified itself
through its hailing of an international public ('Together, we'll show
the world' as the advertising proclaimed), but which served a local
public primarily (as much as 70 per cent of its attendance came
from residents of Brisbane, where it was held). Expo's economic
consequences for Queensland were ambiguous too; while it brought
bumper numbers of tourists to Brisbane, this was at the cost of other
Queensland tourist destinations such as the Great Barrier Reef. As
a national event,[45] Expo was compromised—partly, it has to be said,

by the superior attitude taken by Sydney and Melbourne which refused to believe that their 'country cousin' could pull it off successfully.[46] Although Expo was part of the official Bicentenary program, other States were slow to support it and it took Expo chairman Llew Edwards two years of negotiation to secure their participation. Locally, the planning for the event was dogged by its material effects: giving the lie to public projections of the 'people's Expo'—that is, it was to be more than a trade fair—the development of the site required the demolition of areas of cheap rental housing in South Brisbane and thus impacted most heavily on those who were most vulnerable. As the opening approached, some tenants in the surviving rented accommodation near the site found themselves on the street as landlords looked to let their rooms to Expo visitors at increased rates.

Craik's essay demonstrates convincingly that it is virtually impossible for such an event to be an unqualified success for all citizens in its host city. However, in Craik's account we can detect traces of her own ambivalences: of the same anti-populist distaste which informs Michael Morton-Evans' critique of *Australia Live* and which asks for something more 'substantial', less 'commercial', from its cultural events. Thus the essay harrumphs: 'Expo 88 was a successful party so long as people did not think about it greatly'[47] (it would not be the first party people did not think about!). Craik concludes: 'as a nation-building exercise, Expo 88 was a profound flop; as parochial boosterism, it was at best a flash in the pan'.[48] The jury is still out on the long-term effects of Expo for Brisbane, but it is possible to make the positive case with much more enthusiasm than Craik does. Certainly South Bank—the 'parklands' built on the old Expo site—has been an outstanding success in terms of its popularity with Brisbane residents and few of the fears Craik expresses about its likely design have so far been realised.

What is evident in Craik's essay, and in Trotter's account of the Stockmen's Hall of Fame as well as Cochrane and Goodman's discussion of the Travelling Exhibition,[49] is the substantial distance between the processes and objectives of these exhibitions, the responses from their actual audience, and the expectations of the cultural critic. This distance is only partially explicable through reference to critical reservations about nationalism. Also implicated are the critics' elitist suspicions that the way in which such large-scale public projects produce their audience is especially inauthentic. Hints of such suspicions surface in the critics' frequent incantations of the demonologies of commercialisation, of

Americanisation, of the evils of publicity itself—as if there were ways of constructing an audience for such events which were *less* phony, *more* authentic. Behind all of this lies the critics' intuition of a public which is independent of the media, an intuition John Hartley challenges when he defines the modern 'public' as precisely that which is called into existence *by* the media:

> It transpires . . . that there is a new development in the history of looking: the public has slipped, perhaps decisively, from the disciplinary hands of educational and governmental authorities into the gentler hands of the smiling professions. Smiling has become one of the most important public virtues of our times, a uniform that must be worn on the lips of those whose social function it is to create, sustain, tutor, represent and make images of the public—to call it into discursive being.[50]

By the 'smiling professions' Hartley means the whole domain of publicity, the key medium for which is television. For Hartley, television is a social technology which plays a crucial role in forming the public, not just speaking to it.

Morley and Silverstone also argue that television is more than a means of representing the nation to itself.[51] Drawing on Dayan and Katz's research into the televising of national events, they suggest that television directly 'performs' rituals of community:

> . . . Dayan and Katz are concerned to analyse television's role in constructing (literally 'performing') media events such as the royal wedding. In this connection, they argue, television should not be seen as 'representing' the event but as constructing the experience of it for the majority of the population. . . Television is not simply transmitting such an event (or commenting on it) but is bringing it into existence.[52]

Developing this notion through reference to David Chaney's work, Morley and Silverstone refute the idea that national occasions enacted and broadcast through the mass media are therefore somehow inauthentic. Chaney has argued that television performs a central social function, providing mass society with its rituals— indeed its 'public life'. So, the telecast of the Australia Day celebrations dramatised the nation as a symbolic community and in so doing performed a ritual confirmation of Australians' collective identity. While one might think that the importance of such rituals had diminished in post-industrial society, Morley and Silverstone claim, after Chaney, that their importance has actually increased:

> Contrary to the established view that 'ritual' is less significant in secularised industrial societies than it was in earlier times, Chaney

argues that, because of the scale and nature of these societies (where the entire citizenry simply cannot be personally acquainted and a sense of collective identity must be continually invented), ritual becomes more salient as a mode of dramatising (indeed, constituting) 'community'. Thus, Chaney notes that 'collective ceremonies have patently not disappeared from the calendar of institutional identity and reproduction; indeed they have been made more accessible and less arcane through their dramatisation as media performances'.[53]

This is a radical revision of the idea of the public domain; it has the public seated in their living rooms, experiencing their citizenry primarily through membership of a media event's audience. The boundary between citizen and viewer, between the public and the audience, as John Hartley suggests, disappears.[54]

Such a view of the social function of the media's performance of public events is very different from the view implicit in the three critiques I have referred to that appear in *Celebrating the Nation*.[55] Informing these essays is a nostalgia for a form of national public that Hartley tells us no longer exists (if it ever did): a nostalgia for a place where the national-public could gather, at which we could all be physically present, and for which media representations are a pale and inadequate substitute. Many of the Bicentenary celebrations—certainly the keynote events such as *Australia Live* and the arrival of the First Fleet on Australia Day—were definitively mass media events and virtually all were the subject of vigorous media promotion. As some of the critical distaste for such events (and such promotion) seems related to the imaginary possibility of alternative rituals of collective identity, of more 'organic' forms of community celebration, it is not surprising that some of the resulting accounts are insensitive to those who found these mass-mediated experiences moving and confirming. In Castles et al's *Mistaken Identity*,[56] for instance, the respect for difference which informs the book's discussion of multiculturalism is far less evident in its account of the popular responses to and participation in the Bicentenary.

My aim here is not to recuperate the Bicentenary by emphasising its function as a ritual of collective identity. I am concerned however, given the degree to which criticism of the Bicentenary has itself become ritualised among Australian intellectuals, to maintain a recognition of the complexity of the events and their possible effects, and a respect for the experiences and motivations of those who participated in them. The 'failure' of the Bicentenary has customarily been imputed from the degree to which black and white Australians saw through it, criticised it, refused to participate in it,

91

defied its versions of history. This was a year of highly contested celebrations in which the seamless construction of the nation could barely be sustained for the four hours of *Australia Live*—let alone a whole year. If a nation is assumed to be unitary, its people speaking with one voice, then the Bicentenary certainly failed to produce that kind of nationhood. Far from lamenting that failure, I want to argue that it led to something much more valuable, achieved against the grain of official intentions. The Bicentenary revealed the limits to the official production of nationalism when it made Australia's project of nation-building explicit. Becoming explicit, it rendered itself ever more vulnerable to contestation as new definitions of the nation came into play.

Consequently, most would agree, the Bicentenary was not well contained; it leaked alternative possibilities, shifts in meanings which were consoling because they changed the colour and significance of the program as a whole. I for one am encouraged by this. Nevertheless, if we were to ask whose interests were served by the Bicentenary we would be unlikely to answer: 'the nation'. Foremost among the beneficiaries would be particular commercial interests and the Labor government of Bob Hawke. The benefits to the rest of us may well turn out to be of the kind intimated in my argument in this chapter, but it would be a real optimist who would claim they had already started to arrive. The opportunities taken for material nation-building, for genuine reconciliation with the dispossessed, for the reassessment of issues of equity and justice, were few and far between. Having missed these opportunities, we need to insist even more loudly that they be addressed in the next proposed moment of explicit 'nationing'—the centenary of federation in 2001. For, despite all the encouraging complications one might extract from histories of the Bicentenary, there would be little point in critical analysis of 1988 if it didn't help us avoid an action replay in 2001.

5

Looking to America: the Crocodile Dundee factor

In the preceding chapters, I have built my argument around one or two instances of particular uses of nationalism which have been examined at some length. My procedure in this chapter is more generalised, its examples more dispersed, as I deal with the relationship between Australia and the United States and the implication of that relationship in the construction of Australian national identities. The object ultimately in view is another program of both official and commercial image production—the putatively nationalist project of marketing Australia as a tourist destination.

American Dreams

We saw our big smooth cars cruising through cities with bright lights. We entered expensive night clubs and danced till dawn. We made love to women like Kim Novak and men like Rock Hudson. We drank cocktails. We gazed lazily into refrigerators filled with food and prepared ourselves lavish midnight snacks which we ate while we watched huge television sets on which we would be able to see American movies free of charge and forever. (Peter Carey, 'American Dreams')

In one of his early stories, Peter Carey constructs a fable about Australia's relationship to America. His narrator lives in a small town of no particular distinction; he takes consolation in his 'American

93

Dreams'—'of the big city, of wealth, of modern houses, of big motor cars'.[1] When a recluse who lives outside the town dies, a scale model of the community and its inhabitants is discovered behind the walls around his house. The narrator suspects that the model is intended to reveal the beauty of the place and thus to put a stop to 'the American dreams we were so prone to'.[2] However, the model contains some shocking revelations about people in the town, and so the townspeople are extremely ambivalent about it. Before they can decide what to do, the minister for tourism comes to town:

> The minister for tourism came in a large black car and made a speech to us in the football pavilion. We sat on the high, tiered seats eating potato chips while he stood against the fence and talked to us. We couldn't hear him very well, but we heard enough. He called the model town a work of art and we stared at him grimly. He said it would be an invaluable tourist attraction. He said tourists would come from everywhere to see the model town. We would be famous. Our businesses would flourish. There would be work for guides and interpreters and caretakers and taxi drivers and people selling soft drinks and ice creams.
>
> The Americans would come, he said. They would visit our town in buses and in cars and on the train. They would take photographs and bring wallets bulging with dollars. American dollars.[3]

The Americans *do* come with their dollars but eventually the townspeople become 'pretty sick of the game' of exploiting the local attraction. Crucial to 'the game' is conformity between the town, its people and their representations in the model; the visitors are reluctant to accept that the real life 'characters' might have changed or that they have grown out of the behaviours depicted in their replicas. The narrator is irritated by this but also expresses guilt at having 'let the visitors down' through 'growing older and sadder' than his replica.

'American Dreams' is a sardonic warning about the cultural colonisation of Australia: the people in the town are frozen in time, their mutable identities relinquished in favour of the fixed representations in the tourist attraction. The compensations for colonisation—dollars and dreams—do not sustain them long. Carey has dealt with such themes repeatedly: in *Bliss* and in *Illywhacker* he explores both the seductiveness of American dreams and their corrosive effect on the culture that pursues them.[4] One can see why he is interested: Australia *does* have its American dreams, and it has been repeatedly encouraged to pursue them in return for American dollars. The rhetoric of Carey's 'minister for tourism' is entirely familiar to us now, twenty years after the story was published. Carey's fiction usually examines Australians' ambivalence about their American dreams, but this story's collapsing of the processes of an internationalising capitalism into those of Americanisation is symptomatic of only one side of the ambiguous relationship between the two countries: American domination figures prominently in Australian fears about the erosion of cultural identity. The relationship between Australia and America—in both its negative and its positive aspects—is my starting point for this chapter and it will lead us eventually to consider the industry Carey singles out as especially Americanising, international tourism.

The American model

'I must speak to a boy named Elvis Presley', said the head-mistress of a London comprehensive academy in 1956, 'because he has carved his name on every desk in the school'. (Greil Marcus, *Lipstick Traces*)

Throughout its white history, Australia has obsessively defined itself in opposition to Britain; Australia *was* what Britain was *not* and even those attributes we shared—our 'common traditions'—were said to be inflected differently within an Australian context. In contrast and against the grain of the Carey story, the relation to America has largely been constructed in terms of similarity: our interests often assumed to be, if not identical, then closely aligned. This relationship has certainly become more strained and ambiguous as the twentieth century has unwound, as Australia—like just about every other country in the world—has had to deal with the complex patterns of independence and subjection that the American domination of the world economy has produced. Even today, while the relationship is not a simple one, many Australians find much to admire in what they think of as the United States.

Richard White tells us that the transplanted Anglo-Saxon societies produced by British colonialism during the eighteenth and nineteenth centuries—Canada, Australia, New Zealand—regarded themselves as having much in common. Indeed, their common colonial heritage was established well in advance of their respective claims for nationhood through a shared descriptive rhetoric:

> Words such as brash, young, egalitarian, materialistic, provincial, brag-gart, were applied to all of them. They were commonly thought of as

95

the children of Britain or Europe, as strapping sons, dutiful daughters or juvenile delinquents. Politically they were considered 'in advance' of Europe; culturally they were more often thought to be inferior. Their inhabitants developed a counter-image of Europe or the 'Old World': oppressive and decadent, but also sophisticated and intellectually intimidating, the old world could be sentimentalised or identified with poverty and privilege.[5]

As the individual colonies developed specific mythologies of national character, these common characteristics were folded into the discourses used to define the national 'type'—simultaneously 'nationalised' and naturalised.

Once the colonies began to think of themselves as new societies rather than as outposts of old societies—and this did not take very long at all in Australia's case—the search for an alternative social model almost inevitably led to the United States.[6] By the mid-nineteenth century, the American model was notable for its democratic political system, for its demonstrated capacity for large-scale commercial and industrial development, and, since it too had evolved out of a colonial society, for the apparent ease with which it could be emulated by other similarly situated societies:

> It was the United States which stood out among these new societies. Because of its position as the oldest, biggest, and most advanced of the new societies, it was commonly considered to be, as *The Australian* put it in 1831, 'a model for all new countries and New South Wales (hereafter) in particular'.[7]

It is not America's political system, however, which has become the primary object of Australian desires in the twentieth century: now we dream of an American 'lifestyle'.

Stuart Hall has remarked that the postmodern world 'dreams itself to be American'.[8] Whatever else one might want to say about the various markers of postmodernity, this one at least is not a recent condition: an identification between America and modernity could be posited just as easily. Philip and Roger Bell's *Implicated*, a history of 'the United States in Australia', argues that what is often simplistically thought of as 'Americanisation' is more accurately explained as 'modernisation'. This not only acknowledges the benefits Australia has received from what Philip and Roger Bell describe as the United States' 'implication' in our cultural history, but also emphasises the fact that America was itself caught up in the same modernising process, albeit well in advance of Australia.[9] I think the argument can be pushed a little further in that Australian cultural history, like that of many other countries, suggests that America was

96

generally regarded as the connecting link between modernity and the achievement of material prosperity. The arrival of the supermarket in Australia (Coles offered us a 'New World' in their aisles), the movement from urban semi-detached to suburban housing developments (the spread of the Californian bungalow), the expansion of the suburban block to accommodate a driveway for the car (producing the so-called 'Australian' quarter-acre block), and the progressive introduction of such labour-saving devices as the vacuum cleaner and the washing machine, all provide evidence of an identification between the modern, the American, and the leisured lifestyle of a prosperous middle class. Images of this American lifestyle were naturalised worldwide through the electronic media; not only did the technologies of film and television themselves epitomise modernity, but the representations they carried (especially during the Cold War) were overwhelmingly devoted to rendering as normative the material and cultural consumption patterns of a mythic middle-class America.

Largely due to the success of America's export of its popular culture, Australian and American contemporary popular cultures reflect a close ideological alignment over an idealised image of a desirable way of life. This has been paralleled by other kinds of alignments. There have been many occasions in Australian history when American interests and Australian interests have been represented to Australians as identical. We have a history of military alliances where our shared 'regional interests' (in the case of World War II and Vietnam) have legitimised joint military effort. In trade and foreign policy, Australia's deference to American interests has at times been pretty abject: the nadir of sycophancy occurred, perhaps, when Harold Holt vowed to go 'All the way with LBJ' in Vietnam, but the recent reluctance to criticise revivals of agricultural protectionism in the States was similarly craven. Australians' mixed reaction to Prime Minister Hawke's decision to send an armed force in support of the American-sponsored UN offensive during the Gulf War suggests, however, that while the principle of common interests may be generally acknowledged there are plenty of moments when this principle is questioned in practice. The history of Australian–American foreign policy and trade relations is littered with occasions when critics have argued that American interests have been masked by the ways in which Australian interests have been described.

For example, early in his current term of office, Queensland Premier Wayne Goss travelled to Los Angeles to discuss Queensland's potential as a location for Hollywood film producers.

He was doing so because the industry in Queensland recognised the need to strengthen its infrastructure if it was ever to develop into a viable centre for Australian film production. Some co-production deals were thought likely to achieve this end. When Goss returned, he was flush with excitement after a classic Hollywood snow job. The Americans had promised to come here and work all right, but complained at the costs involved. It was in Queensland's interest, they persuaded him, to attract overseas producers through waiving a range of government charges normally incurred when shooting there. Goss agreed, returning home with the good news that it would now be cheaper for American producers than for Australians to work here, and that this was in the interests of the local industry. It's hard to please some people, it seems, because the local industry was not impressed.

This story is emblematic of a relationship that continually appears to promise benefits to the junior partner while first ensuring that it delivers benefits to the senior partner. Little wonder, then, that despite the seductiveness of the American model in Australia there is more than a little scepticism about the honourableness of its intentions and the desirability of such close alignments between Australian and American interests. For many of my generation, Vietnam is responsible for a residue of leftist anti-Americanism. Paradoxically, and deepening the ambivalences experienced, it is among this generation that certain forms of American culture—popular music, film, contemporary fiction—find their most ardent Australian consumers. In a further contrast, a much more programmatic critique of what is regarded as Americanisation derives from a traditionally conservative resistance to all popular cultural forms. This is by no means a uniquely Australian critique; Dick Hebdige has described its operation in Britain during the 1950s and 1960s in *Hiding in the Light*.[10] As each popular fad turns up from America—be it the 'jungle rhythms' of jazz or rock n' roll, or bizarre one-offs such as the hula hoop, pet rocks or the Teenage Mutant Ninja Turtles—it is met by another moral panic, sparking off newspaper features ('What the Teenage Mutant Ninja Turtles Are Teaching Your Kids!') and 'debates' with Kerry O'Brien on ABC-TV's *Lateline*. At such moments, discourses of anti-populism, moral rearmament and leftist anti-Americanism converge and blur into each other.

Worldwide, America stands for both the best and the worst capitalism can offer: the ultimate fantasy of capitalism's power to deliver on your desires (Disneyland, I guess), and the ultimate nightmare of competitive individualism out of control. This latter aspect has numerous and proliferating forms: it would include Americans' ideological commitment to the right to 'bear arms' or the excessive narcissism of a celebrity like Michael Jackson. As the epitome of modernity, of course, a mythologised America is routinely deployed in media constructions of utopian *and* dystopian futures for Australia, projecting either the 'gleaming promise of modernity or the barbarism of an economically driven consumerism'.[11] During the Gulf War, we could see both kinds of myths in operation.

Initially, it was difficult not to be impressed by the capacity of CNN to bring the war apparently 'live' to our loungerooms; watching the war unfold in this way felt like the cutting edge of modernity. (Definitively, *not* postmodernity; this did not feel like the end of history.) It wasn't long, however, before Australian viewers were voicing concern at the American journalists' apparent militarism: the lack of distinction between the US Defence Department line and that taken by the CNN journalists reporting the war. The mode, rather than the fact, of the coverage became an issue. One Sydney journalist published a series of pieces analysing the jingoistic rhetoric used by journalists and the service personnel they interviewed:[12] for a while there was a genre of post-mission interviews with bomber pilots who talked like footballers—as in 'we sure as hell kicked some ass out there today'. Within a week or two, there was widespread evidence (in the letters pages of the press, for instance) of public distrust of the American military and the American media; Stephen Loosely published an item in *Australian Business* (of all places!) suggesting that it was dangerous to rely so heavily on American news media and calling for more Australian input to 'restore balance'.[13]

It is significant, given the vulnerability of the homology constructed between Australian and American political interests both generally and in this specific instance, that when more Australian input was forthcoming—the ABC were particularly diligent in their attempts to cover the range of points of view, even providing us with samples of Jordanian coverage at one stage—it was sufficiently threatening to warrant prime ministerial intervention. The ABC's primary Middle East expert, Robert Springborg, was subjected to an extraordinary personal attack from Bob Hawke who described him as an object of (among other things) 'contempt'. Hawke's attack was revealing in that it levelled blame for this attempt at informed reporting to an 'anti-interventionist, anti-American, anti-Israeli virus'.[14] And although the prime minister's criticism did lead to an 'independent review' of the ABC's news and current affairs reporting aimed at limiting the contagion from this virus, it is also worth pointing out that the ABC's ratings rose dramatically during this period, that this new audience was concentrated around news and current affairs on radio and TV, and that it has largely stayed with the ABC since.[15]

One could tease out the ambiguities of the American model further through other examples of representations of America(ns)—the Telecom commercials ('We do, Chucky, we do') are almost irresistible texts.[16] At this point, however, it is sufficient for me to say that America has been given multiple meanings at various times and in various contexts within Australian popular culture (I can count at least five categories); although these meanings are potentially contradictory many, if not all, can operate simultaneously. Further, they are meanings which are structurally related in one way or another to notions of, or positions about, Australian national identity. America stands in its most positive light as a model of independence and as a supporter of Australian independence. As the pre-eminent site of modernity, it invites emulation while beckoning to those who want to establish themselves internationally as *the* place to 'make it'. (Which is why Telecom—there, I've succumbed—reiterates its power to impress 'Chucky' with its premier version of modernity, the mobile phone.) On the negative side, America is also a model of those aspects of modernity we would most like to avoid: not only such effects of mass urban existence as high levels of crime but also the discursive regimes of highly 'media-ted' society—those of celebrity, sensationalism and so on which are seen to mark the American media and surrounding industries. Finally, as Australians look for ways to maintain their cultural and political difference they are continually forced to acknowledge their relative powerlessness in a globalised economy that is still dominated by an apparently friendly but nevertheless worrying America. I want to track some of these meanings at work in the Gold Coast theme park, Warner Bros Movie World.

Warner Bros Movie World was established in 1991 as a joint venture between the giant American communications company Warner Bros and the local film distribution and exhibition company Village Roadshow. It shares the site with a working production studio, complete with film processing and post-production facilities, which opened its doors in 1988. The original American partner in the production studios was Dino De Laurentis, who is reputed to have become interested in Australia as a location when Robert Hughes' *The Fatal Shore* hit the American bestseller lists. (There is an industry legend that De Laurentis instructed his lawyers to get an option on the film rights for Hughes' book without knowing that it was a work of history, not fiction.) When De Laurentis hit financial trouble, Warners moved in as the American partner and built Movie World. The studio seems to have established itself as a viable production facility for both the Australian and the American industries. Films produced there include *Fortress, Blood Oath* and *The Delinquents*, while the downmarket TV soap *Paradise Beach* is in production at the time of writing.

Movie World creates the experience of 'Hollywood on the Gold Coast' through a local version of the Hollywood studio tour; by uncovering some of the 'secrets' of film production ('movie magic'); through stunt shows organised around a particular film genre (the wild west show, the 'Police Academy'); through pseudo-funpark rides, organised around a film or television theme (a search for Bugs Bunny via an underground river, for instance, or a tour of the post-production suites pursued by vandalising 'Gremlins'); and by peppering the park with the images of the stars (people in Bugs Bunny suits, 'personal appearances' by Batman). Australian film is, predictably, more or less absent, although there is a replica of Young Einstein's 'Gravity Homestead' as one of the 'blockbuster attractions' (an Australian film in terms of its technical and creative personnel, *Young Einstein* was produced by Warners). More than half of the attractions on offer at Movie World are what the program calls 'shopping adventures' (or what we would call shops): these include merchandising outlets for Warners products (everything from plastic Bugs Bunnies to movie posters to framed original 'cels' from Warners cartoons); recording and video studios ('*You* can be Superman!'); and portrait shops offering 'vintage' portraits or magazine cover shots.[17]

What Movie World offers is the opportunity for Australians to immerse themselves in the culture of American popular cinema without actually going to Hollywood. To this end, the Americanness of the shows and attractions is necessarily unrelenting. The actors, the buildings, the cars, the food on offer, all work towards the construction of an idealised, timeless America through their reiterations of the classic Americana of the movies. This is extremely pleasurable because it manages to be exotic and familiar at the same time. (That is, there is the excitement at the sudden irruption of the American police car, the cartoon character, the Gotham City square,

101

Warner Bros Movie World:
the program. (courtesy of
Warner Bros Movie World)

but this is succeeded by the pleasure of recognition as your movie knowledges allow you to reclaim what you see as part of *your own* cultural inventory.) While the 'Americana' effect is pervasive, it is also often unconvincing; one has the curiously disorienting experience of hearing the actors' Australian accents seeping through the American. Within a theme park aimed at mythologising not only the world of the movies, but also the ways in which that world is industrially constructed (the double possibilities of the idea of 'movie magic'), the sense of artificiality is multi-layered; that the illusion fails to be seamless is not necessarily a significant reduction of the pleasures it produces.

Nevertheless, the experience of Movie World is in its way emblematic. On the one hand, Australian visitors must forget national difference as they submit to their enclosure within the world of Hollywood movies; on the other hand, the palpable phoniness of it all, the cracks which continually remind us of the processes through which these illusions are being produced, comfortably reinforce certain negative preconceptions about American popular culture and reflect a kind of dull authenticity back onto our own domestic culture. Contrastingly, at a time when the Australian film industry has begun to flex its muscles again, a visit to Movie World is a sobering reminder of just how comprehensive a hold Hollywood has on the popular imagination of this country. Movie World's stunt shows continually draw on and reinforce the audience's knowledge of and affection for Hollywood cinema; the enthusiasm with which the audience responds is telling. If anyone doubted that Hollywood film and television provided the *lingua franca* of story and fantasy for at least the English-speaking western world, a visit to Movie World would convince them.

One has to be wary, though, of viewing the Movie World audience's enthusiastic participation only through the lens of cultural imperialism. John Caughie has argued that 'commonsense notions of the colonisation of the unconscious or the imaginary, a notion which informs quite persistent national anxieties about the seductiveness of American popular entertainment', misunderstands some aspects of the pleasures and ironies implicit in the kind of audience activity I have recorded—an activity very like those he describes as 'playing at being American'.[18] Drawing on feminist screen theory's postulation of the female spectator's 'double identification' with film narrative—her capacity to identify with both subject and object, seer and seen or, in Movie World's case, American and Australian—Caughie explores the possibility of film and television viewers 'playing' with their apparent subjection to American texts and genres. They do this, he suggests, through an 'ironic knowingness':

> . . . which may escape the obedience of interpellation or cultural colonialism and may offer a way of thinking subjectivity free of subjection. It gives a way of thinking identities as plays of cognition and miscognition, which can account for the pleasures of playing at being, for example, American, without the paternalistic disapproval that goes with the assumption that it is bad for the natives.[19]

103

Caughie differentiates his description of an audience's 'games and tactics' from utopian celebrations of the progressive resistance of 'naturally oppositional readers who will get it right in the end'.[20] He emphasises that his is merely an attempt to retain the sense of the 'double edge' in the production of cultural identities, not to discount the power of the structures within which cultural identities are produced.

Caughie's argument helps refine the ideological texture of what happens for the visitor at Movie World, and of the nature of the Australian/American relations structuring that experience. At another level of analysis, and further illustrative of the complex, even paradoxical, negotiations between Australian cultural nationalism and American economic power, is the relation between Movie World, the Warners production studios and the development of the Queensland film industry. The Warners studios are central to the policies adopted by Film Queensland to build up a local production infrastructure that will include a fully commercial sector. In comparison to most of the other States, Queensland has been a very late starter in the development of a film culture and a local production industry, and it has been difficult for policy-makers to decide just how to assist this development best. While government financial support for the Warners production studios has been contentious—few of the productions have been entirely local in origin, after all—there have been no alternative commercial ventures they might have supported instead. It remains an American operation and is rarely talked about as an integral part of Queensland film culture by other local participants in that culture—such as the independent film makers or Cinematheque.

Nevertheless, while Movie World, for its part, barely even acknowledges the existence of an Australian industry, it is possible to see its operations as providing significant support for it. I am not privy to the precise financial relation between the theme park and the production studios, but it is clear that Movie World's cash flow has been critical in buffering the studios against hard times. As for the studios, while they have depended on American productions or co-productions in order to survive in the past, this will not necessarily be the pattern in the future. Currently, the studios are thriving with both wholly local projects and co-productions booked in over the next twelve months and they may well provide a stable basis for industry growth and employment further down the track. Ironically, the significant benefits which should flow from this to the Queensland industry are at least partly due to the money earned by a theme park bent on reinforcing mythologies about the cultural universality of the American industry. This is a case where 'playing at being American' is serving what are usually conflicting objectives. The pleasant symbiosis I have described here is not typical. Mostly, our cultural industries find themselves asking the question Caughie offers as the nagging counterpoint to his critique of the assumptions behind the cultural imperialism thesis: 'what if playing at being American is the only game in town?'. What happens then to what Caughie calls 'the embarrassingly persistent category of the nation'?[21] Despite the inroads made by economic rationalist policies, most of our cultural industries still have regulatory structures which protect them, up to a point, against competition from outside. Regulations which prescribe a minimum level of local content have become standard and often extremely effective components of the context within which the Australian cultural industries operate. Without the local music quota which has operated in Australian radio since the 1940s it is very unlikely that we would have an Australian music industry now.[22] Without the (recently modified) regulation that all advertising screened in Australia should be shot by Australians (and despite the scams that this regulation legitimised, involving dummy crews of Australians on foreign shoots and so on), most Australian film historians believe that we would not have been able to establish a local film production industry in the 1970s.[23] The implied—indeed, often the explicit—object of such culturally nationalist and industrially protectionist strategies is the American popular entertainment industry. While one might think that this should place our cultural industries in opposition to the Americans, the fact that the marker of success for Australian cultural products is acceptance within the American market actually encourages industrial partnerships with the Americans—like that at the Warners Movie World studios.

This creates some complex cultural politics. In a recent edition of SBS's *Movie Show*, David Stratton commented on the casting of American actor Jimmy Smits in the Australian film, *Gross Misconduct*. He saw the rewriting of the part (the film was loosely based on the Orr case at the University of Tasmania in the 1950s) in order to accommodate an American star with box office appeal as 'cheapening' the film, and he regarded Smits' performance as the film's only significant flaw. Stratton's co-host, Margaret Pomerantz—characteristically—disagreed; she thought Smits was 'pretty cute', and that the choice of actors with international pulling power was often justified. Her point of view was supported by the film's director, George (*Snowy River*) Miller, who maintained that this casting decision virtually guaranteed greater success with sales and distribution. It is, of course, a familiar and longstanding source of controversy in the Australian industry; the dispute between what Dermody and Jacka called 'Industry 1' and 'Industry 2'—roughly, between cultural nationalism and internationalism.[24] The internationalist side of the dispute thinks about itself through the discourses of business that we met in Chapter 2: it represents hard-nosed industry wisdom against the wishy-washy impracticalities of cultural nationalism. There is actually very little empirical evidence to support such a construction. Dermody and Jacka wrote in 1987 that it 'is difficult to think of a case where overseas personnel, particularly actors, have enhanced a film's artistic or box-office performance, or conversely where a film's failure is attributable to the absence of such personnel'.[25] It is still difficult to think of such a case, although one can easily provide instances of the reverse: films in which a cynical casting decision has had disastrous effects on the film's artistic or commercial success (the casting of Charlie Schlatter in *The Delinquents* would head my list). Nevertheless, as Pomerantz pointed out, Stratton had not objected to the casting of Holly Hunter and Harvey Keitel in Jane Campion's film, *The Piano*.[26] The point of criticising the casting of one American but not another was both aesthetic *and* ideological, and thus not entirely contained by arguments about exactly where—indeed, *if*—one does draw the line against the American influence.

While I am suggesting that simple accusations of American cultural imperialism cannot adequately explain the cultural politics here, it is undeniable that in film and television production in Australia today the dominance of the American industry is still perceived as a genuine practical problem. As production and promotion budgets escalated through the eighties, the chances of a return to investors from an Australian film's local box office alone— always a pretty remote possibility—became even more negligible. In the nineties, getting a run in the American market, either in cinemas or through television release, necessarily figures in Australian producers' sales and marketing plans as a key objective. During the Uruguay round of GATT talks, 'free trade' in film and video became an area of dispute between Australia and the United States, with the States accusing Australia of protectionism. The Australian industry's resistance to suggestions that we drop local content requirements for television or loosen the eligibility requirements for state funding, at a time when our government was advocating the

106

mythical 'level playing field' in other commodities, is of course motivated by their fears that the American industry could obliterate our own if we left it to the market.[27] For, despite the US producers' claims of Australian protectionism, the Australia/United States traffic in film and television is grossly in the United States' favour. While our industry is dominated by American product (up to 70 per cent of the local cinema market goes to American films[28]), we have had very little success selling into their market. This is unlikely to change. Although we might think of the American as an internationalised (and therefore 'open') market—probably because the two processes, Americanisation and internationalisation, have become effectively identical in non-American cultures—the American market in film and television is actually excessively parochial. There has never been a foreign-made ratings success on American network TV, and the few major foreign films which achieve an American distribution deal (only 1 per cent of the US market in 1989[29]) rarely achieve the patterns of widespread simultaneous release enjoyed by even relatively modest American features.

In other cultural industries, such as popular music, the story is similar. While America is the largest market and thus offers the largest returns to bands who are unable to make a living out of record sales alone in Australia, it is notoriously difficult to crack. Australian popular music would find it hard to claim that it has an 'Australian sound'[30] of the specificity achieved by the 'Australian look' of 1970s and 1980s film and television products, and so one would imagine that there would be fewer obstacles to its acceptance by the American industry. There is not the problem, for instance, of the Australian accent so often nominated by film and television distributors as a negative factor for Australian film to overcome with American film audiences. Nevertheless, what we find is that while Australian bands remain part of the local industry—living here, recording here, performing primarily here—they have little success in the United States. When they move, becoming a *de facto* part of an American industry (just as is the case with individuals in the film and television industries), their chances improve.

As a consequence of such factors, Australian producers in the culture industries have developed a degree of realism about their potential for American success. Nevertheless, where they believe Australian national interests are to be protected or even advanced, many Australian culture industry producers have maintained their loyalty towards their origins. Sometimes this involves significant commercial costs; subsidising the local industry while attempting to operate at both the local and the international level is not the best way to succeed in contemporary market capitalism. Sometimes, fortuitously, the commercial and the local coincide, as in the success of Midnight Oil, Peter Carey, *Strictly Ballroom* or *Crocodile Dundee*.

Crocodile Dundee is probably the most contentious as well as the most significant of these examples because of the way it has highlighted the ambiguities in the Australia/America relation. On the face of it a simple, popular narrative, the film's cultural meaning has turned out to be far from self-evident: after an initial burst of silliness,[31] Australian analysis has tended to hedge its bets:

> Perhaps the film offered a fantasy for the popular audiences of both Australia and the US; perhaps it was a gesture that Australia 'knew its (natural) place'. In both cases it showed how complex the cinematic relationships between the outback/natural Australia and city/cultural US were. If this film represented cultural domination, it was to some extent actively produced by the dominated.[32]

I am not so much interested in following up these competing possibilities here,[33] however, as in considering *Crocodile Dundee*'s contribution to a little burst of desire that travelled in the opposite to the customary direction: that is, Australia became an object of desire for Americans. If *Crocodile Dundee*'s narrative provided a new way of 'reconciling American money and culture with Australian nature',[34] this reconciliation has been played out in the most uncomplicatedly commercial and, significantly, the least nationalist of the cultural industries, tourism. (I admit that calling tourism a cultural industry is to push the category to the limit but that is how I want to place it in this discussion. As I will suggest later, the business of tourism produces certain kinds of consciousness and needs to be thought of as within the domain of cultural, not just economic, policy.) The film's prehistory is, of course, embedded in Australia's recent development as a tourist destination—particularly for Americans—through Paul Hogan's Australian Tourism Commission television commercials. For these, Hogan, one of the purest living examples of Russel Ward's 'national type', offered his time *gratis* as a patriotic gesture—so the story goes—in order to help develop the local industry (and to establish his persona in the United States). The irony is, of course, that tourism—notwithstanding its grateful appropriation of this national icon—is possibly the last industry one should look to for a defence of national difference, wherever it might be found.

Australia World: tourism and the nation

*Shick also had that peculiar deafness that Americans adopt
towards Australians (not dissimilar to the deafness city
people adopt when listening to country people). It comes
from not understanding the rhythms of their speech and
assuming they would not live where they did if they were
more resourceful.* (Peter Carey, Illywhacker)

Between 1980 and 1988, international arrivals in Australia increased
by over 150 per cent to more than 2 million. According to a Bureau
of Industry Economics (BIE) report in the mid-1980s, tourism had
become a major industry in Australia 'rivalling the value of mining,
or of the combined value of textiles, clothing, footwear and motor
vehicles as employers and in terms of generating revenue'.[35] These
days, tourism is *the* industry which is most frequently held up as a
model for the future of Australian commercial development.
Tourism's attraction for many who would regard Australia's manufacturing prospects as dead is that it is a labour-intensive service
industry in which Australia enjoys some 'natural' market advantages.
Despite such advantages, however, those trumpeting the benefits of
tourism usually see the need for significant change in Australia if
international tourism is to 'take off' here. Just as Peter Carey's
fictional minister for tourism implied, Australians have to accept
some sacrifices if they are to succeed. Many of these sacrifices turn
out to be cultural. Not only is the physical environment altered
when it is geared towards tourist needs, but other aspects of our
everyday lives are affected too. Jennifer Craik notes that among the
'institutional changes' targeted by the BIE in their 1984 inquiry were
penalty rates, restrictions on shopping hours, fares for public trans-
port and school holiday periods.[36] These are justified, as in Carey's
story, because once they occur 'the Americans will come'.

The boom in tourism is often regarded as an instance of
Americanisation even though America is not in fact the largest
source of international visitors.[37] A case in point is the Queensland
Travel and Tourism Commission's 'Yo! Way to Go' campaign. This
campaign is a rich site for all kinds of arguments against contemporary practice in tourism promotions. The flagship commercial
used lots of suntanned bodies on beaches, including two notoriously sexist shots of a woman's G-string-clad bottom being sprayed
with oil and pinched. (The production company's defence against
criticism was that the pincher was the model's husband!) As the
campaign was dedicated to promoting Queensland, the use of

American urban slang in the slogan 'Yo! Way to Go' seemed especially inappropriate—and, to those members of the market outside the targeted age group, probably even incomprehensible. Previous QTTC slogans—'Queensland: beautiful one day, perfect the next', for instance—had been enormously successful, surviving the campaigns that produced them and entering popular speech (if not always in precisely the original formation or with the original implications). The widely perceived Americanness of the 'Yo! Way to Go' campaign does seem to have been implicated in the series of controversies that led up to the resignation of Peter Laurence as head of the QTTC in mid-1993. His replacement, Jim Kennedy, cancelled the campaign as one of his first acts in office and announced that he would be looking for a more distinctively Queensland image—'not America, not Florida'—for QTTC promotions in the future.

The expansion in tourism from America is customarily connected to the success of *Crocodile Dundee* and the complementary strategies of the Australian Tourism Commission ads and the Qantas 'koala' commercials. Jennifer Craik suggests that tourism's expansion involves more than the American market but agrees that the rapid growth in international visitor numbers to Australia over the last decade has been due, 'in part, to international publicity about Australia and the popularity of Australian films such as *Crocodile Dundee* and other cultural products'.[38] Tom O'Regan has noted that tourism expanded more rapidly in Australia 'than in any other nation in the developed world in 1987' (the year after the film's release), and quotes tourism officials who also attribute much of this to the interest generated by *Crocodile Dundee*.[39] A little later in this section, I will address the nature of this interest more directly, but first I want to consider some of the implications of the tourism boom. While Australia's heightened visibility overseas—its status as an object of desire rather than indifference—is flattering, there are worrying dimensions to this apparent success.

There are important arguments to be had about the specific environmental and social effects of particular tourist facilities in Australia, as well as about tourism's mobilisation of familiar developmental rhetorics aimed at constructing Australia's social future as within the gift of market economics. There is serious doubt about tourism's potential as a long-term industry and about the strategies of development currently in play. The history of tourism developments in our region—in Bali, Fiji, the Hawaiian islands—offers plenty of evidence of the economic and cultural dangers ahead.

Jennifer Craik's *Resorting to Tourism* offers a much more informed critique of such issues than I could provide. My interest here is both more generalised and more restricted to a consideration of the cultural effects of the improbable enclosure of tourism within an apparently nationalist commercial project.

As I remarked at the end of the previous section, tourism is a particularly unlikely champion of national difference. The discourses of tourism are thoroughly internationalised, and operate as a means of translating existing cultural differences into a transnational code of the exotic, of the leisurely, and of the familiar; a code that results in a consoling crosscultural sameness—what Meaghan Morris has called a 'consistent indistinction'.[40] As it markets Australia's attractions, tourism's promotion and publicity is also aimed at controlling the multiplicity of meanings released by the word 'Australia', and at reprocessing the signifiers of nation and place into the signs of familiar modes of consumption. Such representational strategies carry consequences.

At a local level in Australia, there have been significant shifts in specific meanings as a consequence of their subjection to the discourses of tourism. Jon Stratton describes how the tropical Northern Territory has been made 'safe'—at least rhetorically—for white westerners: the 'untamed' becomes the 'beautiful' and the 'scenic' as the genuine and still present dangers of the physical environment are 'sanitized and reconstructed in traditional Romantic terms'.[41] While on the one hand the tourist promotions emphasise that we are at one of Nature's last frontiers (the exotic), on the other hand they must also reassure us that civilisation has established a beachhead here (the familiar). In a telling example, Stratton notes how the legendary 'mental degeneration and lassitude' so long identified with living in the wet tropics has been positively 'reworked into the idea of the Top End as having a relaxed atmosphere'.[42] 'Going troppo' no longer means what it did as it becomes enfolded into the discourses of leisure and desire which dominate tourist promotions for the Top End.

The acceleration in the promotion of Australia as a tourist destination has resulted in a multiplication in the volume of representations but not in the varieties of their content. In order to market its product, tourism has to perform selections from a restricted repertoire. If it is allowed a sense of place at all, the tourist destination most easily becomes a theme park—Australia World—defined by a generic list of attractions. In our case, the genre is natural rather than social—kangaroos, koalas, beaches, crocodiles,

The tourist's Australia: the reef, the wilderness, the beach and the outback. (reproduced courtesy of Creative Tourism Publications Pty Ltd)

Uluru and, the significant exception, the Sydney Opera House. In America, Japan and in Britain, Australia's desirability as a tourist destination has grown dramatically on the back of promotions which almost exclusively foreground 'the outback, wilderness areas,

112

the Reef' as quotations from Australia World's 'distinctive way of life'.[43]

The 'distinctive way of life' represented in *Crocodile Dundee* was literally a joke, but not everyone seems to have got it. O'Regan lists just a few of the ways in which the motif of the crocodile has been taken up in the Northern Territory subsequent to *Crocodile Dundee*'s success. These include an international hotel in the shape of a 250-metre crocodile now doing business in the heart of the Kakadu National Park (guests enter through its jaws); the use of the cute crocodile logo for the Northern Territory's pavilion during Expo 88; and the opening of Club Crocodile at Airlie Beach in Queensland where guests can apparently share their swimming pool with real crocodiles.[44] Crocodile farms are becoming an indispensable part of any northern tropics tourist venture, it would seem, and in the process the crocodile's meaning is undergoing a certain amount of modification:

> Crocodiles, which have signified the threat of Northern Territory's nature by means of stories of people being taken and eaten, are now visitable by tourists at a farm 40 kilometres out of Darwin and are to be found 'smiling' in welcome in cartoon form on postcards. One radio advertisement for the Crocodile Farm invites people to pop down and visit the crocodiles and 'keep the snappy chappies happy'.[45]

As Jon Stratton goes on to remark, the key to the change of the crocodile's meaning is their being turned into food as a new market for crocodile meat opens up—in a resonant reversal, where once the crocodiles preyed on the tourist, the tourist now preys on them.

At the end of his survey of museum and heritage sites in Australia, including theme parks like Timbertown, Old Sydney Town and Sovereign Hill, Tony Bennett notes the 'truly remarkable' increase in the numbers of such institutions over the last couple of decades.[46] Also remarkable, he found, was the extent to which tourist sites in Australia are subject to a 'rural gerrymander'. What he refers to is a concentration on 'the lives of pioneers, explorers, settlers, goldmining communities and rural industries in the nine-teenth century at the expense of twentieth century urban history'.[47] Bennett argues that because tourism will always want to offer 'a trip away from the everyday' (the slogan used by Dreamworld, another theme park on the Gold Coast), it is always more likely to 'focus on the country rather than the city, and the nineteenth rather than the twentieth century'.[48] Fair enough, but for an emerging postcolonial nation like Australia, actively involved in a complex process of nation formation which necessitates explicit recognition

AUSTRALIA CROCODILE COUNTRY

Mick Dundee has a lot to answer for.

---

of the multiple identities of the present, this tendency is a conservative one. Bennett goes on to make an even more worrying point. As tourism becomes increasingly orientated towards the foreign tourist, the current strategies of representation run a substantial risk:

> . . . of fashioning a past which meets the demands of foreign visitors for tourist locations which seem to embody the virtues of the exotic, the eccentric and the authentic—in short, which seem to be the antithesis of the metropolitan centres from which they travel. The more the Australian past is fashioned to meet this demand, the greater will be its tendency to represent Australians to themselves through the cracked looking-glass of the Anglo-American gaze in its tendency to cast the national character in the form of a heroic and primitive simplicity—the Crocodile Dundee factor.[49]

It is worth thinking some more about what this 'Crocodile Dundee factor' might be.

Tony Bennett is invoking a relatively generalised image; for his purposes, Crocodile Dundee works as a metaphor for a genre of representations of Australianness. It's an interesting choice, however: the film and its star are locations where various discourses of cultural identity compete. The film's success is seen as especially comprehensive because it happened most dramatically in America;

its celebration of Kakadu established the area as a tourist destination for Australians as well as for Americans, and both nationalities probably find it equally exotic; while Hogan may be the perfect example of the 'national type', his Crocodile Dundee character reveals an awareness of also being something of an anachronism—in Australia, as well as in New York; and finally, Hoges may have beaten the Yanks at their own game in his films but he is widely depicted as having sold out in 'real life'—to judge from the popular press, most spectacularly by leaving his wife Noelene for 'curvy co-star' Linda Koslowski. It is a pattern of ambiguities entirely consistent with the history of Australian/American cultural relations—and also with the history of an internationalising, modernising, postcoloniality. The aspect I want finally to develop here, though, relates to evidence of the highly particularised interest that Americans have expressed in the 'Crocodile Dundee factor': the idea of Australian life they have evidently constructed from their experience of Australian film.

To many American filmgoers, it would seem, Australian films speak not so much of Australia itself as of a highly idealised, deeply nostalgic vision of America. Repeatedly, in their interviews with American publicists and critics, Peter Hamilton and Sue Matthews found Australian movies being talked about as if they were slightly refracted representations of 'American Dreams'. What the American interviewees find in these films is a world that no longer exists in America, but which they definitely recognise:

> These movies are comforting in this time of terrible pessimism and depression when we've reached a level of cynicism which leads us to appreciate your naive optimism and vigor. Since the best of your films have been set in your colonial period, they recall the frontier spirit which we have lost. We wish that we could return to the 'good old days' when America seemed as robust and unsophisticated as Australia appears in these buoyant movies.[50]

Recorded in 1982 in response to such films as *Picnic, Breaker Morant, Caddie* and *My Brilliant Career*, Kathleen Carroll's remarks are strikingly similar to those of *New York Times* critic Vincent Canby when he reviewed *Crocodile Dundee* in 1986. He, too, noted the presence of 'old frontier values', claiming that Australia stood to be the 'beneficiary of a worldwide loss of confidence and nostalgic yearning for utopias'.[51] Summarising his survey of American reviews of Hogan's film, Stephen Crofts suggests that Canby's is typical of American responses in that he sees Australia merely as the 'ideal set for U.S. frontier myths':

In Robert Hughes's gloss: 'Australia has sold itself as this nostalgic picture of a lost frontier, and Americans, yearning after their primal innocence, have bought it'. Canby thus celebrated Australia as America refinding itself: 'As I understand it, the Australians would have us believe [that Australia] is the only place left on earth where one might still be able to find the kind of character once popularly identified as 'American'. They may well be right . . . *Crocodile Dundee* successfully creates the impression that there is something approaching a smogless, egalitarian American heaven on earth, though it's called Australia. . . It's possible that we're now importing an ideal that we used to think was exclusively American'.[52]

The encouraging dimension to these remarks is their validation of the canniness of *Crocodile Dundee's* assumption that Americans are vulnerable to having their own dreams sold back to them. But it is impossible for an Australian to read the quote with complete equanimity: its omnivorous ethnocentrism highlights the risks involved in setting out to penetrate this market by tailoring representations of our national image to its demands. Canby shows us how effortlessly Australian difference might be appropriated to American ends.

It is never that simple, of course; I know that cultures are not effortlessly swamped, not all culture lives in the mainstream media, no moment of hegemony is permanent and culture is never simply imposed from above or outside. Furthermore, the *Crocodile Dundee* analogy can cut both ways. As I suggested earlier, it is by no means self-evident that this film's meanings serve only American interests. Rather, *Crocodile Dundee* perfectly exemplifies Caughie's 'ironic knowingness', the pleasure that comes from playing at being American. Meaghan Morris has described the film as a 'takeover fantasy', of 'breaking into the circuit of media power', and as such it operates as anything but a mere slavish imitation of the American model.[53] It is important to acknowledge the film's deadly aim at the preferences of *both* its major markets and its ability to survive simple appropriation by either. As the revival of domestic tourism in the Top End and the beginnings of a gradual movement towards Aboriginal control of tourism management in some areas might suggest, it is even possible to think of the film's implication in Australian tourism developments as serving more than one set of interests:

The outback maneouvres in *Crocodile Dundee* are situated not only in relation to colonial and nuclear politics but also to contemporary practices of tourism, safari holidays, theme parks, locality environmentalism, that can now conflict with mining, as a reason for conservation . . .[54]

As Morris goes on to say, no matter how steeped in American film genres *Crocodile Dundee* may seem to a Vincent Canby, to most Australian audiences the film is *not* about 'home-longing for the world of Davy Crockett', but precisely the reverse. Finally, and as this last remark implies, the meanings generated through films are more negotiable than those generated through tourism advertising; there are significant differences between the cultural and political function of a popular film narrative and an official campaign of commercial image production.

Given all of that, it is not always easy to establish who is exploiting whom in the 'representation wars' between Australia and America.[55] They do take their place within a history of, largely, American cultural domination, but within that history Australians have often fancied their chances at the short-term con. Mick Dundee adopts his colourful name to help the tourist trade, lies about his exploits and, in *Crocodile Dundee II*, pretends to be the noble savage in New York to enhance his survival. Similarly, our tourist image may contain something of the 'ironically knowing' con, taking part in the game of playing at being American. Ultimately, though, this may not be enough to prevent the commercial (and perhaps even the official) construction of Australian identities moving off-shore. Rather than challenging or complicating foreign under-standings of Australian cultural identities, the unlikely national project of tourism is recycling them. Through our tourism advertising, perhaps more than through any other cultural products, we are supplying a narrow selection of images, simulacra of Australian life to be replayed through the mass media all over the world. As the images eventually recirculate back home, Australians' visions of leisure, fashion, lifestyle and cultural identity must in turn be shaped through, among other things, these same tourist promotions. And on it goes, each successive image ever more distant from its orig-inating referent.

As it pursues its international markets, Australian tourism adver-tising is peddling precisely those singular versions of national identity that in other contexts we have spent at least two decades contesting. While we are arguing at home about blurring and broadening our definitions of national identities, our identity over-seas may have actually sharpened and narrowed. In committing itself to tourism as *the* national project of economic restructuring, Australia has also committed itself to a national image which directly inhibits if not reverses the movement towards multiple or hybrid definitions of the nation. Australians' chances of complicating our shared imaginings must be compromised by the seductiveness, the reductive uniformity and even the canny fictionality of media constructions of Australia as a frontier tourist paradise. It is not enough, however, to deal with this by thinking of it as merely an instance of Americanisation or even internationalisation. We should also acknowledge its local roots: as yet another short-term alliance between business and the discourses of nation which works against competing, broader, cultural conceptions of the national interest.

6

Redefining the nation: from purity to hybridity

*It seems clear that, despite the often over-rationalist
expectations favoured by the internationalist perspectives of
the left, nationalism is not only not a spent force; it isn't*
necessarily *either a reactionary or a progressive force,
politically.* (Stuart Hall, 'Culture, community, nation')

Caught in the act: constructing the nation

Informing this book's analyses is an argument for a reappraisal of
Australian nationalisms. A quick route to changing the current
versions of Australian nationalism might seem to be to jettison the
idea of nation completely (the route usually offered by multiculturalism), but I am not suggesting that we do this. I am suggesting,
however, that we change some of the things the nation currently
means so that the ends its representations most easily serve are less
regressive, discriminatory and exclusivist. One of the ways we can
begin, and I hope this book plays a part in such a project, is by
examining more closely how and in whose interests the established
discourses of nation actually operate within our culture.

To some, this may still seem like a pretty pointless task. Nationalism is often regarded as something that needs to be eradicated
rather than interrogated; since its effects will always be anti-democratic and oppressive, why bother examining the specifics? The
authors of *Mistaken Identity* are far from alone in their calls for a
'nation without nationalism'.[1] Australian cultural critics have been

arguing long and persuasively that nationalism is no longer a plausible means of articulating a common identity for those living within the geo-political entity called Australia—this, due to the narrow definitions of national character currently under licence. In such arguments, nationalism is regarded as a nineteenth century ideology administratively dedicated to the flattening of cultural and political differences within the modern nation-state. This opinion is supported by the fact that the dominant versions of Australian nationalism over the last century could hardly be said to have promoted tolerance of cultural or political differences.

The case against nationalism also maintains that nationalism is now in decline throughout the western world. As capitalism globalises, it is argued, the boundaries between nation-states matter much less than they did. Instead of mediating usefully between the local and the international, the national has now become irrelevant. Thus, the crucial distinction in the future will not be between the national and the international but between the global and the local. The ease with which some globalising cultural industries have crossed national boundaries, pay TV in Europe for instance, has lent considerable empirical weight to such propositions. Consequently, they have been taken up by many communication theorists in Europe, America and Australia who regard the acceleration of the processes of globalisation within the media as paradigmatic of a new economic and political order.[2]

I have reservations about both these arguments. As I said in Chapter 1, my criticism is not so much of nationalism *per se* as of the uses to which it is put in specific instances. My view of the standard case against nationalism is that its assumptions about the political potential of the idea of the nation are too simple. I'm not alone in this. Tom Nairn argues that one of the consequences of what he calls the 'demonisation' of nationalism is the erasure of its historical relationship with the expansion of democracy and western modernity.[3] Following Benedict Anderson, Philip Schlesinger describes nationalism as the fundamental social process through which modern collective identities are formed (or in Anderson's case, 'imagined'), but emphasises that this process must always be the subject of contest and negotiation—its 'strategies and mechanisms' exposed to analysis.[4] Homi Bhabha reminds us of the 'inherent ambiguity' of the idea of 'nation'; he is referring both to the contradictions at the heart of the nation-state (the imperative to reconcile the interests of the individual and the state) and to its dual political potential. Writing about the function of 'the nation' within postcolonial societies, he maintains that its political potential need not necessarily be conservative. Rather, within the postcolonial context where it operates as a means of resisting domination by (for instance) the colonial power, the idea of the nation retains the potential for multiplying possibilities and supporting articulations of difference.[5] It is not difficult to find Australian evidence to support Homi Bhabha's argument. As we noted in the previous chapter, there are certain areas in which the strategies of nation formation pursued by the Australian state over the last few decades have had progressive effects. The establishment of the film industry, the support of the live and recorded popular music industry and the expansion of Australian literary publishing are among the outcomes of nationalist cultural policies.[6]

My second reservation comes from the conviction that we are not witnessing the 'demise of nationalism' in Australia or anywhere else. Much of the enthusiasm for the notion that multinational capitalism has wiped out nationalism came from the late-1980s euphoria whipped up around the idea of a united Europe. Once projected to achieve complete union in 1992, Europe looks even further away from that objective in 1993 than it did in 1990. There are actually more independent nation-states on the European continent now than there were four years ago (although I am not suggesting that this, in the circumstances, is cause for celebration). Early accounts of the globalisation of the media industries represented the process as irresistible, extinguishing cultural difference as it constructed a single international market. The process certainly has sufficient force to necessitate such measures of resistance and containment as many Australian cultural industries have employed to protect local industries and identities. However, to see it as an utterly incontestable force is to oversimplify the process of globalisation and the various contexts within which it has to operate.[7] For one thing, as Giddens has pointed out, globalisation has been both dialectical and uneven: the 'loss of autonomy on the part of some states or groups of states has often gone along with an *increase* in that of others'.[8] It is also possible to argue that globalisation has, far from eradicating nationalism, actually served to produce it:

> For the first time in human history, the globe has been effectively unified into a single economic order under a common democratic state model—surely, the ideal, dreamt-of conditions for liberal or proletarian internationalism. Actually these conditions have almost immediately caused the world to fold up into a previously unimaginable and still escalating number of different ethno-political units.[9]

121

There are now different kinds of nationalism; perhaps there always were. Giddens coins the term 'state-nation'[10] to accommodate the decline in importance of 'natural' ethnic or cultural identities and the correspondingly increased importance of explicitly 'constructed' political and territorial factors in the modern nation-state. The political function of the idea of the nation in Australia, where it still retains some radical potential, is dramatically different from that in Britain, where largely it does not. It is unwise to assume that nationalism will always mean the same thing, will always serve the same kinds of interests, and will always operate as a conservative ideology, no matter where and under what circumstances it operates. As Stuart Hall puts it in the epigraph to this section, nationalism 'isn't *necessarily* either a reactionary or a progressive force, politically'.[11] One needs to pay close attention to the way it is used.

This is not to recuperate the idea of the nation as an ideal, but to suggest that certain formations of the nation may be strategically useful in a postcolonial society such as ours. As Suvendrini Perera puts it, with some emphasis to catch the speed readers:

> This is *not* to reinstall nation, 'race' or ethnicity as absolute, unified given categories, but to see them as strategic and provisional responses produced at both international and local levels by a range of needs and practices.[12]

That said, to make use of the power invested in the discourses of nationalism, we must first do something about their currently licensed meanings and their dominant patterns of use. Rather than waiting for the 'end of nationalism' to *really* come around, we should be thinking about interrogating and expanding the range of discourses employed in its representations.

As a first step, we need to examine the kind of nationalism Australia has taken on—a particularly exclusive, Eurocentric definition of the nation. Most European discussions of nationalism assume as their object a nation-state composed of individuals drawn from a single ethnic, religious and cultural source. National identity is synonymous with cultural purity. Against such a model, a nation such as Australia looks bogus, artificially constructed through the migration of polyglot cultural traditions into and over the putatively singular traditions of the original inhabitants.

There is every reason why we should contest such a construction of national identity. Indeed, I regard the dominance of the 'cultural purity' model of national identity as a trap laid for the new nations by the old nations: it proposes the old nations' primacy, endowing them with a naturally coherent identity which throws ours into negative relief as especially constructed and spurious. Of course, *all* nations are 'constructed'[13]—indeed, all forms of collective identity are culturally produced. The older nations, however, have more densely mythologised histories from which explanations or legitimations can more implicitly emerge. The newer nations have to undertake the process of nation formation explicitly, visibly, defensively, and are always being caught in the act—embarrassed in the process of construction. Traditional definitions of nationhood deny the legitimacy of such societies and of such processes.

Finding an alternative more appropriate to a postcolonial collective identity, however, is difficult. Settler/postcolonial societies face enormous problems in articulating a common identity across competing forms of ethnicity and against a history of occupation and dispossession of the original inhabitants. The more we become aware of these internal differences and ambiguities, the more problematic becomes any simple affirmation of collective identity. As we saw in Chapter 4, as a consequence of the contradiction between the assumptions underlying the Bicentenary's projection of national identity and those informing the competing ethnic, social and racial groups within Australia, the Bicentenary did pretty much the opposite of what it set out to do: it demonstrated the inadequacy of earlier, traditional definitions of Australian national identity and the futility of offering a singular, consensual explanation of that identity to the Australian people.

The task before alternative formations of collective identity is much more complex. Among other things, they must be plural: identities rather than identity. They must be built on the recognition rather than the overriding of cultural difference, and they must accept and negotiate Australia's dual history as colonised and coloniser.[14] This does not have to be impossible just because it is contradictory. Indeed, new ways of thinking about the nation would necessarily involve the acceptance of a degree of inherent contradictoriness: for instance, the need to acknowledge cultural differences at home while presenting a more cohesive political identity in our relations with other nation-states.

So far, the best indications of what alternative formations of Australian national identities might look like have come from multi-culturalists. Con Castan, drawing upon Benedict Anderson, describes it this way:

> An Australian imagined community . . . would not be based on

123

ethnicity, language or religion, would be inclusive rather than exclusive, pluralistic rather than monolithic, multicultural rather than nationalistic. While within the community, there would be a majority 'ethnicity of destination' (which would constantly be evolving and assented to by more and more citizens), there would also be room for minority ones (including the English, I would add); and while there would be a national language, there would also be room for community languages and useful roles for these to play in the lives of groups of citizens. Such a nation is based on a territory and on citizenship; it would conceive of itself as a community which has force and validity in spite of the divisions that exist in it and the uneven distribution of power; it would not need to gloss over these, to practice historical forgetfulness to secure the polity from internal divisions.[15]

This is a pluralistic model, definitively tolerant of cultural difference. I think we can go one step further and suggest that difference should not just be tolerated as an accepted deviation from a stable core identity, but that difference should actually be *constitutive* of identity.

Australian national identities can be grounded in the heterogeneity and hybridity of Australian culture. In postcolonial literary theory, a key strategy for the postcolonial critic bent on challenging Eurocentric definitions of nation and the postcolonial subject is to embrace the contradictions inherent in the construction of a new nation.[16] This involves proposing a national identity which celebrates its hybridity rather than its purity. Such a strategy turns the postcolonial condition to advantage and alters the ontological status and political potential of the category of the nation. The construction of collective identities becomes a creative, resistant, cultural and political process of becoming—rather than a conservative, already completed, project of exclusion. As a means of liberating postcolonial writing from the overdetermining aesthetic and political constraints which had kept it permanently on the margins of the English canon, this has proved a useful strategy; we should deploy it more widely to deal with what I called earlier the 'tired and irrelevant' discourses of traditional Australian nationalism. In the next section, I want to suggest a few locations at which this seems to be happening already.

Before doing that, though, and as a final point here, it is worth emphasising that this notion of hybridity is very different from 'the superficiality of old style pluralism where no boundaries are crossed, and from the trendy nomadic voyaging of the postmodern or simplistic versions of global homogenization'.[17] It is not simply the multiplication of difference, or as Hall puts it, 'one damn thing after another or the difference that makes no difference'.[18] While the hybrid retains its links to and identification with its origins, it is also shaped and transformed by (and in turn, shapes and transforms) its location in the present. Belonging at the same time to several 'homes', it cannot simply dissolve into a culturally unified form. The complex achievement of the hybrid is a product of its obligation to 'come to terms with and to make something new of the culture' it inhabits, 'without simply assimilating to it'.[19] The result, argues Hall (quoting Salman Rushdie), is a celebration of cultural impurity, a 'love-song to our mongrel selves'.[20]

Against homogeneity

SBS television is probably our most radical example of a genuinely heterogeneous public institution. Unlike most other television channels, SBS emphasises its lack of unity, its multiplicity of objectives, its refusal to construct its audience as unified, singular, conceivable. SBS defies the norms of television programming in that it doesn't 'play'; one program does not easily lead into the next because of the wide range of genres and languages. There is probably no such thing as an SBS viewer—despite the press's perjorative descriptions that has them all drinking Perrier, driving Volvos and living in Balmain. What SBS has done is multiply possibilities; it has produced audiences for German detective drama, Brazilian soap opera, Italian soccer, classic world cinema, without (so far) becoming itself the victim of such a menu of choices. As a cultural institution which is funded by the state but almost never appears to think of itself as addressing an audience defined by membership of that state, SBS is a startlingly original achievement.

Where else do we look, though, for examples of the hybrid national formations suggested in the first half of this chapter? SBS is unique among our cultural institutions in that the nation it sets out to form is defined by its lack of homogeneity. While no other institutions come to mind as performing similar functions, there are signs of change in other areas of Australian popular culture—for my purposes here, in film and in popular music—which lead us in a similar direction. Since the revival of the 1970s, Australian cinema has been criticised for its conservative representations of national identity.[21] In some of the recent crop of Australian films, however, the nation is represented in much less conservative ways indicating a growing commitment to the ethic of multiculturalism. Australian popular music, although given a spurious radical tinge by its enclosure within the mythologies of the rock music industry, has largely aligned itself alongside conventional white, masculine definitions of the Australian character. Indeed, in Australian rock music's primary site of performance—the pub—this relationship is almost seamless.[22] The commercial success of the multiracial band Yothu Yindi may not have changed all that but the band does provide us with an example of the hybrid text: a new music constructed out of two distinct traditions.

In an article on 'heterogeneity' in Hong Kong and Taiwan cinema in 1992, Chris Berry describes how the films from both these countries have resisted the temptation to fit into a 'national model'. Instead their films have drawn on an extraordinary range of generic, aesthetic and cultural influences, constructing identities which are 'paradoxically based on particular configurations of hybridity and difference'. Such a tradition is far in advance of current Australian practice, he argues:

> In Australia, we have strained to mould our postcoloniality to fit the mould of the homogeneous nation, with a token nod in the direction of multiculturalism and aboriginality. Forms of cultural hybridity are an inevitable result of the forces of international trade and imperialism that create postcoloniality, but we have preferred to ignore this. In Australian cities, Vietnamese bakeries abut Halal butchers, but this is only slowly appearing in a movie industry still dominated by Anglo-Celtic last names.[23]

While we are still a long way from the situation Berry describes in Hong Kong and Taiwan, I think that we have gone beyond the 'token nod', at least in regard to multiculturalism (despite the appearance of both *Blackfellas* and *Bedevil* in 1993, there is still a long way to go with Aboriginality).

As I noted in Chapter 1, recent films such as *Death in Brunswick*, *The Big Steal*, *Strictly Ballroom* and *The Heartbreak Kid* are set in a multicultural Australia where Vietnamese bakeries *do* 'abut Halal butchers'. A further example, *Romper Stomper*, is brave (or naive) enough to address the tensions produced in such a world directly. While *Romper Stomper* is an extremely confronting drama and the other films mentioned are comedies, it still shares significant attributes with them. They are all urban, contemporary, highly generic in their narrative structures, and they reflect something of the mix of cultural differences and ethnicities current in Australian society. The vast majority of films made between 1973 and 1981 (after which there is evidence of a gradual modification of the revival's conservative representations) were none of these things. The representation of Australia's distinctiveness in these earlier films employed precisely those discourses of Australian nationalism that this book has criticised. In defence of the films from the seventies, the preceding long hiatus in Australian film production must have made it seem that there was something of a backlog of cultural iconography to work through. Given the demand to develop a visual mythology for the nation, in what was virtually a new medium for Australian audiences, it is little wonder that the versions of Australian identity offered for our recognition were nostalgically masculine, rural and colonial.

It is different now. There is a new, much younger, audience attending and being addressed in contemporary Australian film. The big domestic successes of the last few years, with the exception of *The Piano*, have been 'youth' films: *The Big Steal, The Heartbreak Kid, Romper Stomper, Strictly Ballroom, Flirting*. The national iconography one might abstract from these films would not be at all homogeneous. Just in terms of the representation of the male leads, for instance, instead of the early revival's reiterations of Jack Thompson or Bryan Brown the current batch offers us Ben Mendelsohn, Alex Dimitriades, Russell Crowe, Paul Mercurio and Noah Taylor. On the evidence of this selection alone, the semiotics of Australian ethnicities and masculinities would seem to have changed.

The representation of Australia as a social context for narrative has also been modified over the last decade. John Ruane's *Death in Brunswick* grounds its narrative within a richly detailed, ethnically inflected, contemporary urban context. The 'Australian' context in *Death in Brunswick* is signified through its *lack* of cultural purity and through the patterns of collision, competition and collaboration between multiple, often contradictory, cultural formations. While the film certainly doesn't deal with such issues in any depth, it does have a thematic interest in the complexity of the cultural mix that audiences are expected to recognise as characteristic of but not necessarily unique to Australian life. *Death in Brunswick*'s plot involves a weak but sympathetic hero, Carl, whose attempts to get his life in order involve him in (among other things) the accidental death of a Turkish kitchenhand, a battle between a group of Turkish avengers and the Greek owners of the nightclub where the death occurs, a risky but rewarding romance with a Greek-Australian girl, Sophie, and the attempted murder of his dominating mother. The film places Sophie's ethnic/sexy vitality ('She looks like Gina Lollobrigida', says an awestruck Carl) in direct opposition to the

Sam Neill as Carl in *Death in Brunswick*. (courtesy of Meridian Films Pty Ltd)

dead hand of Anglo values symbolised by Carl's elderly middle-class mother; inasmuch as that opposition is resolved, it opts for the sexually bountiful multicultural over the desiccated Anglo. Comically qualifying this, however, is the repressive masculinity of the Greek culture Carl must enter as Sophie's husband, its patriarchal sexism utterly at odds with the bewildered gratitude with which Carl regards his awesome Sophie.

In the past, there have been occasional films which have examined Australian multiculturalism seriously and directly—Paul Cox's *Kostas*, for example. What is significant now is so many mainstream popular films routinely taking their multicultural social contexts for granted as they get on with their plots. *Strictly Ballroom* is one such film. While its over-the-top theatrical visual style requires it to unfold against the most minimal of social backgrounds, *Strictly Ballroom*'s plot line leads us to a resolution that may hold a little more than the standard romantic resonances. In the final dance, the blending of cultural traditions is enacted through the hero's and heroine's performance. Again, it is the European tradition which is seen as the richer one,[24] Scott's appropriation of the *paso doblé* breathing life into a conventional and backward Anglo-Australian institution. However, Scott and Fran's performance has its roots both in Fran's Spanish family and in Scott's father's repressed history of attempting to challenge the dance competition's conventions himself. What is seen as individually expressive for Scott is grounded in apparently contradictory socio-cultural origins. Again, what we are offered is not the submerging of difference within a consensual model—the cultural purity model of nationalism—but the much more difficult task of maintaining differences even as they are blended to form something new: a hybrid dance form.

While such a reading of *Strictly Ballroom* pushes it in directions most audiences would probably resist—I would admit that the film's multiculturalism is not its primary attribute—Michael Jenkins' *The Heartbreak Kid* clearly and unselfconsciously foregrounds ethnicity. A light romantic comedy about the affair between a young school teacher, Christina, and her problem student, Nick, it takes place within a Greek-Australian community in Melbourne. Multiculturalism is explicitly invoked in the film when Nick's small sister asks for help to prepare some food for 'multicultural day' at her school. To Nick, this is all phony liberal 'crap': 'what kind of wog do you want to be?' he asks parodically. Nick's cynicism comes from his experience at school where the 'ethnics' are subject to systematic discrimination. Southgate, the sports master, shuts the soccer-playing

Claudia Karvan and Alex Dimitriades in *The Heartbreak Kid*. (courtesy of View Films Pty Ltd)

'wogs' out of school sport in favour of the presumably purebred Australian Rules football players. The film depicts Southgate as emblematic of a vigorously masculinist Australianness (he is flabbergasted when Christina announces that she intends to coach the soccer team)—an Australianness which is hostile to cultural difference, threatened by multiculturalism's challenge to cultural purity and (in Southgate's case) by Christina's refusal of his authority over her.

Like *Death in Brunswick* and *Strictly Ballroom*, *The Heartbreak Kid* endorses multicultural values. Ethnicity is not seen unambiguously, however. The film constructs a richly detailed social context and in it there are differences within ethnicities as well as between them. Indeed, Christina's story—ultimately about the gaining of

Schoolyard scene from *The Heartbreak Kid*. (courtesy of View Films, Pty Ltd)

personal independence—is tied up in the network of conflicting expectations her behaviour is supposed to satisfy as she attempts to extricate herself from a complacently patriarchal tradition without renouncing her ethnicity, loyalties and sympathies.

The Heartbreak Kid is not a tale of a unique, diasporic culture surviving within an ersatz host culture—the generic model one might have expected. The social world in which this film takes place—which incorporates a Greek community undeniably altered by its migration to Australia—is instantly recognisable as Australian. When I first saw the film, the cinema was full—largely with teenage girls. I was impressed by their enthusiastic response to the film; not only did they make loudly appreciative noises when Alex Dimitriades took his shirt off, but their involvement with the classroom scenes in particular was vigorously identificatory. Gasps of indignation at the sports master's racism and sexism, hoots of appreciation at the behaviour of the classroom lairs, snorts of derision at 'teacher talk'. This was not an 'ethnic' film; it was a film about the social world of this audience.

Probably the key moment in *The Heartbreak Kid*, where the social context is most dramatically made visible, is our first view of the classroom. This is a highly detailed series of shots which relies upon audience recognition for it to make all its possible sense.

Dilapidated, disorganised, peopled by kids clad in the shambling, many-layered, multi-signed garb of urban teenagers, the classroom speaks eloquently of the school and the kids in it. The students' behaviour and language, their sense of themselves and their relation to the teacher, the combination of Anglo-Australian accents and Australian accents inflected with other ethnicities—all of these invited and received recognition from the cinema audience. Again, as with *Death in Brunswick*, what is 'Australian' about this context is not its cultural purity but the *mix* of identities and accents—the play of ethnicities and class positions audible in the dialogue or legible in the clothing and physical appearances. More than *Death in Brunswick* does, though, *The Heartbreak Kid* actually celebrates Australia's heterogeneity, a heterogeneity implicit in the multiple possibilities Christina faces as the narrative ends.

One can always get carried away by noting positive trends in cultural formations, but it does seem to me that the representation of Australian ethnicities in film (and TV) does go, in these examples, beyond the 'token nod' and does move towards an internalised acceptance of the multicultural character of Australian society. To move from multiculturalism in film to the hybridity of the music of the multiracial band Yothu Yindi is to move to a much more complicated phenomenon where it is more difficult to be sure of the significance of the changes one notices. Furthermore, and to our discredit, Australians are arrested at an earlier stage in the process of understanding and accepting Aboriginality than occurs in the case of multiculturalism. Take two snapshots from Yothu Yindi's most successful year, 1991. Their single, 'Treaty', won the Human Rights Commission's Award for Songwriting; it was named Song of the Year by the Australasian Performing Right Association (APRA); and it won awards for Australian Song of the Year, Best Australian Single, and Best Engineer for the Filthy Lucre dance mix from the Australian Record Industry Association (ARIA). The video for 'Treaty' won MTV and Australian Music awards, and the album *Tribal Voice* won Best Indigenous Record and Best Album Cover Artwork awards.[25] On the other hand, however, on the night before accepting the ARIA award on national television, Mandawuy Yunupingu, the band's leader, was refused service in a St Kilda bar in Melbourne allegedly on the grounds of his colour. The uproar which this event created eventually wore down an initially unrepentant proprietor, but the fact that it could happen at all gave the lie to claims that Yothu Yindi's success was a sign of the end of racial prejudice. From what one saw on subsequent television

132

coverage, Mandawuy Yunupingu handled this outrage with both anger and dignity. His ARIA acceptance speech, significantly, pushed an appropriating white culture back in the queue: it was delivered in the Yolngu language of his own people.

Yothu Yindi have achieved a level of visibility and acceptance far in excess of that achieved by any previous Aboriginal musicians.[26] This is not always held to be a good thing. Some critics of the band argue that because their image is less threatening than that of, say, Bart Willoughby and Mixed Relations, it is therefore more assimilatory. Phil Hayward criticises the video which promotes the second version of 'Treaty' as constructing a view of Aboriginality that displaces it onto joyful children dancing on a beach in Arnhem Land—or as he puts it, 'safe, exotic and somewhere else'.[27] As Hayward's remarks indicate, there are various assessments of what Yothu Yindi's success might mean for Aboriginals generally. The January 1993 issue of the music and popular culture journal, *Perfect Beat*, is dominated by articles debating the politics of the band, in particular the politics of the remixed dance version of 'Treaty'.

Although my primary concern is with the music itself, it would be futile to try to separate this from such debates. The original version of 'Treaty' was released in February 1991. It got some radio airplay but failed to reach the Top 100 in the national charts. A remix aimed at the dance-club audience was made by the Melbourne producers Filthy Lucre (and there have been lots of comments about *that* name). The rhythm track was boosted, the didjeridu put higher in the mix, the English lyrics all but disappeared (the English lyrics claim that the promises of the Bicentenary had come to nothing, and call for Hawke's promise of a treaty to be honoured), and the song became a European techno-pop dance track with exotic 'World Music' overtones. The remixed 'Treaty' entered the charts at number 44 within a month of its release in June 1991 and peaked at number 11 in September.[28] In Adelaide, it hit No.1—the first record by an Aboriginal artist to do so since Jimmy Little's 'Royal Telephone' in 1964.

This little industrial history just begs to be understood in terms of an 'authentic' traditional culture selling itself out to market capitalism and popular success. This is pretty much how Phil Hayward sees it in his discussion of how the band has been represented, particularly in the video for the Filthy Lucre remix:

> To note the nature of their [Yothu Yindi's] representation is not to foist a white radical project upon them but to recognise the white hegemonic discourses which have created their cultural identity and thus

Multiracial band, Yothu Yindi, in promotional mode. (courtesy of
Mushroom Records)

context of reception. There is, after all, a consensual convenience to
their elevation as Australian cultural ambassadors in the post-Bicen-
tennial period. Their lack of overt political threat or 'edge' and their
colourful ethnicity has rendered them highly 'media friendly' in an
environment whose institutions are, more than ever before, aware of
the political correctness of including *occasional* representations of
Aboriginal material.[29]

To the insistence that white critics *are* in fact 'foisting their
project' upon these musicians, and that these professional musicians
are being required to maintain a political legitimacy we would never
demand from INXS or Jimmy Barnes, Hayward replies that ' "Treaty"
is not just any old song or video, it's a new highwater mark for
Aboriginal culture's access to the popular cultural mainstream'.[30]
Thus it is the band's political significance which matters most.
Conversely, Chris Lawe Davies cautions in the same journal that
'Yothu Yindi should not be fetishised to the point that they alone
constitute Aboriginality'. This overestimates their importance and
oversimplifies 'Aboriginality'. As to their political credentials, Lawe

Davies says phlegmatically, 'They do their bit'.[31] And they do. At the most obvious level, they have maintained the practice of recording traditional music and of performing their traditional dances and music as integral parts of their live shows; they have even pressed this point by performing such items as encores.

Obviously, there must be a minefield of political sensitivities here. And that is just for the white critics, to whom this is pre-eminently a theoretical issue. For Aboriginal bands themselves, the politics of race must determine their choices at the most practical, or the most industrial, level: finding work and venues, addressing an audience, securing recording possibilities and airplay, selecting management and so on. Over the years, white racism has actively inhibited Aboriginal bands' access to mainstream audiences. Now, white critics' more benign but still naive expectations that some kind of cultural authenticity should be audible in Aboriginal rock music do not make it that much easier for Aboriginal bands to reach this mainstream audience. Faced with such expectations from whites, and faced with even more complicated expectations from an Aboriginal community which is far more culturally diverse than simple constructions like 'Aboriginal rock music' would imply, Aboriginal musicians must 'steer a course between the cliffs of essentialisation on one side and assimilation on the other' in deciding what to play and where to play it.[32]

Given all of this, to talk of Yothu Yindi's music as an example of hybridity is possibly to blunder into an already overcomplicated field of argument. However, it does seem important to challenge the demand that the rock music played by Aboriginals must adopt a prescribed relation to traditional indigenous musics. As John Castles points out, 'white encouragement of the category of 'Aboriginal music' as a reconnection with and expression of a prior Aboriginal community continues to hold a dangerously essentialising potential'.[33] That is, it assumes that Aboriginality is a uniform category; it assumes that cultural expressions derive their legitimacy only from a racial, genetic, source; it assumes that whites still know what are the 'right' politics for Aboriginal bands; and it assumes that the only thing Aboriginal bands have to offer is their 'Aboriginality'. The implications of such a politics are discriminatory. The search for the authentic 'Aboriginality' of Aboriginal rock music leads to an endless 'tracing backwards'[34] of sources and origins. The result must be a progressively narrow definition of 'Aboriginality' which marginalises all competing definitions. Indeed, the idea of 'authenticity' has been used in racist politics in the past as a means of containing and limiting the claims of Aboriginality: privileging the tribal over the urban Aboriginal, for instance, or more recently asking for proof of 'continuous occupation' in order to validate Aboriginal land claims.[35]

Rock music is a highly globalised industry. While its dominant industrial and discursive structures are continuously contested, it still makes little sense to talk of there being an 'authentic' Australian rock music, in my view, let alone an 'authentic' Aboriginal rock music. Textually, rock music is a 'dirty' cultural form, full of excess and appropriations. The task of interpellating an indigenous musical culture into such a discursive and industrial regime is not to be underestimated. Where it happens at all, it will happen by way of interpretive translation rather than unmediated transmission. The generic traditions of the music and the structures of the industry will always intervene, shaping and influencing the eventual product. In their rock (rather than their traditional) music, Yothu Yindi seem comfortable with the processes of negotiation, incorporation and appropriation so fundamental to the operation of the popular music industry. Their music thus takes the risk of being seen as assimilatory. To many this is a risk worth taking; as Tony Mitchell says, again in connection with the remixed 'Treaty':

> While the loss of the original version of the song's elaboration of an Aboriginal view of the British invasion of Australia is important, the way in which groups of young Aboriginals have adopted the remixed version of the song and dance to it on street corners offers a legitimation of Yunupingu's openness to a hybridization of Aboriginal culture and Western music technology.[36]

Which brings us back to hybridity. John Castles talks of Yothu Yindi's music as 'fusion' and makes use of a metaphor from the band's 'Mainstream' as a means of describing it; the mainstream is where the two streams, black and white, meet and become one:

> For Yothu Yindi the mainstream is both presence in white society and continuing to flow with Aboriginal traditions. Their rhetorical points tie in more with a post-Bicentenary politics of Aboriginal *renaissance* than with an earlier style of struggle and contestation. . . They say: we are sovereign in our own country, but we can play your musical game too.[37]

Here the idea of 'fusion' does not quite catch what interests me about Yothu Yindi; Castles' emphasis is on the potential for homogeneity, as the two cultural forms become one. In the hybrid, the two forms retain their distinctiveness but their combination produces something startlingly new. Listening to Yothu Yindi's albums, one does hear the contributing traditions: the Aboriginal traditions which provide wholly Yolgnu material as well as influencing the instrumentation and tonal qualities in the contemporary repertoire; and the western rock music traditions which provide the musical framework for the contemporary numbers (for instance, the post-punk thrash of 'Gapirri' and 'Dharpa', or the reggae influence on 'Matjala'). However, to fully appreciate the hybridity of their music, I suspect, one needs to see Yothu Yindi perform live.

Yothu Yindi is a big band, with a highly theatrical show: the painted dancers, the backup singers, the backdrops and the contrasting performances of traditional and contemporary material all contribute to the effect. It is also a very distinctive band. The multiracial rhythm section creates an unusual sound. The bass, drums and guitar work like a dance-band rhythm section: stylishly tight, tonally narrow, and pushy. The effect of the didjeridu is to provide a richer but slacker tone, to complicate or suffuse the beat, meanwhile releasing all the resonances of the exotic, of World Music, of constructions of the 'primitive'. Band members see the didjeridu's expansive sound wave operating so as to tie the lower register of the band's sound together and to give a variety to the bottom end no other instrument can give: as drummer Hughie Benjamin puts it, 'the bottom end of the didj is fantastic, it rattles your ancestors'.[38] Surprisingly, the didjeridu works especially well on the more vigorous, 'thrash', numbers where its modal and unmelodic effect seems complementary. What is most striking about the live performance, however, is the apparent unity of the material. Yothu Yindi's music has a stylistic coherence that appears to emerge fully formed, with no rough edges, from this presumably quite complicated but obviously thorough processing of a cocktail of cultural influences.

The best rock bands have always put their own stamp on their music; they invent a small section of the field of rock and roll. In concert Yothu Yindi do that through a group of songs that share an anthem-like character: they have choruses which lift under the impetus of rising chord structures and the sudden addition of four or five voices to the mix; the effect is enhanced by the use of harmonies which are slightly exotic and therefore arresting to western ears. Such songs as 'Mainstream', 'Djapana', 'Hope', 'Tribal Voice' and 'Treaty' delivered in quick succession in a concert feel like a wholly new kind of music, bred from a recognisable combination of sources but winding up sounding nothing like them. What is produced is a celebration of hybridity which works on and transforms its various competing and interlocking histories and cultures in order to produce something like Rushdie's 'love-songs to our mongrel selves'.[39]

As Phil Hayward suggests, Yothu Yindi *have* been taken up by the media and by government as the marketable face of contemporary Aboriginality. Part of this, I am sure, has to do with their place of origin[40] and with the relaxed exoticism of their visual representations—even of some of their music. International interest in Aboriginal music, like international interest in Aboriginal art, 'gravitates towards the isolated locale': 'it seeks artists isolated enough to lay claim to authentic lines of tradition'.[41] In Yothu Yindi's case, as we have already seen, the relation to 'authentic lines of tradition' is quite complex and its significance debatable but they do fit the paradigm that John Castles describes. Such being the case, a degree of cynicism about the long-term implications of this band's public success is probably justified. However, what should be acknowledged is that another component of Yothu Yindi's attraction—particularly to a government rhetorically committed to reconciliation with indigenous Australians—is that they are an explicitly political band genuinely committed to using their music and their organisation to further their people's cause. I would see the appropriation of Yothu Yindi as at least partly due to their capacity to represent the acceptable face of reconciliation rather than to their putative performance of a model of assimilation.

Nevertheless, it is true that the 'nationalisation' of Yothu Yindi has been largely media-driven, given impetus by Mandawuy Yunupingu's appealing media personality as well as by the newsworthiness of the commercial success of their music. The processes which have installed Yothu Yindi as a new symbol of Australian culture are the same as those which installed Alan Bond as a new symbol of Australian capitalism—the processes we examined in Chapter 2. Accordingly, one should acknowledge that this construction may well be serving interests that have little to do with those of Aboriginal people. That said, there are important differences between the two cases of Alan Bond and Yothu Yindi. Bond's nationalisation mythologised a recklessly individualist form of capitalism which actively worked against the interests of most Australians; it was made possible through the use of established, traditional myths of Australianness. The nationalisation of Yothu Yindi is made possible by the mythologising of very different constructions of Australianness: these constructions—among other things—admit the centrality of Aboriginality to Australian culture, value difference above conformity, and regard the maintenance of an indigenous culture as essential to future Australian identities. The content of the Australian nationality projected onto Yothu Yindi seems to me light years away from that projected onto Alan Bond; in the distance between them, I see some hope for a revision of the dominant forms of Australian nationalism.

The debates around the meaning of Yothu Yindi's success have been preoccupied with sources and origins, leaving little time to consider the musical utterance itself. If future nationalisms in this country will celebrate our hybridity and take advantage of the heterogeneity of the cultural forms we produce, then there is every reason to see Yothu Yindi's music as the perfect example of the kind of national cultural expression we should be celebrating now. Notwithstanding how the band is taken up in other domains, in their performances to date and in their *Tribal Voice* we can see how the movement from purity to hybridity opens up possibilities rather than closes them down.

7

The media, the nation
. . . and conclusion

And the winner is . . . Sydney! (Olympic president, Juan Antonio Samaranch)

This is a win for the people of Sydney, not for a group of politicians; it's a win for the Australian people. (NSW Opposition leader, Bob Carr)

Here we go again: Sydney 2000

As I was completing this book, Sydney was selected as the host city for the Olympic Games in 2000 ('the games of the millennium', television repeatedly called them). The announcement was greeted with extraordinary celebrations in Sydney. Thousands had gathered at specially organised events in Sydney Cove, partying on until the announcement was due at 4.20 a.m. When giant video screens delivered The Result, people went beserk: there was dancing, cheering, even tears, as the party continued through the dawn and into the next day. Sydney newspapers had their special editions on the street with staggering speed; the *Sydney Morning Herald* had a colour wraparound announcing that 'we' had won. The *Australian* (somewhat bathetically, a day later) abandoned all pretence of being a newspaper by adopting a Ken Done T-shirt-styled picture of Sydney framing the statement 'We did it!' as its entire front page. All TV channels, except SBS which was off the air anyway, suspended their normal programming in order to cover the

140

announcement and the subsequent celebrations in Sydney and in Monte Carlo. Rivalry between competing TV channels evaporated in the heat of the occasion; Channel 9's Ray Martin and Channel 7's Bruce McAvaney teamed up to ask Paul Keating what he would think of a boss who fired anyone for being late to work today (an allusion to Bob Hawke's emotional outburst at the Royal Perth Yacht Club when *Australia II* won the America's Cup). Comparisons with the America's Cup victory, one might have thought a fairly tenuous connection,[1] proved irresistible once it was noted that the announcement had come within a day or two of the tenth anniversary of Bond's victory at Newport.

One had only to turn on the radio or the television to find out that this was a major national event. For those Australians who did not live in Sydney, the Sydney bid had not really been an object of keen interest until it looked like winning. Even then, it still seemed primarily a Sydney matter. However, and while Sydney-siders responded with much greater enthusiasm than anyone else, Samaranch's words immediately changed the nature of the event for the rest of the country. Within minutes, Sydney's success was nationalised. Keating told Ray and Bruce that the IOC's vote proved we were now taken seriously by the rest of the world (at least he didn't say it put us on the map!). On breakfast television, State premiers were fielding reporters' questions on 'what this means' for Queensland (or Victoria, South Australia and so on), and survivors from Brisbane's and Melbourne's unsuccessful bids were wheeled in to hear that they had helped prepare the way and thus shared the glory now heaped upon Sydney. From every perspective canvassed on that morning, this was a Great Day—not just for Sydney, but for Australia.

Of course, before the Great Day arrived, the Sydney bid had not been entirely free of critics. Wendy Bacon has noted that before the New South Wales government accepted the proposal that Sydney make a bid there was significant public and official scepticism (notably, from the then Premier, Nick Greiner). Bacon quotes the *Sydney Morning Herald*'s editorial warning in 1990 that an Olympics bid could develop its own momentum, irrespective of its merits: '[the] tendency to wrap a flag around a bid for the Olympic Games makes it difficult for opponents to establish a rational debate about the bid's financial merits', the paper suggested.[2] Once the bid was endorsed, however, such warnings disapppeared. From that moment on, any public criticism could be regarded as providing ammunition for Sydney's competitors and thus as actively threatening the city's chances. Given such a scenario, it was easy to represent any criticism as 'un-Australian'. Some dissenting voices were raised on 2SER and ABC radio[3] while, on television, *Four Corners* and the *7.30 Report* made short and under-researched attempts to investigate the budget and to predict what might be the likely economic effects. As the date of the decision approached, the internal politics of the International Olympic Committee itself was subject to more sustained interrogation than the details of the Sydney bid's budget. The most developed critique I encountered was on ABC Radio's weekend sports program, 'Grandstand', where Max Walsh and John Valder engaged in a lengthy if unilluminating debate. To date, there has been virtually no significant media consideration of the socio-economic effects of staging the Games in 2000, although as I write there *are* stories surfacing which suggest that the process of the budget 'blowing out' has already begun.

While the lack of critical media attention is alarming, it is not surprising. The ability of the Sydney news media to cover the bid and its implications in a critical or even interrogative way was effectively nullified by its co-option onto the organising committees. Both the *Sydney Morning Herald* and the *Telegraph-Mirror* were represented on the bid committee, while Kerry Packer—owner of Consolidated Press Holdings and Channel 9—was also a member.[4] In a graphic demonstration of the effect of media monopolies, once Sydney's two daily newspapers had abandoned their public responsibilities in favour of commercial responsibilities there was no local press outlet capable of serving them. As for television, it would probably be naive to expect a network which hoped to supply the Games coverage for Australia and maybe sell that coverage on to other countries to do anything other than offer its wholehearted support. The remaining commercial networks, of course, had their hopes too and in any case could hardly be expected to singlehandedly take on the bid Committee; some of their major advertisers were sponsors of the bid. Once Sydney's bid succeeded, canvassing the likely socio-economic effects on inner urban Sydney looked like raining on John Fahey's parade in just the way the *Sydney Morning Herald* had predicted. Humphrey McQueen tried, on Radio National's *Life Matters* on the day of the announcement, to suggest that we needed a lot more scrutiny than had so far occurred. Pitted against a euphoria so widespread that we even had Prue Goward literally whooping with delight before commencing her political report from Canberra on Radio National's *Daybreak*, such sensible warnings were bound to go unheeded. The unfortunate fact is that such stories are still years off for the local media; they will come, but only when they are too late to make a difference.

So, here we go again. All the familiar discourses I have been discussing throughout this book have been moved into position once more. The success of a small group of politicians and businessmen acting in the name of an entire city, whose specific long-term interests have never been publicly evaluated, has been claimed as a national triumph. The seamless identification of Australian national interests with those of Australian business has been once again immediate; the Games were introduced on at least one radio broadcast as a 'recession-buster', and in the short time I have been following their representation their importance has been connected more routinely with economic than with sporting development. (The *Bulletin's* 19 October 1993 cover story was '35 Ways to make money from the Olympics'.) As the history of the Olympic Games is that, on balance, they tend to impoverish the cities which host them, this is a connection which media representations ought to have found difficult to maintain. They haven't. Rather, the process of making the Sydney Olympic Games national has worked with depressing predictability. It has worked to protect them from criticism and scrutiny; to dismiss their impact on specific social groups and interests as secondary to their national significance; and to mobilise support around a narrow, almost colonial, index of national achievement—that of actually hosting the event. Sport, and Australia's possible sporting achievements at the Games, are running a distant second in the race for the dominant meanings of this event.[5] Indeed, it is already appearing as if Australia World is likely to push sport into third place as the Games are used to sell Sydney as a tourist destination.

Despite all of this, one has to admit, many of us felt a nice warm glow when Sydney won. The improbability of a Southern Hemisphere success coupled with the threat of a cynical decision favouring Beijing made the announcement surprisingly pleasing. It is likely that most Australians will derive great pleasure and pride from the Games themselves. As someone who is old enough to remember the 1956 Melbourne Olympics, I still recall my special affection for the names of Betty Cuthbert, Marlene Matthews and Shirley Strickland as they became my first Australian heroes on the athletics track. Furthermore, it is undeniable that modern nations are built through such moments of high spectacle. As Sydney 2000 *is* going to happen, then, it is worth thinking about how it could

143

be turned in a progressive direction. As a nation-building exercise, the Games provides an opportunity for Australians to activate the 'use by' date on our traditional nationalisms and attempt to establish a more heterogeneous and socially grounded set of signifiers for the nation. I would like to think that the opening ceremony—traditionally the place where the host nation signifies its identity through spectacle—is the location where this could occur.

While this might seem a slightly romantic fantasy, the alternative is hard to contemplate without shuddering. If the reader feels some ambivalence about the Bicentenary in 1988, try thinking back a little further—to the Commonwealth Games of 1982, held in Brisbane. These were the Games where Norman May's celebrated burst of nationalist repetition produced the immortal phrase, 'It's gold, gold, gold—gold for Australia!'. The opening ceremony featured a performance by Rolf Harris, and had lots of schoolchildren running from the pouch of a giant mechanical kangaroo which completed the spectacle by winking at the audience. For the television coverage, a classic media shotgun wedding was arranged. The then ABC current affairs anchorperson Geraldine Doogue joined sportscaster Norman May to comment on the proceedings and produced one of the most uncomfortable performances I have ever witnessed; she clearly had no idea what one should say about such a gormless spectacle and had trouble making sense of anything Norman said. While this was comic, there were other aspects that were not. Australian Aboriginals were acknowledged through the incorporation of a corroboree into the event, but the respect this might have signified was denied by the Aboriginal rights demonstration outside the stadium. If we are not to repeat this spectacle, we will need to find other ways of representing the nation.

These are unlikely to eventuate if we leave it to the Australian news and current affairs media. Throughout this book, I have been concerned to emphasise the structural importance of the Australian print and electronic news media in the process of 'making it national'. Unfortunately, their performance in this crucial structural role has all too often been ill-informed, sycophantic, shortsighted and opportunistic. If we were to generalise from the media's mythologisation of Alan Bond, the ability of specialist and editorial writers to provide an accurate analysis of current events must be seriously doubted. Similarly, the coverage of Maralinga was trivialising, actively diverting readers from the most important aspects of the issue. As we saw with Malcom Turnbull, the media routinely disconnects individuals from their social or political significance by treating them as 'personalities', most often as renditions of the national type. It would be a bewildered Australian who relied only on the local news media to tell them what was an important event and what was not. When the Mabo decision was first passed down it made barely a ripple in the daily press because its implications were simply not understood. A year later, it dominates the headlines and is finally acknowledged as a landmark in the history of Australian race relations. In contrast, Sydney's Olympic bid—notwithstanding its massive scale, a less significant event—dominated all news outlets for days immediately after the decision's announcement. Even in this case, though, the nature of the coverage belied the apparent importance of the event in that it was superficial, uncritical and highly personalised.

The inadequacies in the coverage of the Olympic bid only serve to highlight systemic problems which are firmly embedded in the normal operation of the Australian news media. As Wendy Bacon suggests, when all the 'shouting about the Olympic bid has died down' and most of its stories have finally been told, serious issues will still remain which relate to the structure and performance of the news media in Australia:

> These include the weakness of our independent media, the importance of maintaining a public ABC, the political hostility to dissenting voices, the disappearing line between advertising and editorial, the co-option of the media (news, promotion and advertising) into the political mobilisation of public opinion and action, and last but no means least, the lack of time and resources for journalists to investigate and analyse rather than merely quote press releases and prominent sources.[6]

While I have already dealt with certain structural problems within the media and popular culture at various junctures in this book, I want to discuss some of these issues—albeit briefly—in this final chapter.

Feeding the chooks: the independence of the news media

The newspaper is an active cultural technology for elaborating and consolidating what actually counts as society and how 'what counts' gets incorporated and individuated in modes of behaviour and forms of identification and affiliation. (Colin Mercer, *Celebrating the Nation*)

The media are among the institutions through which the nation is

145

constructed and they constitute the primary processes through which discourses of nationalism are deployed and disseminated. Benedict Anderson claims that the growth of the print media, in particular, is one of several determining factors in the origins of modern western nationalism.[7] Colin Mercer argues that the techniques and genres which constitute the newspaper, and the crucial role these techniques have played in forming definitions of the individual, the citizen, and the national population, actually make it very difficult for modern newspapers to handle 'that which does *not* [my emphasis] fit the national'.[8] As for television, Morley and Silverstone describe it as a central mechanism for connecting the 'familiar' or domestic domain with the national or international spheres: for sustaining 'both the image and the reality of the "national family" '.[9]

In his history of 'the creation of the public' through the popular media, John Hartley describes the cultural role of the news media in this way:

> The news media function, at the most general level, to create a sense of belonging for the population of a given city, state or country. Their readers and audiences are an 'imagined community'; in the case of popular (or monopoly) outlets these readers or viewers are assumed to be coterminous with the nation or state, and they are encouraged by each newspaper or TV channel to see the news as part of their own identity, while the news strives to identify with them. So news includes stories on a daily basis which enable everyone to recognise a larger unity or community than their own immediate contacts, and to identify with the news outlet as 'our' storyteller.[10]

As Hartley's explanation implies, a rarely noticed consequence of the increasing concentration of media ownership in Australia is that, as more media outlets hold monopolies in their market, more media outlets address their readers or viewers as a national—rather than a local, a metropolitan, a regional or even a State—audience. The consequent reduction in the variety of opinion and access is accompanied by another consensualising editorial imperative as the media companies respond to commercial demands that they become identified with what counts as 'the national'.

There is little point in my rehearsing here the customary arguments against the increasing concentration of ownership and the shrinking of the whole domain of news and current affairs production. These arguments have been outlined often enough elsewhere,[11] and their representation during the federal government's inquiry into the print media in 1991 seemed to have the usual effect (that is, none) on the eventual recommendations. Media critics can recite an ever-lengthening list of alternative or quality news outlets which have bitten the dust over the years, unable to operate in a field dominated by three major players. *Nation, Nation Review, The National Times* and *Times on Sunday* provide a mythic prehistory for the gallant but ultimately doomed attempts of *Australian Society, Modern Times* and *Australian Left Review* to represent new voices and opinions. The failure of such magazines and the mainstream press's lack of interest in the independent opinions that *do* manage to get aired—say on public radio—are major factors in the discursive unanimity which marks the representations of most of the cases examined in this book. The concentration of the media in Australia is a structural impediment to free expression of opinion, to investigation and analysis; and it exercises a well-orchestrated, anti-democratic influence on the processes of nation formation.

I am interested in highlighting some other structural problems, however, which also affect how the media participate in the processes of nation formation. The degree to which the media maintain (or fail to maintain) their independence from government and commercial interests, for instance, is an issue raised by the Sydney 2000 bid. The relationship between the media and government was the subject of a review by the Electoral and Administrative Review Commission (EARC) in Queensland and its report (published in 1993) provides useful empirical evidence of the interdependence of the two institutions. The Commission's terms of reference were actually quite narrow in that it was directed to confine itself to 'systemic problems' and not to consider particular 'allegations of inefficiency, dishonesty or partiality'. The Commission *was* concerned, however, with assessing how the media discharged its public responsibilities and how government attempted to direct the media's performance to its own ends—to manipulate or, less perjoratively, to 'manage' the media.

The EARC report makes interesting reading on both counts. It outlines an institutional symbiosis between the media and government so established that it routinely delivers journalists into press relations jobs with government ministers and departments. The most telling evidence of the close relationship between government and the media comes from EARC's 'Media Release Study', which tracked the fate of government press releases. Initiated as a result of suspicions that the news media routinely ran government press releases without further investigation or in some cases even without rewriting them, this study attempted to assess how rigorously the Queensland news media scrutinised government-sourced information. In the four-week period of the study, the fate of 279 individual government media releases was followed up. 'Of these 279 releases', the report says, '220 of them were reproduced virtually unchanged in at least one newspaper and 140 of them—almost exactly half— ran virtually unchanged in a large circulation newspaper'.[12] The percentage of stories which, though rewritten, were considered to be 'highly influenced' by the media releases was 55 per cent.[13] Regional newspapers were particularly culpable, accounting for 85 per cent of the instances in which media releases were run unchanged.[14] Television and radio fared better, although this may be a consequence of the reduced news content of the electronic media in comparison to the print media. However, although television news only had a take-up rate of 6 per cent, almost 60 per cent of the press release stories they did run carried no evidence of any independent corroboration.

In his evidence to the Commission, Jack Waterford, the deputy editor of the *Canberra Times*, claimed that 'in Queensland, as in all too many places, relations between politicians, press secretaries and the media are altogether too cosy and too pally for words'.[15] Clearly, this situation is not confined to Queensland. EARC reported on a survey of television news in three State capitals which found that, for example, in Sydney only 24 per cent of political news stories were the result of interviews initiated by journalists. British and American studies referenced by the Commission contain even more alarming results than the EARC study. One American analysis, covering a twenty-year period, found that 46 per cent of stories in the *New York Times* and the *Washington Post* originated with government officials or sources. In England, a study of county press outlets found that locally generated government information enjoyed a take-up rate of 96 per cent![16]

While journalists and their organisations must be accountable for such results, many submissions to the Commission made the important point that governments have learned to 'manage' the news very skilfully and journalists are at some disadvantage in their attempts to resist. In particular, political journalists' dependence on their government sources discourages critical treatment of government information and fosters a sycophantic, 'cultivating' relationship. Governments are aware that there may well be limits even to such a relationship, and do what they can to further limit journalists' ability to investigate (this was the case with Maralinga, for instance). Warren Clarke, a reporter for Channel 9 in Brisbane, described the journalist's predicament in the following way:

> The way many government media conferences are handled is also conducive to the media often being unable to pump out much different to the government line. It works like this: Media conference at 2pm, Media turn up, Minister arrives with minder, minder provides media with a page or two about some major issue which the government often has spent months working on. The journalists, who most likely have not even had time to read to the bottom of the press release, are asked 'Any questions?'
>
> In an almost lunatic attempt that fools no one except the public and usually the journalist's own conscience, you then run around to the Opposition to get its impression of this latest earth-shattering initiative by the Government, bearing in mind the Opposition has probably put about as much thought into the process as you have. After getting their response you put it all together for public consumption and somehow kid yourself that you have balanced the story. . . It is a joke, but it is also the system at work.[17]

Clarke is right to emphasise the systemic nature of the dilemma he describes. The media depend on their ability to systematically produce what is an unpredictable and unmanageable commodity, cheaply and quickly. Government is a predictable source, readily accessible to journalists. While the public might think of journalists, first and foremost, as writers, the professional skills of the journalist must also include the ability to maintain good contacts with government sources and thus keep the line to news open. Ian Ward goes so far as to suggest that the job of the journalist today is primarily that of 'cultivating and harvesting sources'.[18] Often, events suggest, there is some truth in this view.[19]

The media's independence is compromised not only by the institutional alignment with government which the EARC report describes, but also by the media's industrial identification with the interests of business. Without explicitly jettisoning the responsibilities of the Fourth Estate, media proprietors routinely talk of their interests in purely commercial terms. A former editor of the *Age* told EARC that most media proprietors today face conflicts between their commercial interests and the public interest:

> Gone for the most part are the days when newspaper publishers were merely publishers: strong-willed men of powerful prejudice perhaps, but men with no other commercial barrows to push. Today most media proprietors are caught, whether they admit it or not, in conflicts of interest which undermine their credibility and that of contemporary journalism.[20]

The co-option of the media onto the Olympic bid committee and the notorious $400 000 payment to the premier of Queensland, Sir Joh Bjelke-Petersen, made by Alan Bond when head of Channel 9 (in order that he 'continue to do business successfully in Queensland') are only two examples of conflicts of interest which undermine the credibility of contemporary journalism.

The alignment with business does not involve only the proprietors. Chris Lawe Davies has argued that the 'corporate yoke' which now overdetermines news operations engenders an identification between individual journalists and their employing organisation. This corporate loyalty suggests a 'compliance with the corporate aims of the organisation' that is 'a danger to the independence of the press'.[21] In some cases (tabloid journalists, say, or those working in the more populist magazines), the identification with the corporate yoke may extend beyond the specific organisation to a redefinition of the journalist's role into that of a member of what John Hartley called the 'smiling professions'—those of publicity and entertainment. To the extent that this occurs, it helps explain the effortlessness with which the ideological alignment between the media and business traced at various points through these chapters has been constructed, and the degree to which this alignment has worked to privilege 'corporate speech' and the world view of certain sections of Australian private enterprise. What is also notable about this ideological alignment is how 'medium-specific' it is. Some years ago, I researched the representation of work and business in 1980s Australian TV soap operas. My reading of the news media at the time led me to expect that I would find substantial ideological or discursive support for the white collar high-flyer, the larrikin capitalist or the 1980s yuppie in these soaps. I didn't. Instead, a traditional working-class valorisation of family, community and non-material ideals was repeatedly and convincingly articulated. For all the congruence my research uncovered, *Neighbours* and *Home and Away* on the one hand, and the *Australian* and *Business Review Weekly* on the other, could have come from different planets. One would have to conclude that the news media's ideological positioning was not a reflection of a widespread cultural shift but of their own sectional interests.

'The meanest intelligence': journalism and ethics

The twentieth century inaugurated a new phase in journalism, a new chapter in the history of looking. The education of the population turned from democratization to domestication. The editors of the day went in for popular instruction, reconfiguring their mass readership from class to family. They wrote not for their peers, as the organic intellectuals of the pauper press had done; now, readerships were divided along class, not community lines, with the new generation of literates produced by the establishment of universal elementary schooling in 1870 forming a new market for simple, home truths. Journalists themselves were taught that they were 'writing for the meanest intelligence', as Kennedy Jones, one of Lord Northcliffe's senior editors, reminded his staff in 1919. (John Hartley, *The Politics of Pictures*)

Hartley suggests that journalism today takes place in a 'post-truth' society; where the 'politics of pictures' are no longer overlooked but vigorously contested. The shift from a democratising, universalising 'truth' happens much earlier, according to Hartley, than most media analysts would have it. The current enthusiasm for 'infotainment', for tabloid news, and the shift away from providing public information and towards the occupation of domestic leisure is only the end of a process that began in the mid-nineteenth century. Today, journalism's ethics, idealistically hooked up to discourses of truth and objectivity, are in constant contradiction with journalism's practice. As anyone who watches CNN or *Hard Copy* will know, this is not peculiar to Australian journalism—although Australian journalism has held on to the myth of objectivity longer than most and thus lives with some pretty stark contradictions between ideals and practice.

It is to the practices of the news media that I want to address my attention in this section. The EARC's Media Release Study revealed how routinely print journalists fail to follow up stories, to corroborate information received from official sources, or even to pursue an alternative opinion. While television and radio do better, they have their failures too. Many of these failures are due to the lack of resources devoted to investigations; many are not. A particularly chilling example was broadcast during 1993 on the ABC Radio National *Media Report*, whose team spent a week with the *Hinch* current affairs TV program. During their visit, Derryn Hinch delivered one of his 'Shame File' attacks (in which an individual or

151

organisation in the news is 'exposed' by Hinch and denounced in a piece straight to camera). The provocation for this particular attack turned out to be a two-paragraph item lifted from a Brisbane newspaper. No independent attempt was made to investigate the story, the individual concerned or the legitimacy of the position adopted by the Brisbane report before the Shame File piece went to air. When the *Media Report* questioned Hinch about the lack of corroborating research, he seemed nonplussed; this was evidently normal practice.

The media's treatment of the Mabo debates is a further example of uncorroborated, irresponsible reporting. During the peak of the media beat-ups around this issue, May and June of 1993, alarmist stories were routine in the daily press. Headline after headline warned of takeover claims, legal chaos, investor panic. Press releases from interested parties were printed without any investigation and allowed to stand uncontested. Some reports were unashamedly inflammatory. On one slow news day, 17 June, the *Courier-Mail* ran with 'Blacks to sue Britain: James Cook "a criminal"' as its contribution to informing its readers about the progress of the debate. The *Australian's* headline on the same day, 'Banks warn of Mabo fallout', ran above a story which hinted at threats to domestic home loans. The *Australian* was well aware that ordinary homeowners were in no danger from Aboriginal claims or (in this respect, at least) from the banks. Indeed, the paper had published a letter from Ian Barker QC several days before which had made this point in response to an earlier, similarly alarmist, report. But there was no attempt to provide either balance or accuracy in the front page story. On 29 June the *Australian* published a front page story which repeated BHP's warning of the day before that Mabo was forcing it to defer projects, and a business column written by Bryan Frith also reiterated BHP's position. Page 2 of the *same* edition, though, carried BHP's retraction of the warning! Buried halfway into the page 2 report, readers might have found the information that 'The managing director of BHP, Mr John Prescott, acknowledged that no BHP projects were being held up by the High Court's Mabo decision'.[22]

Such was the barrage of misinformation over this period, such was the pre-eminence given to the opinions of the banks and the mining industry over those of the government and, most of all, Aboriginals, and such was the outcry from both the Right and the Left of politics, that the media's treatment of the Mabo debates became itself an issue in the media. Mike Willessee, of all people, devoted most of one edition of *A Current Affair* to serving up Dorothy Dix-ers to Paul Keating so that the prime minister could reassure Australians that 'their backyards were not in danger' and correct the false impressions people had been receiving from the print media. However, as many researchers have established, journalists by and large do not really know much about their readers or audiences, and seem to care even less.[23] Their response to criticism of their work is hostile, and so even the articles which acknowledged public concern about the coverage of the Mabo debates quickly became apologias for the local industry and its practices—usually by means of brandishing a British tabloid as a point of comparison. Errol Simper's piece on the 'feeding frenzy' around Mabo cited numerous criticisms only to dismiss them through the accommodating nostrums of Clem Lloyd, professor of journalism at Wollongong and former press secretary to Bill Hayden:

> The media has not had much help from government in the form of a clear, firm line over Mabo. So under the circumstances I'd say it's done a reasonable job. Certainly it's avoided the irrational, sensational line you would expect in, say, UK tabloids.[24]

Characteristically, Simper's piece ends up with a personal attack on one of the harshest critics of media performance on this issue, former Hawke press secretary, Colin Parkes.[25]

Paradoxically, as public confidence in journalists declines—it is now customary to point out that they poll just ahead of union leaders and car salesmen, and their institution only just ahead of the political system[26]—journalists' confidence in the myths of their own trade seems to grow stronger. Indeed, the low regard in which journalism is held can be a source of 'malicious satisfaction': 'one interpretation is that the nature of their job makes it impossible for the public to love them—that the poll figures *should* be low, if journalists are doing their job properly'.[27] It has been suggested that contemporary journalists have abandoned their 'natural' alliance with their readers and thus their place in the public sphere, shifting allegiance 'not only to corporate and government power bases' but also to a narcissistic celebration of their own professional standing:

> There was a recent example of this narcissism at a media conference in Brisbane. During the conference David Fagan of *The Courier-Mail* defended journalistic practices of representing Australian cultural diversity, in the face of criticism from those who claimed to be misrepresented. Fagan used the phrase 'working journalist' to underline the veracity of the professional/industrial expert, in the face of mere social subjects.[28]

As Lawe Davies goes on to suggest, the fetishisation of the 'working journalist' is a bid for lost authority, the authority to dismiss the judgements of anyone outside the trade and thus 'outside the loop' of privileged knowledges.[29]

The claim for the political and cultural authority of the journalist, and indeed for the overarching authority of 'the media' within the public sphere, is struck on a number of fronts. The advent of so-called 'tabloid TV' (*Hard Copy*, in one formation; *Cops*, in another), with its invasive, exploitative and lurid representational strategies masked by the label of 'reality TV', does represent an extension of television into 'real life'. Television current affairs anchorpersons routinely occupy key structural positions in the debates they present: they become the voice of the audience's common sense, and thus carry more authority than either of the positions they are setting out to 'mediate'. At times, their confidence in this (purely semiotic) power is almost comic; Peter Couchman, for example, seemed genuinely disappointed at times that he couldn't persuade his studio guests, despite their years of campaigning on opposite sides of a complex issue, to agree 'in front of the cameras'. Couchman's constant beckoning movement with his arms, as if gathering a brood of chooks, dramatised his frustration at not being able to exert any material influence on the debates beyond the studio. And then there is the occasional moment of complete narcissistic excess when television succumbs to the temptation to stop being television and become the 'real world'—which means getting the two domains hopelessly confused. The Hanging Rock seige with *A Current Affair*'s irresponsible transition from reporting, to becoming, the news is the most grotesque example of this.[30] Not that journalism's tendency towards industrial *hubris* has gone unnoticed by those within its ranks; leading figures such as Jana Wendt, columnist Sam Lipski and the chief executive of Fairfax, Stephen Mulholland, have all recently attacked their profession for low journalistic standards and for self-importance.[31]

What has really worried me in the research for this book is the fact that a key location for low journalistic standards and self-importance is a very significant one: the newspaper editorial. As journalism's authority has declined, the various media have attempted to repair the effects of this in different ways. In television, there has been the obsession with 'colour and movement' and the construction of viewer identification with the program presenter. While the profession as a whole may not be credible, individual performers within it certainly are; instructive here is the effect of

Jana Wendt's departure on both the quality and the ratings of *A Current Affair* during 1993. In the print media, the repair job is much more difficult. Fundamental to that difficulty is the fact that, despite print journalists' ritualised invocation of their location within 'the real world', their work is almost entirely rhetorical. The authority of the editorial has to be constructed rhetorically, rather than through the mobilisation of the knowledge or expertise it has brought to bear on particular topics. This is achieved through a kind of 'high ventriloquism', uttering what passes for the common sense of the readership through a discursive construction of lofty objectivity. Stylistically, it manages to be pompous and populist at the same time. This editorial voice is, of course, a total fraud and we have already seen how ill-informed and misguided its judgements have been in particular instances.[32] The trick does seem to work, however, as readers (especially other journalists) accept the authority of the editorial in much the way that churchgoers accept the authority of the priest—through an act of faith.

The points made in the preceding paragraph qualify the argument made elsewhere in this section, in that they presume a media which actually want an audience. While those who work in the news media are not likely to want to *meet* their audience, they do *need* them. The simplest way to conceptualise that audience, and the simplest mode of address to adopt when speaking to them, is through the idea of the national. As we have seen in earlier chapters, the use of a restricted repertoire of nationalist discourses offers a ready mechanism for boosting a story's newsworthiness; once published, such an angle can guarantee at least initial interest and assent. At its most populist, this angle forms a strategy which endlessly produces stories about renditions of the national character. Events, places and personalities are all incorporated into the continuing narrative of the development and refinement of the national type. Paul Hogan, Evonne Goolagong Cawley, Elle McPherson, Nicole Kidman (and 'Australia's favourite son-in-law' Tom Cruise), Olivia Newton-John—it would be hard to list a mass-mediated celebrity who was not eventually understood in relation to national identity. (It can also happen to much less populist figures, too—Patrick White and Peter Carey are two who come to mind.[33]) At times, this can be problematic; Australians' recognition of Noelene Donaher from TV's *Sylvania Waters* was actually compromised by the embarrassing proposal that she was 'typical'. At such points, the media simply orchestrate the consequent debate, once again, around consensualised definitions of national identity. The problem with this is not just the versions of nationalism employed although, as we have seen, that *is* a problem; it is that it goes on largely uncontested by other voices, other points of view. It is the singularity of the view of the world we receive through our news media that is so impoverishing and so politically manipulable.

We should be critical of the Australian news media's participation in the formation and dissemination of our understandings of the nation. As the analyses in this book repeatedly demonstrate, the media's deployment of the discourses of Australian nationalism— their constant interest in 'making it national'—almost inevitably works to protect its subjects from criticism or analysis, to mask the interests being served or to expose those regarded as outside the ambit of nationalist discourse to attack. Given its potential—still—to organise support for a heterogeneous, socially democratic society, these are pretty disreputable uses for the idea of the nation. As Chapter 6 is meant to suggest, however, the situation is not entirely bleak, and I should stress that I have been more concerned with analysing those aspects of the circulation of the national within popular culture which worry me than with those which give me hope and pleasure. But there is much to be done in interrogating the terms through which Australian nationalisms are represented and put to use, and in challenging the structure and performance of the media which carry these representations.

Finally . . .

This book has drawn its stories, largely, from the 1980s. During that decade we saw business ascend to a position of cultural authority despite the excesses of the larrikin capitalists, the concentration and decline of the national news media, and the installation of the economy as the central category in the political conceptualisation of the nation. Since the 1980s, Australians have become used to hearing the nation talked about as if it were a brand name, rather than a social community whose interests politics should protect. While the excesses of the larrikin capitalists seem unlikely to be repeated in the near future, the other cases I have examined in the preceding chapters could easily be (or are being) replayed, one way or another, in the 1990s. The case studies are not quotations from a past we are unlikely to revisit; they are products of deep-rooted patterns in media representations of the national culture—patterns that need to be continually foregrounded if they are ever to be revised.

If a national community comes into being through the collective imaginings of its citizens, the cynical and self-interested deployment of the discourses of nation surveyed in this book suggests that our ability to find the terms through which we might better (that is, more appropriately or more democratically) imagine our common-alities is itself seriously depleted. How can Australians imagine their collective identity in the 1990s? Buried under the detritus of nine-teenth century definitions of a masculinist national type, bombarded with tourism imagery that offers impossible dreams of an Australian lifestyle, and diverted by complacent invocations of national identity which deliberately obscure the material relations within which we all live, Australia's national imagination is looking pretty groggy. As I said earlier, I don't think we deal with this by dispensing with Caughie's 'embarrassingly persistent category of the nation'. The revival of the national imagination must proceed from a thorough renovation of current definitions of Australian nationalism so that they more accurately reflect and respond to the interests of all Australian citizens.

James Walter has written a piece for *Australian Quarterly* in which he looks at the failure of another, but related, kind of imagination. Struck by similarities between the British general elec-tion of 1992 and the Australian federal election in 1993, Walters sets out to describe what he calls the failure of political imagination apparent in the two campaigns—and its implications:

> The British and Australian elections of the past year make manifest a failure of political imagination in both countries, and on both sides of politics. What has been lost is the ability to imagine the links between civil society, state and economy, and to see politics as the negotiation of collective benefit for a definable community. Notwithstanding Keating's retrospective reference to the people's common values, their compassion and their resistance to ripping the social fabric apart, politicians have lost the art of addressing people in terms of shared interests. At base, politics has become a debate not about the kind of community we want, but about the kind of economy we should have. The swing from persuasion to prescription in the political rhetoric of the past decade has been enormous.[34]

While Walter does address himself to the kind of issues we met much earlier in this book—the territory of Pusey's attack on econ-omic rationalism, for instance—he is not concerned only with the privileging of the economy in public discourse. He also considers the relation between institutional politics and the community.

Politicians, he argues, 'no longer know how to address their constituents' but, like the journalists criticised in the preceding section, 'it seems not to matter to them'. As was the case with the senior economic advisers Pusey studied, this is because British and Australian politicians of all persuasions are afflicted by their failure to 'conceptualise the community'. There is, Walter implies, no model of society, no unifying set of community interests or identities, no overarching social or civic ideals which these politicians recognise as the proper motivation for their actions. In place of such conceptions we find the familar elision of market and society, and the simple-minded appeal to consumer instincts—individualistic ethics, with no 'moral valency'.

Walter draws on Judith Brett's *Robert Menzies: The Forgotten People* to make the point that even in the bad old days of Menzies the relation between politics and the community provided a better model than the current situation:

> . . . in the 1940s, there was sustained debate about the correct mix of state action and private enterprise—with Labor and non-Labor differing on which element should dominate—but with planners and politicians clearly indicating of whom and for whom they spoke. Judith Brett's study of Menzies' appeal to an audience, *Robert Menzies: The Forgotten People* (1992), provides a detailed instance of this. Political rhetoric then conventionally drew on notions of the proper role of the state, and of how politics should serve the community. It was addressed to an audience conceived as located within and having commitments to civil society, and not just a market.[35]

Walter's argument is directed towards reviving the kind of political imagination that Brett's book describes, reclaiming a more socially grounded notion of the collective (national) interest, and redefining Australians as citizens rather than consumers. Above all, he says, Australians need to demand more vigorously that the agencies of the state act in the people's interest. To do this we need first to find ways of imagining this 'people' and their varying, competing, interests. As Walter concludes, the task before the Australian political imagination today is that of constructing such a 'unifying discourse'.

Australians do have their 'unifying discourses', of course, but the evidence I have put forward in this book would suggest that they do not serve us well. I have paralleled Walter's diagnosis of the failure of the Australian political imagination with Australia's failure to imagine the nation through anything other than the discourses this book has critiqued as regressive or exclusivist. Despite the continued efforts of intellectuals and others, these discourses have not yet been superseded by the official ideology of multiculturalism—perhaps because of its emphasis on diversity rather than hybridity. It would seem undeniable, though, that 'the capacity to *live with difference* is . . . the coming question of the twenty-first century'.[36] What will be needed to displace established ways of seeing the nation is more than just a spruced-up version of the old nationalisms. This is quite a challenge, particularly for intellectuals of the Left: how to adapt and transform the discourses of the national to better deal with our current historical circumstances. One thing is clear. We are going to have to come up with a particularly radical kind of unifying discourse: one that accepts the multiplicities and contradictory natures of the interests in whose names it speaks.

In this book I have examined the uses of nationalism in contemporary Australian popular culture in order, primarily, to help counteract their effects—but also to highlight the progressive potential being squandered. While I maintain that the category of the nation remains essential for the construction of community within our current political structure, this book also demonstrates that it is all too easy for nationalist discourses to build a consensus which masks the specialised interests that stand to benefit from their use. If Walter's unifying discourse is to develop, if we are to come up with a way of identifying with difference, it will have to happen through constant negotiation with the kind of critical scrutiny I have presented here. It is my hope that critiques such as this will bring us closer to the kinds of discourses which will enable us to imagine a heterogeneous, hybridised and socially inclusive Australian society.

Notes

Chapter 1

1   'Birth of a post-modern nation', *The Weekend Australian*, 24–25 July 1993, p. 21.

2   Bill Hayden's interview with Bob Hawke on *Four Corners* in September 1993 stiffened the resolve of the monarchists and added legitimacy to the idea that this was a party-political issue after all. As a payback from Hawke to Keating, the program was nicely targeted.

3   I do not think it is necessary to provide an elaborated definition of this type here. The classic construction of Australian identity around the mythologies of the bushman is Russel Ward's *The Australian Legend* (Melbourne, Oxford University Press, 1958) and a more recent account of the history of Australian identities is Richard White's *Inventing Australia* (Sydney, Allen & Unwin, 1981).

4   S. Magarey et al. (eds), *Debutante Nation: Feminism Contests the 1890s*, Sydney, Allen & Unwin, 1993, p. xix.

5   M. Lake, 'The politics of respectability: identifying the masculinist context', in S. Magarey et al. (eds), op. cit., pp. 11–12.

6   See John Docker, 'The feminist legend: a new historicism?', in S. Magarey et al. (eds), op. cit.

7   S. Magarey et al. (eds), op. cit, p. xx.

8   At this point, I should note that 'Australian nationalism' could well be made plural here. Traditional Australian nationalism is not monolithic, and there are competing versions which are buried within the generalised description I have given. I am content to stay with such a description for my purposes here, though, in order to move on to a closer analysis of contemporary formations. In the subsequent chapters, the argument will be more detailed. Suffice it to say here that all

of the older versions of nationalism are unitary, proposing a single and homogeneous culture. The break with this model of nationalism is what marks the contemporary critiques.

9   See Sneja Gunew, 'Denaturalizing cultural nationalisms: multicultural readings of "Australia"' in Homi Bhabha (ed.), *Nation and Narration*, London, Routledge, 1990; Susan Magarey et al. (eds) op. cit. Kay Schaffer, *Women and the Bush: Forces of Desire in the Australian Cultural Tradition*, Melbourne, Cambridge University Press, 1988; Eric Michaels, 'Aboriginal content: who's got it, who needs it?', *Art and Text*, 24, 1986; Elizabeth Jacka, 'Australian cinema: an anachronism in the 1980s?', in Graeme Turner (ed.) *Nation, Culture, Text: Australian Cultural and Media Studies*, London, Routledge, 1993.

10 Peter Cochrane and David Goodman, 'The great Australian journey: cultural logic and nationalism in the postmodern era', in Tony Bennett et al. (eds), *Celebrating the Nation: A Critical Study of Australia's Bicentenary*, Sydney, Allen & Unwin, 1992, p. 175.

11 Benedict Anderson, *Imagined Communities: Reflections on the Origins and Spread of Nationalism*, London, Verso, 1983, p. 14.

12 Benedict Anderson's *Imagined Communities* is known for developing this argument, and Philip Schlesinger also deals with the idea in *Media, State and Nation: Political Violence and Collective Identities*, London, Sage, 1991.

13 Anderson, op cit., pp. 11–16.

14 Towards the end of Chapter 4, I refer to John Hartley's idea that there is no such thing as a 'public' in modern societies; but there is a public audience. The media actually bring the public into being. See *The Politics of Pictures: The Creation of the Public in the Age of Popular Media*, London, Routledge, 1992.

15 John Frow and Meaghan Morris, *Australian Cultural Studies: A Reader*, Sydney, Allen & Unwin, 1993, p. xiii.

16 For a discussion of this see Graeme Turner, 'Suburbia Verite', *Australian Left Review*, 144, October, 1992, pp. 37–9.

17 Consider the contributions of some of the high profile entrepreneurs of the eighties once claimed to be leading us into prosperity. Alan Bond is responsible for a significant proportion of the national debt through his offshore borrowing; his brief sojourn as a media mogul while owner of the Nine network served to run up the price of overseas programming to all the networks, and thus exacerbated the sudden financial crisis which gripped the television industry at the end of the eighties; his period as owner of Castlemaine XXXX resulted in the loss of the company's Queensland monopoly and ultimately of the whole company to the New Zealand brewer, Lion Nathan. Christopher Skase ran down the Seven network before abandoning the country his exploits were supposed to benefit; he is alleged to owe his Australian creditors over $170 million. Rupert Murdoch has monopolised the press to the point where there is virtually no

possibility that any new competitor could launch a successful challenge in any of his metropolitan markets. At the same time as his control over the print media has extended to 67 per cent of the Australian market the total number of Australian metropolitan newspapers has dramatically declined. Tabloids have all but disappeared, while Brisbane, Adelaide and Perth are victims of press monopolies. Kerry Packer, easily the most responsible citizen of the lot, has nevertheless been accused of being the principal industry influence on a whole raft of more or less egregious government policies on media networking, the aggregation of regional television markets, the purchase of AUSSAT and the final makeup of the pay TV system.

Chapter 2

1 Gabrielle O'Ryan and Brian Shoesmith, 'Speculation, promise and performance: businessmen as stars', *Australian Journal of Cultural Studies*, vol. 4, no. 2, 1987, p. 163.
2 M. Pusey, *Economic Rationalism in Canberra: A Nation Building State Changes its Mind*, Sydney, Cambridge University Press, 1991, p. 10.
3 O'Ryan and Shoesmith, op. cit., p. 163.
4 John McManamy, *Crash!: Corporate Australia Fights for its Life*, Sydney, Pan, 1988, p. 44.
5 H. Grace, 'Game boy: serious business and the aesthetics of logic', in John Frow and Meaghan Morris (eds), *Australian Cultural Studies: A Reader*, Sydney, Allen & Unwin, 1993.
6 Helen Grace, 'Business, pleasure, narrative: the folktale in our times', in Roslyn Diprose and Robyn Ferrell (eds), *Cartographies: Poststructuralism and the Mapping of Bodies and Spaces*, Sydney, Allen & Unwin, 1991, p. 115.
7 'Business, pleasure, narrative', op. cit., p. 118–9.
8 See Helen Grace, 'Game boy', op. cit.
9 J. McManamy, op. cit., p. 5; following quote, p. 15.
10 See, for instance, Neil Lawrence and Steve Bunk's *The Stump Jumpers: A New Breed of Australians*, Melbourne, Hale & Iremonger, 1985. The book charts the exploits of a number of successful Australians and grounds their achievements within the national character. 'Stump jumpers' are defined on the book's title page as: '1. One who or that which jumps stumps, i.e. overcomes obstacles by innovation and independence, to attain high achievement. 2. A self-made, resilient Australian achiever of vision'.
11 Matthew Stevens and David Uren, 'Bond's great gamble', *Business Review Weekly*, 11.11.1988, p. 60.
12 Rod Tiffen, *News and Power*, Sydney, Allen & Unwin, 1989, pp. 41, 45, 47.
13 ibid. p. 46.

14 ibid. p. 47
15 M. Emmison, ' "The economy": its emergence in popular discourse', in Howard Davis and Paul Walton (eds), *Language, Image, Media*, London, Basil Blackwell, 1983, pp. 139–55.
16 ibid. pp. 142–3.
17 ibid. p. 154.
18 ibid. p. 152.
19 Meaghan Morris has characterised economics as a 'totalitarian discourse', motivated by a 'fantasy of social control'. Within this fantasy, she says, 'the natural order of the market' assumes an explanatory importance comparable to the 'genetic order of nature in the neo-Darwinian household'. See *Ecstasy· and Economics: American Essays for John Forbes*, Sydney: EmPress, 1992, pp. 61–2.
20 Meaghan Morris (op. cit., p. 52) makes this point at some length:

> Proponents may say calmly that economic rationalism is just a belief that 'markets usually allocate resources better than planners'—on the surface, a simple post-Keynesian proposition. But for all of its modern history, Australia has been governed by the opposite assumption: 'laborism', a social contract upheld in various forms since 1904, exchanged trade protection and currency controls for a state-regulated wage fixing system and compulsory arbitration; as a capital/labor deal for redistributing national income primarily between white men, laborism was sustained by a massive immigration policy legitimated and administered on racist principles until the 1960s—but by forms of multiculturalism thereafter. So the process of internationalising the Australian economy has had a devastating intellectual . . . as well as social effect; as the political alignments of a century slowly begin to shatter, even those 'new social movements' most critical of the history and practices of laborism—feminism, anti-racism, environmentalism—find themselves recast by its decline as 'entrenched' and 'vested' interests now obstructing *radical* change.

21 ibid.
22 See Stephen Castles, Bill Cope, Mary Kalantzis and Michael Morrissey, *Mistaken Identity: Multiculturalism and the Demise of Nationalism in Australia*, 3rd edn, Sydney, Pluto Press, 1992. They point out that while net debt as a proportion of GDP doubled (from 15 per cent of GDP to 30 per cent), the level of investment in new plant and equipment as a proportion of GDP rose less than 2 per cent between 1983 and 1988.
23 See Michael Pusey, *Economic Rationalism in Canberra*, op. cit., p. 240. Pusey notes an 'upward redistribution of national income' of 3 per cent from wages and salaries to profit share. This may not seem much until we recognise, as Pusey points out, that 'since the business

163

and managerial beneficiaries of this redistribution are such a small fraction of the population, the redistribution represents a massive increase in wealth for them'.

24 Meaghan Morris, *Ecstasy and Economics*, op. cit., p. 60.
25 Ben Elton, *Stark*, London, Sphere, 1989, p. 10.
26 ibid. p. 11.
27 J. McManamy, *Crash!*, op. cit., p. 11.
28 The *Age*, 28.9.1983, p. 13.
29 *Rydges*, editorial, January 1984, p. 3.
30 Peter Stirling, 'The entrepreneurs: how 25 Australians strove for success', *BRW*, 11.1.1985, p. 29.
31 *Rydges*, April 1986, p. 20.
32 M. Hartwell 'First entrepreneurs flourished in freedom', *BRW*, 18.12.1987, pp. 58–62.
33 *Time*, 12.10.1987, pp. 52–3.
34 *FEER*, 8.8.1985, p. 50.
35 D. Uren, *ALR*, no. 96, Winter, 1986, p. 9.
36 P. James, 'Australia in the corporate image: a new nationalism', *Arena*, 63, 1983, pp. 65–106.
37 Bill Bonney, too, has analysed the uses of nationalism in the naming and marketing of the new banks which followed deregulation—again, campaigns in which multinational companies attempted to claim a position within the Australian marketplace by representing themselves through the discourses of nationalism. See 'Naming and marketing the new banks', *Australian Journal of Cultural Studies*, vol. 1, no. 1, 1983, pp. 92–106.)
38 Amazingly, there are those in big business who still believe that they have not been given a fair shake in the Australian media. Hugh Morgan, executive director of Western Mining, has been quoted by Boris Frankel as saying that 'there is no society in the history of the human race, to my knowledge, where the intellectual class, the priests, the scribes, the teachers, the TV personalities on the one hand are so set against the economic class made up of entrepreneurs, the managers, the businessmen, on the other'.
     As a cultural commentator, Morgan makes a credible mining executive. This is the opposite of what has in fact been the relationship between the media and business in Australia. As Frankel goes on to say in response to Morgan's claim, there are far too many 'scribes, TV personalities, priests and intellectuals who have gone overboard in their celebration of business . . . or who by remaining silent in public affirmed greed and profit making'. See *From Prophets the Deserts Come*, Melbourne, Arena, p. 135.
39 The *Age*, 28.9.1983, p. 8.
40 ibid.
41 The *Weekend Australian*, 11–12 September 1983, p. 4; The *Australian*, 28.9.1983, p. 36.

42 The *Australian*, 27.9.1983, p. 1.
43 The *Australian*, 22.9.1983.
44 The *Australian*, 28.3.1983, p. 36.
45 See Jim McKay, *No Pain, No Gain? Sport and Australian Culture*, Sydney, Prentice Hall, 1991, p. 29.
46 See Jim McKay, op. cit, p. 123.
47 Mackay analyses the 'They said you'd never make it' campaigns in some detail in *No Pain, No Gain?* (pp. 117–23), so I don't intend to repeat that here. For those who need reminding, though, the ads used a number of Aussie 'battlers' who had survived the critics to succeed (Ken Done, Greg Norman, Brad Hardy)—to establish persistence, macho courage and upward mobility as the Australian way. It should go without saying that the campaign was only possible because of the way in which the meanings of the Cup had been already been constituted. The spuriousness of the narrative being offered as a national mythology is apparent if you look at these ads today. To the refrain, 'They said you'd never make it', one is irresistibly drawn to reply, in Bond's case anyway, 'and they were right'.
48 B. Stannard, *The Bulletin*, 9 August 1988, pp. 122–8.
49 Alan Atwood, 'The tottering tycoons: the 80s, decade of the entrepreneur, is ending in an agony of debt', *Time*, 6.11.1989, p. 34; Carolyn Simmonds, 'Wheeler and dealer who couldn't stop', The *Australian*, 27.9.1990, p. 17.
50 Tom O'Regan, 'The rise and fall of entrepreneurial TV: Australian TV 1986–1990', in Graeme Turner (ed.) *Nation, Culture, Text*, London, Routledge, 1993, p. 99; Jim McKay, op. cit., p. 34.
51 Philip Rennie, 'A form guide to the entrepreneurs', *BRW*, 30.10.1987, pp. 49, 52, 57.
52 See, for instance, *BRW*'s sycophantic report on Bond's purchase of the English village of Glympton (18.11.1988, p. 116).
53 Les Carlyon's column on the 'Age of the predator', which repeats the arguments Henry Bosch had presented three years earlier; *BRW*, 18.1.1988, p. 160.
54 Sydney, Transworld and ABC, 1990.
55 The *Australian*, 1.12.1988.
56 *BRW*, 'Dissecting Bond Corp', 3.3.1989, pp. 22–5.
57 Charles Boag, 'Bond is just a four letter word' (11.4.1989, pp. 96–8) deals with Bond University; Bruce Stannard, 'I can go to the US, says Bond', (18.4.1989, pp. 36—7) deals with the media licence inquiry; Bruce Stannard, 'Why single out one company?' (25.4.1989, pp. 134–7) is a long and very defensive interview with Bond himself.
58 F. Robson, 'King Bond: portrait of a man under siege', The *Weekend Australian Magazine*, 21–22 April 1990, pp. 24–39.
59 The media construction of Eileen Bond—as a national hero in the stoic mould of 'The Drover's Wife'—is another story; as is the media's apparent 'tactfulness' in keeping Bond's extra-marital relationships

relatively private until his hero status had fully declined. There does seem to be a degree of male 'bond-ing' here too which offers further insight into the alignment between Bond's values and those of the media.

60 Terry McCrann, quoted in Jim McKay, *No Pain, No Gain?*, op. cit., p. 30.
61 The *Australian*, 1.1.1990, p. 8.
62 J. McManamy, *Crash!*, op. cit., p. 163.
63 M. Pusey, *Economic Rationalism in Canberra*, op. cit., p 240.

Chapter 3

1 Editorial, *Rydges*, January 1984, p. 3.
2 I am thinking of, for instance, recent proposals that the profession come under the auspices of the Trade Practices Commission.
3 The *Australian*, 28.11.1986, p. 8.
4 The *Australian*, 21.12.1986, p. 6.
5 Tony Stephen, 'How sweet it is for Malcolm Turnbull', *Sydney Morning Herald*, 14 March 1987.
6 *Business Review Weekly*, 11.12.1987, p. 56.
7 *The Weekend Australian*, 3–4 September 1988, p. 4.
8 ibid.
9 *Good Weekend*, 13.4.1991, p. 21.
10 Quoted in Malcolm Turnbull, *The Spycatcher Trial*, Melbourne, Heinemann, 1988, p. 168.
11 Stephen Castles, Bill Cope, Mary Kalantzis and Michael Morrissey, *Mistaken Identity: Multiculturalism and the Demise of Nationalism in Australia*, 3rd edn, Sydney, Pluto, 1992.
12 ibid. p. 153.
13 Castles et al., op. cit., p. 1.
14 ibid. p. 11.
15 I am thinking here of Meaghan Morris's protest in response to a paper of mine, that 'the last time I can remember Britain as a real influence was when I was seven years old and we had our last Empire Day bonfire'. See Larry Grossberg, Cary Nelson and Paula Treichler (eds), *Cultural Studies*, New York and London, Routledge, 1992, p. 651.
16 Castles et al., op. cit., p. 196.
17 ibid. p. 195.
18 Ken Sweetman, 'Brits pay for nuke mess', *The Courier-Mail*, 30 June 1993.
19 Lindy Woodward, 'Buffalo Bill and the Maralingerers', *New Journalist*, 43, April 1984, p. 18.
20 ibid. p. 22.
21 A. Tame and F.P.J. Robotham, *Maralinga: British A-Bomb, Australian Legacy*, Melbourne, Fontana/Collins, 1982, p. 10.

22 Janine Perrett, 'Diamond Jim shuts up the London shop', the *Australian*, 20.3.1985, p. 9.

23 N. Sanders, 'The hot rock in the Cold War: uranium in the 1950s', in Ann Curthoys and John Merritt (eds), *Better Dead than Red*, Sydney, Allen & Unwin, 1986, pp. 155–69.

24 ibid. pp 155–7.

25 ibid. p. 162.

26 Deborah Smith and Deborah Snow, 'Our atomic cover-up', *The National Times*, 4–10 May 1980, p. 3.

27 Brian Toohey, 'Plutonium on the wind: the terrible legacy of Maralinga', *The National Times*, 4–10 May 1984, p. 3.

28 There are a number of accounts of the history of the tests and their implications. See Robert Milliken, *No Conceivable Injury* (Melbourne, Penguin, 1986) and Denys Blakeway and Sue Lloyd-Roberts, *Fields of Thunder: Testing Britain's Bomb* (London, George Allen & Unwin, 1985).

29 These articles were written by Paul Malone and Howard Conkey and ran daily from 28 September to 1 October 1984. The titles: 'Inquiry into nuclear tests has great deal to consider' (p. 2, 28.9.84); 'Impact on Aborigines: the loud bang and black cloud linger' (p. 15, 29.9.84); 'Confusion on contamination' (p. 12, 30.9.84); and 'Mosaic tests: were they H-bombs?' (p. 12, 1.10.1984).

30 See Jim McClelland, *Stirring the Possum: A Political Autobiography*, Melbourne, Viking/Penguin, 1988, p. 210.

31 See Robert Milliken, *No Conceivable Injury*, op. cit., pp. 334–5.

32 Robert Milliken, for instance, quotes this comment from the *Guardian*, which had been particularly positive about the 'refreshingly informal' but 'persistently inquisitive Australians': 'The whole story amounts to another swingeing indictment of British official secretiveness, and it is to our shame that it was left to the Australians to expose it' (op. cit., p. 319).

33 *Sydney Morning Herald*, 5.1.1985, p. 4.

34 See Robert Milliken, op. cit., pp. 330–8 for an account of the deterioration of relations between the British and Australian counsel.

35 Robert Milliken, 'The nuclear fallout in St James's Square', *National Times*, 11–17 January 1985, p. 4.

36 ibid. p. 3.

37 The Australian government was careful to maintain a low profile to avoid being cast as a defendant, while the British put off appointing a counsel until it was clear that there was nothing they could do to avoid being cast as a defendant.

38 Papers which ran lead stories using this headline include the *Australian* (5.1.85), the *Sydney Morning Herald* (5.1.85) and the *Sun-Herald* (6.1.85).

39 For example, see Sue Morgan's front page story in the *Sydney Morning Herald* on 10 January 1985, headlined 'Atomic Tests: How UK Lied'.

40 See Robert Milliken, *No Conceivable Injury*, op. cit., pp. 316–7.
41 K. Palmer, 'Dealing with the legacy of the past: Aborigines and atomic testing in South Australia', *Aboriginal History*, vol. 14, nos. 1–2, 1990, p. 205.
42 ibid. p. 200.
43 A. Downer, 'McClelland's Royal Commission: an exercise in practical politics', *Quadrant*, vol. 30, no. 3, March 1986, pp. 33–8.
44 The *Age*, 6 December 1985, p. 13.
45 *SMH*, 6 December, 1985 p. 16.
46 S. Alomes, *A Nation at Last? The Changing Character of Australian Nationalism 1880–1988*, Sydney, Angus & Robertson, 1988, p. 230.
47 Robert Cockburn, 'Maralinga tribal lands for war games park', *The Bulletin*, 25 July, 1989, pp. 35–6.
48 See also Max Hawkins, 'Defence update', *Australian Aviation*, September, 1989, pp. 82–4. The office of the Minister of Defence responded to my enquiries as to future plans of this kind in a letter dated 12 December 1991. It largely endorsed the outline given in Hawkins' article but denied that any use of ordnance was intended. At that date the Maralinga people had not responded, nor was there any 'planned development' of the war games park on a commercial basis.
49 David Lague, 'US may shift bomb ranges to Australia', *Financial Review*, 7.11.91, p. 6. The French connection is made in the SBS *Dateline* story referred to in my next paragraph.
50 See, for example, 'Australia keeps wraps on UK bomb fall-out report', *The Times*, 5.7.1989; 'Maralinga Aborigines want Britain to pay for clean-up', *The Times*, 9.3.1991.

Chapter 4

1 P. Buckridge, 'Canon, culture and consensus: Australian literature and the Bicentenary', in Tony Bennett, Patrick Buckridge, David Carter and Colin Mercer (eds), *Celebrating the Nation: A Critical Study of Australia's Bicentenary*, Sydney, Allen & Unwin, 1992, p. 85.
2 I am grateful to Tony Bennett for pointing out that most nationalisms are 'understated' in this way; furthermore, the idea that a nationalism might be understated is an instance of nationalist discourse itself. The point I am highlighting, however, is the specific problem facing a program of nation formation in a new nation where the invention of ritual has to be so explicit, so apparently 'inorganic'.
3 P. Spearritt, 'Australia Day, Australia wide: a *Sydney* spectacle', *Australian Society*, December 1988/January 1989 p. 38.
4 This notion, that the nation is a cultural–historical invention rather than a natural phenomenon, has achieved wide currency now, particularly through Benedict Anderson's *Imagined Communities* (note 11,

Chapter 1). In Australia it was argued most directly and influentially in Richard White's *Inventing Australia*, Sydney, Allen & Unwin, 1981.

5   At this point, I thought it necessary to acknowledge that although it is fast becoming customary—and it is often convenient—to refer to those of British or Anglo-Saxon stock in Australia as 'Anglos', it is probably as reductive a term as any other ethnic label. Hence, 'so-called' here to at least suggest that an Anglo-Saxon ethnic background does not entirely overdetermine one's politics or attitudes.

6   The history of the ABA itself is a complex one, and I have no room to go into it here. Those interested might look at the discussion of the conflicting aims and objectives of the ABA from 1980 onwards in Peter Cochrane and David Goodman, 'The great Australian journey: cultural logic and nationalism in the postmodern era', in Tony Bennett et al., *Celebrating the Nation*, op. cit.

7   This point is developed further in the last section of the chapter.

8   P. Buckridge, 'Canon, culture and consensus', op. cit., p. 70.

9   *SMH*, Bicentennial Special, 27 January 1988, p. 1.

10 'Introduction: national times', in Tony Bennett et al. (eds), *Celebrating the Nation*, op. cit., p. xvii.

11 P. Cochrane and D. Goodman, 'The great Australian journey', in *Celebrating the Nation*, op. cit., p. 175.

12 ibid.

13 P. Spearritt, 'Australia Day, Australia wide', op. cit., pp. 38, 40.

14 M. Morris, 'Panorama: the live, the dead and the living', in Graeme Turner (ed.) *Nation, Culture, Text*, London, Routledge, 1993.

15 Barbara Hooks, 'From belfry to basement, a modern Cook's tour ends in triumph', the *Age*, 2 January 1988, p. 4.

16 P. Adams, 'It's Carleton, saying cheese', the *Weekend Australian Magazine*, 16–17 January 1988, p. 10.

17 M. Morton-Evans, 'Celebrating the cliche of eternal larrikinism', the *Australian*, 6 January 1988, p. 10.

18 M. Morris, 'Panorama: the live, the dead and the living', op. cit., p. 161.

19 ibid.

20 'Australia live—1988: the birth of a major broadcast', *Broadcast Engineering News*, February 1988, pp. 6–7, 22–23.

21 'Introduction', in Homi Bhabha (ed.), *Nation and Narration*, London, Routledge, 1990, p. 3.

22 ibid. p. 2.

23 Tony Bennett in *Celebrating the Nation*, op. cit., p. xvii.

24 Kevin Robins, 'Tradition and translation: national culture in its global context' in John Corner and Sylvia Harvey (eds), *Enterprise and Heritage: Crosscurrents of National Culture*, London, Routledge, 1991, p. 24.

25 ibid. pp. 42–3.

26 P. Cochrane and D. Goodman, op cit., p. 175.

27 As he is not named in the film, it is probably unfair to name him here;

suffice it to say that he was in many ways an astute choice. A prominent Sydney doctor and property investor (now *that's* an eighties combination if ever there was one!), he has been reported as having lost more than $6 million over failed development deals since the eighties bubble burst.

28   It might help convey the flavour of the YPO to note that its Western Australia chapter once included Alan Bond, Laurie Connell and Dallas Dempster.

29   S. Lawson, 'Voices of dissent around Sydney harbour', *Australian Society*, March 1988, p. 23.

30   ibid. p. 54.

31   Phil Jarratt, 'What the blacks demand for 1988: no treaty—no party, they warn', *The Bulletin*, 22 September 1987, pp. 18–20.

32   Michael Cordell and Tony Hewett, *SMH*, 9 January 1988, pp. 37, 42.

33   Asahi Shimbun, 'The media cast'; Kim Langley, 'What the reporters will see', *SMH*, 9 January 1988, p. 42.

34   'The year of black protest', *SMH*, 4 January 1988, p. 8.

35   Tracey Maurer, 'First protest buses show their battle colours', the *Weekend Australian*, 23–24 January 1988, p. 6.

36   S. Lawson, op. cit. p. 54.

37   K. Brass, 'A march of mourning ends with rejoicing', the *Australian*, 27 January 1988, p. 10.

38   Norman Abjorensen, 'Day of contradictions', *SMH*, Bicentennial Special, 27 January 1988, p. 1.

39   Annette Young, 'Veterans of black struggle take to Sydney streets', the *Age*, 27 January 1988.

40   ibid.

41   See Cochrane and Goodman, op. cit., p. 177.

42   M. Morris, 'Panorama', op. cit., p. 186–7.

43   ibid. p. 162.

44   See J. Craik, 'Expo 88: fashions of sight and politics of site', in Bennett et al. (eds) *Celebrating the Nation*, op. cit., pp. 142–59.

45   It should be noted that Expo could only *be* a national event through vigorous masking of its incompatibility with nationalist celebrations. Normally, expositions and national celebrations would not coincide; as Tony Bennett puts it, while 'centennial celebrations and the like tick to the clock of the nation', expositions 'tick to the international time of modernity itself'. ('The shaping of things to come: Expo 88', *Cultural Studies*, vol. 5, no. 1, 1989, p. 30.)

46   One can see traces of this attitude even in an academic study of the preparations for Expo which seems to have been written without the aid of a single visit to the site: Tony Fry and Anne-Marie Willis's 'Expo 88: backwoods into the future', *Cultural Studies*, vol. 2, no. 1, 1988, pp. 127–38.

47   J. Craik, op. cit., p. 155.

48   ibid. p. 159.

49 'Pioneering the past: the Stockmen's Hall of Fame', in Bennett et al. (eds), *Celebrating the Nation*, op. cit., pp. 160–74.
50 J. Hartley, *The Politics of Pictures: The Creation of the Public in the Age of Popular Media*, London and New York, Routledge, 1992, p. 122.
51 David Morley and Roger Silverstone, 'Where the global meets the local: notes from the sitting room', in David Morley, *Television Audiences and Cultural Studies*, London and New York, Routledge, 1992, p. 283.
52 ibid. p. 285.
53 ibid. p. 284.
54 J. Hartley, op. cit., especially chapters 1 and 5.
55 Bennett et al., op. cit.
56 See note 11, Chapter 3.

Chapter 5

1 'American Dreams' in Peter Carey, *Exotic Pleasures*, London, Picador, 1981 (first published by University of Queensland Press, 1974), p. 160.
2 ibid. p. 158.
3 ibid. pp. 159–60.
4 See Graeme Turner, 'American dreaming: the fiction of Peter Carey', *Australian Literary Studies*, vol. 12, no. 4, 1986, pp. 431–41.
5 Richard White, *Inventing Australia*, Sydney, Allen & Unwin, 1981, p. 48.
6 John Frow has pointed out that there are in fact severe limitations to the homology normally assumed to exist between 'settler colonial capitalist formations'—particularly where nations were not based on the importation of slaves. See 'Response to Michael Denning', in David Bennett (ed.), *Cultural Studies: Pluralism and Theory*, University of Melbourne: Department of English, 1993, p. 100).
7 R. White, op. cit., p. 49.
8 S. Elizabeth Bird et al., 'On postmodernism and articulation: an interview with Stuart Hall', *Journal of Communication Enquiry*, vol. 10, No. 2, 1986, p. 46.
9 P. Bell and R. Bell, *Implicated: The United States in Australia*, Melbourne, Oxford University Press, 1993.
10 'Towards a cartography of taste 1935–1962', in Dick Hebdige, *Hiding in the Light*, London, Comedia, 1988, pp. 45–77.
11 Bell and Bell, op. cit., p. 203.
12 P.D. Jack did a piece for the *Australian Financial Review* which dealt with the euphemisms used, primarily, on the American side (24.1.1991, p. 35.); and Tony Walker also wrote on the quality of the coverage and the euphemisms used by Americans interviewed, in the *Sydney Morning Herald* (4.2.1991, p. 26).
13 *Australian Business*, 13.2.1991, p. 2.

14 Peter Young, 'The ascendancy of the military over the media in the Gulf', *Australian Studies in Journalism*, 1, 1992, p. 79.

15 In a 1993 interview on *MediaWatch*, the head of ABC news and current affairs pointed out that now, whenever a 'big' news story broke, the ABC's ratings shot up.

16 Matthew Allen has published an analysis of these ads: 'Telecom adverts, Telecom Australia: national identity and information technology', *Australian Journal of Communication*, vol. 20, no. 2, 1993, pp. 97–113.

17 Ruth Barcan has an interesting chapter in her PhD thesis on the Gold Coast, 'Site/countersite: a semiotic study of the Gold Coast' (University of Queensland), which presents a detailed analysis of the park through notions of mimicry.

18 J. Caughie, 'Playing at being American: games and tactics', in Patricia Mellenkamp (ed.), *Logics of Television: Essays in Cultural Criticism*, London, BFI, 1990, p. 48.

19 ibid. p. 54.

20 ibid. p. 55.

21 ibid. p. 47.

22 See Marcus Breen, 'Magpies, lyrebirds and emus: record labels, ownership and orientation', in Philip Hayward (ed.), *From Pop to Punk to Postmodernism*, Sydney, Allen & Unwin, 1992 pp. 45–7.

23 See Stuart Cunningham, *Framing Culture: Criticism and Policy in Australia*, Sydney, Allen & Unwin 1992; especially Chapter 3.

24 See Susan Dermody and Elizabeth Jacka, *The Screening of Australia*, Vols 1 and 2, Sydney, Currency Press, 1987 and 1988.

25 Susan Dermody and Elizabeth Jacka, *The Screening of Australia: The Anatomy of an Industry*, Sydney, Currency Press, 1987 p. 152.

26 In Stratton's defence, Campion's film is a different case in that it was a three-way funding split between New Zealand, France and Australia. Australia's claim on the film is not strong from that perspective as well as the casting.

27 See Toby Miller, 'Splitting the citizen', *Continuum*, vol. 4, no. 2, 1991, pp. 193–205.

28 See the Australian Film Commission's submission to the 'Moving Pictures Inquiry': 'Analysis of the performance of Australian films since 1980', 1991.

29 ibid.

30 See my 'Australian popular music and its contexts', in Philip Hayward (ed.), *From Pop to Punk to Postmodernism: Popular Music and Australian Culture from the 1960s to the 1990s*, Sydney, Allen & Unwin, 1992.

31 Typical would be the Ruth Abbey and Jo Crawford article '*Crocodile Dundee* or Davy Crockett?' in *Meanjin* vol. 42, no. 2, 1987, pp. 145–52.) Their essay demonstrated little understanding of how popular cinema was financed, produced, marketed and distributed—let alone how it made sense to its audiences.

32 Philip Bell and Roger Bell, *Implicated*, op. cit., p. 194.

33 Meaghan Morris's 'Tooth and claw: tales of survival, and *Crocodile Dundee*' in her *The Pirate's Fiancee* (London, Verso, 1988) is essential reading in this respect. See also my '*Crocodile Dundee*, 10BA and the future of the Australian film Industry', *Australian Studies*, 2, 1989, pp. 93–103.

34 Bell and Bell, op. cit., p. 194.

35 See Jennifer Craik, *Resorting to Tourism: Cultural Policies for Tourism Development in Australia*, Sydney, Allen & Unwin, 1991, p. 228.

36 ibid. p. 230.

37 New Zealanders are the largest national group, but in recent times the Americans have moved into second place—just ahead of Asia and the UK. See J. Craik, *Resorting to Tourism*, op. cit., p. 20.

38 ibid. p. 16.

39 See 'Fair dinkum fillums: the *Crocodile Dundee* phenomenon', in Susan Dermody and Elizabeth Jacka, *The Imaginary Industry: Australian Film in the Late '80s*, Sydney, AFTRS, 1988, pp. 172–3.

40 M. Morris, 'Panorama', in G. Turner (ed.) *Nation, Culture, Text*, op. cit., p. 21.

41 Jon Stratton, 'Deconstructing the Territory', *Cultural Studies* vol. 3, no. 1, 1989, p. 50.

42 ibid. p. 54.

43 J. Craik, op. cit., p. 16.

44 'Fair dinkum fillums', op. cit., p. 173.

45 Jon Stratton, op. cit., p. 50.

46 Tony Bennett, 'Out of which past: critical reflections on Australian museum and heritage policy', Occasional Paper No. 3, Institute for Cultural Policy Studies, Griffith University, Brisbane, 1988, p. 16.

47 ibid. p. 21.

48 ibid.

49 ibid.

50 Kathleen Carroll, quoted in Peter Hamilton and Sue Matthews, *American Dreams, Australian Movies*, Sydney, Currency Press, 1986, p. 37.

51 See Stephen Crofts, 'Cross-cultural reception studies: culturally variant readings of *Crocodile Dundee*', *Literature/Film Quarterly*, vol. 21, no. 2, 1993, p. 161.

52 ibid.

53 M. Morris, 'Tooth and claw: tales of survival, and *Crocodile Dundee*', in her *The Pirate's Fiancee*, London, Verso, 1988, p. 250.

54 ibid. pp. 264–5.

55 The phrase is drawn from John Frow and Meaghan Morris's anthology, *Australian Cultural Studies: A Reader* (Sydney, Allen & Unwin, 1993), where it is used in the title of Suvendrini Perera's excellent essay on the diplomatic furore around the TV series, *Embassy*: 'Representation wars: Malaysia, *Embassy*, and Australia's *Corps Diplomatique*', pp. 15–29.

Chapter 6

1 Stephen Castles, Mary Kalantzis, Bill Cope and Michael Morrissey, *Mistaken Identity: Multiculturalism and the Demise of Nationalism in Australia*, 3rd edn, Sydney, Pluto Press, 1992.
2 A typical example of this kind of argument can be found in Richard Collins' book, *Television: Policy and Culture*, London, Unwin Hyman, 1990.
3 Tom Nairn, 'Demonising nationalism', *London Review of Books*, 25 February 1993, p. 6.
4 P. Schlesinger, *Media, State and Nation: Political Violence and Collective Identities*, London, Sage, 1991, p. 160.
5 'Introduction', in Homi Bhabha (ed.) *Nation and Narration*, London, Routledge, 1990, pp. 3–4.
6 For a fuller development of such an argument, see Stuart Cunningham's *Framing Culture: Criticism and Policy in Australia*, Sydney, Allen & Unwin, 1992.
7 See Marjorie Ferguson, 'Globalisation of cultural industries: myths and realities', in *Cultural Industries: National Policies and Global Markets* (Proceedings of the CIRCIT Conference, December 1992), Melbourne, CIRCIT, 1993, pp. 3–12.
8 Giddens, *The Consequences of Modernity*, Stanford, Stanford University Press, 1993, p. 67.
9 Tom Nairn, 'Demonising nationalism', op. cit., p. 5.
10 Giddens, op. cit., p. 74.
11 Stuart Hall, 'Culture, community, nation', *Cultural Studies*, vol. 7, no. 3, 1993, p. 355.
12 S. Perera, 'Representation wars', op. cit., p. 21 (see note 55, Chapter 5).
13 See Richard White's *Inventing Australia*, (Sydney, Allen & Unwin, 1981) and Benedict Anderson's *Imagined Communities* (London, Verso, 1983).
14 And they must break forever with that tradition of cultural analysis which addresses the nation as a psychological rather than a political entity—the latest example of this being Hugh Mackay's diagnosis of Australia as an 'adolescent society' in *Reinventing Australia*.
15 C. Castan, 'Multiculturalism and Australia's national literature', paper presented at the Postcolonial Formations conference, Griffith University, Brisbane, July 1993, p. 3.
16 See Bill Ashcroft, Gareth Griffiths and Helen Tiffin, *The Empire Writes Back: Theory and Practice in Post-Colonial Literatures*, London, Routledge, 1989.
17 Stuart Hall, op. cit., p. 362.
18 ibid.
19 ibid.
20 ibid.

21 See, for instance, the Epilogue to Susan Dermody and Elizabeth Jacka's *The Screening of Australia, Vol. 2* (Sydney, Currency Press, 1988).

22 See my Chapter 1 in Phil Hayward (ed.), *From Pop to Punk to Postmodernism*, op. cit. (note 30, Chapter 5).

23 C. Berry, 'Heterogeneity as identity: hybridity and transnationality as foundation myths in Hong Kong and Taiwan cinema', *Metro*, 91 (Spring, 1992), p. 48.

24 Pat Gillespie's review is, possibly justifiably, critical of the predictability of this. She sees it as a cliche: 'ethnic family life and its down-to-earth values versus the tacky technicolour of the Australian ballroom'. (*Cinema Papers*, 91, p. 52.)

25 Lisa Nicol, 'Culture, custom and collaboration: the production of Yothu Yindi's *Treaty* videos', *Perfect Beat*, vol. 1, no. 2 (January) 1993, p. 28.

26 It should be noted that while Yothu Yindi is a multiracial band—the rhythm section is partly divided into the two traditions: whites playing drums, bass and guitar, and blacks playing didjeridu, bilma or clapsticks, and guitar—it is usually referred to as if it were a wholly Aboriginal band. This is possibly because the content of its songs places its concerns as wholly Aboriginal.

27 P. Hayward, 'Safe, exotic and somewhere else: Yothu Yindi, *Treaty*, and the mediation of Aboriginality', *Perfect Beat*, vol 1, no. 2 (January) 1993, pp. 33–42.

28 L. Nicol, op. cit., p. 26.

29 P. Hayward, op. cit., p. 39.

30 ibid. p. 40.

31 Chris Lawe Davies, 'Black Rock and Broome: musical and cultural specificities', *Perfect Beat*, vol. 1, no. 2 (January), 1993, p. 51.

32 John Castles, 'Tjungaringanyi: Aboriginal rock', in Philip Hayward (ed.), *From Pop to Punk to Postmodernism*, Sydney, Allen & Unwin, 1992, p. 32.

33 ibid.

34 C. Lawe Davies, op. cit., p. 49.

35 I am indebted to a conversation with Chris Lawe Davies for this point.

36 Tony Mitchell, 'World music, indigenous music and music televison in Australia', *Perfect Beat*, vol. 1, no. 1 (July) 1992, p. 14.

37 J. Castles, op. cit., p. 38.

38 See Karl Neuenfeldt, 'The didjeridu and the overdub: technologising and transposing aural images of Aboriginality', *Perfect Beat*, vol. 1, no. 2 (January), 1993, p. 70.

39 See Stuart Hall, 'Culture, community, nation', op. cit., p. 362.

40 By this I mean that the fact that they are not urban people disconnects them from the way in which urban Aboriginals are seen as slightly anomalous; having lost contact with their land, they are seen to have sacrificed claims to authenticity.

41 J. Castles, op. cit., p. 26.

Chapter 7

1 After all, this was a victory in a public relations exercise, not a sporting event. To see Australia as having 'won' anything that depended upon the demonstration of superior performance was to stretch credulity to the limit. The vote had more in common with a lottery than with a boat race.

2 See Wendy Bacon, 'Watchdog's bark muffled', *Reportage*, September 1993, p. 3.

3 Wendy Bacon, 'Win or lose: media's role questioned', *Reportage*, September 1993, p. 1.

4 Wendy Bacon, 'Watchdog', op. cit., pp. 3–4.

5 Rather comically, Mike Munro's interview with Paul Keating for Channel 9's *A Current Affair* almost forgot sport altogether ('Yes . . . and not to mention what happens to our sport'). It came up as the very last question, prompting a one-sentence reply ('Well, for our sport it will be marvellous, because Australian sport, as we know, has been marvellous') before Keating moved back to 'all the other things', like Aboriginal reconciliation and what he called 'the nation-building quality'.

6 Wendy Bacon, 'Win or lose', op. cit., p. 2.

7 See B. Anderson, *Imagined Communities*, op. cit. (note 13, Chapter 6).

8 C. Mercer, 'Regular imaginings: the newspaper and the nation', in Tony Bennett et al. (eds), *Celebrating the Nation*, op. cit. (note 1, Chapter 4), p. 46.

9 Morley and Silverstone, 'Where the global meets the local: notes from the sitting room', in David Morley, *Television Audiences and Cultural Studies*, op. cit. (note 51, Chapter 4), p. 283.

10 J. Hartley, *The Politics of Pictures*, op. cit. (note 50, Chapter 4), p. 207.

11 See, for example, David Bowman's *The Captive Press*, Melbourne, Penguin, 1988 and Julianne Schultz, 'Failing the public: the media marketplace', in Helen Wilson (ed.) *Australian Communications and the Public Sphere*, Melbourne, Macmillan, 1989, pp. 68–84.

12 Electoral and Administrative Review Commission, *Report on Review of Government Media and Information Services*, April 1993, p. 70.

13 EARC, p. 71.

14 EARC, Appendix, p. N.4.

15 EARC, p. 73.

16 EARC, Appendix, p. N.10.

17 EARC, p. 99.

18 EARC, p. 14.

19 In Brisbane in 1993, *7.30 Report* presenter Pamela Bornhorst was allegedly dumped for, among other things, failing to observe this obligation sufficiently. Immediately after she left, a flood of govern-

ment personnel hitherto 'unavailable'—most notably the premier, Wayne Goss—became available to the program for interview.

20 EARC, p. 17.

21 Chris Lawe Davies, 'Relations with the media', in John Wanna (ed.) *Goss and the Labor Government: Promise and Performance in Queensland*, Brisbane, Centre for Australian Public Sector Management, 1993, p. 8.

22 By October, the *Australian* seemed to have changed its mind; it was promoting Keating's proposed legislation just as actively as it had earlier fed public alarm. Neither tack, in my view, constitutes responsible reporting.

23 See Chris Lawe Davies, op. cit., p. 9.

24 Errol Simper, 'Feeding frenzy', the *Australian*, 12 July 1993, p. 7.

25 Similarly, in a recent attack on *MediaWatch*'s Stuart Littlemore the *Australian*'s Frank Devine spent at least the first third of his column making fun of Littlemore's bald head! And when *Sixty Minutes* ran its final program for the year in 1993, a special called 'Has the Media Gone Too Far?', protests about the behaviour of the media after the rescue in the Himalayas of the so-called 'iceman', James Scott, provoked an extraordinarily vicious and ugly attack upon his sister by members of the media.

26 John Henningham, 'Journalism's threat to the freedom of the press' (University of Queensland Inaugural Lecture), St Lucia, University of Queensland Press, 1992, p. 13.

27 ibid., pp.13–14.

28 C. Lawe Davies, op. cit., p. 9.

29 It can reach ludicrous dimensions. In 'Has the Media Gone Too Far?' *A Current Affair*'s Mike Munro was confronted by a former hostage from a seige in which Munro had irresponsibly intervened: he had telephoned the gunman for a chat and thus probably put all the hostages' lives at risk. Asked what expertise he possessed to enable him to usefully negotiate such a dangerous situation, Munro seemed happy to rely on his experience as someone who could talk to anyone—'from the Pope to Neddy Smith' as he put it. With the notable exception of George Negus, few of the other journalists present appeared to find this arrogant or stupid.

30 For those who don't remember, the Hanging Rock seige involved several gunmen with children as hostages who were surrounded by police in a northern New South Wales farmhouse. Police negotiations aimed at securing the children's release were hampered by repeated intervention from the media: phone lines to the house were jammed with reporters' calls, a television crew landed its helicopter between the police and the house, and Mike Willessee even phoned the children 'live' on television. Police angrily condemned the behaviour, but it had little effect; some months later *A Current Affair*'s Mike

Munro did much the same thing during the Eagle Street seige in Brisbane.

31 The *Australian*, 21 November 1992, p. 3; Sam Lipski writes a regular column in the *Australian* where this criticism is repeatedly put; the *Sydney Morning Herald*, 13 December 1992, p. 2. On the evidence of the *Sixty Minutes* special referred to earlier, their opinions are not shared by many of their peers.

32 Indeed, it can be downright hypocritical. As the details of the Sydney 2000 budget finally made it into the press over the week of 11–15 October, revealing that the cost is likely to be almost double that which had been promised earlier, the *Australian* ran an editorial which applauded the collapse of the earlier 'bipartisan' approach and welcomed the chance for such information to be scrutinised by the public. As News Ltd had actually been part of the bid Commitee and had therefore cooperated in the media's silencing of criticism in the lead-up to Monte Carlo, the editorial must be regarded as disingenuous humbug.

33 See my 'Nationalising the author: the celebrity of Peter Carey', *Australian Literary Studies*, vol. 16, no. 2, 1993, pp. 131–9.

34 J. Walter, 'The failure of political imagination: reflections prompted by the 1993 federal election', *Australian Quarterly*, Autumn 1993, p. 549.

35 ibid.

36 Stuart Hall, 'Culture, community, nation', *Cultural Studies*, vol. 7, no. 3, 1993, p. 361.

References

Abbey, Ruth and Jo Crawford '*Crocodile Dundee* or Davy Crockett?', *Meanjin*, 42:2, 1987

Allen, Matthew 'Telecom adverts, Telecom Australia: national identity and information technology', *Australian Journal of Communication*, 20:2, 1993

Alomes, Stephen *A Nation at Last?: The Changing Character of Australian Nationalism 1880–1988*, Sydney, Angus & Robertson, 1988

Anderson, Benedict *Imagined Communities: Reflections on the Origins and Spread of Nationalism*, London, Verso, 1983

Ashcroft, Bill, Gareth Griffiths and Helen Tiffin *The Empire Writes Back: Theory and Practice in Post-colonial Literatures*, London, Routledge, 1989

Barcan, Ruth 'Site/Countersite: A Semiotic Study of the Gold Coast', unpublished PhD thesis, University of Queensland

Bell, Philip and Roger Bell *Implicated: The United States in Australia*, Melbourne, Oxford University Press, 1993

Bennett, Tony 'Out of Which Past: Critical Reflections on Australian Museum and Heritage Policy', Occasional paper No. 3, Institute of Cultural Policy Studies, Griffith University, Brisbane

——'The shaping of things to come: Expo 88', *Cultural Studies*, 5:1, 1989

Bennett, Tony, Patrick Buckridge, David Carter and Colin Mercer (eds) *Celebrating the Nation: A Critical Study of Australia's Bicentenary*, Sydney, Allen & Unwin, 1992

Berry, Chris 'Heterogeneity as identity: hybridity and transnationality as foundation myths in Hong Kong and Taiwan cinema', *Metro*, 91, 1992

Bhaba, Homi *Nation and Narration*, London, Routledge, 1990

Bird, S. Elizabeth 'On postmodernism and articulation: an interview with Stuart Hall', *Journal of Communication Enquiry*, 10, 1986

Blakeway, Denys and Sue Lloyd-Roberts *Fields of Thunder: Testing Britain's Bomb*, London, George Allen & Unwin, 1985

Bonney, Bill 'Naming and marketing the new banks', *Australian Journal of Cultural Studies*, 1:1, 1983

Bowman, David *The Captive Press*, Melbourne, Penguin, 1988

Breen, Marcus 'Magpies, lyrebirds and emus: record labels, ownership and orientation', in Philip Hayward (ed.) *From Pop to Punk to Postmodernism*, Sydney, Allen & Unwin, 1992

Buckridge, Patrick 'Canons, culture and consensus: Australian literature and the Bicentenary', in Tony Bennett *et al* (eds) *Celebrating the Nation*, Sydney, Allen & Unwin, 1992

Castan, Con 'Multiculturalism and Australia's National Literature', paper presented at the Postcolonial Formations conference, Brisbane, 1993

Castles, John *'Tjungaringanyi:* Aboriginal rock', in Philip Hayward (ed.) *From Pop to Punk to Postmodernism*, Sydney, Allen & Unwin, 1992

Castles, Stephen, Bill Cope, Mary Kalantzis and Michael Morrissey *Mistaken Identity: Multiculturalism and the demise of nationalism in Australia* 3rd edn, Sydney, Pluto, 1992

Caughie, John 'Playing at being American: games and tactics', in Patricia Mellenkamp (ed.) *Logics of Television: Essays in Cultural Criticism*, London, BFI, 1990

Cochrane, Peter and David Goodman 'The great Australian journey: cultural logic and nationalism in the postmodern era', in Tony Bennett *et al* (eds) *Celebrating the Nation,* Sydney, Allen & Unwin, 1992

Collins, Richard *Television: policy and culture*, London, Unwin Hyman, 1990

Craik, Jennifer 'Expo 88: fashions of sight and politics of site', in Tony Bennett *et al* (eds) *Celebrating the Nation*, Sydney, Allen & Unwin, 1992

——*Resorting to Tourism: Cultural Policies For Tourism Development in Australia*, Sydney, Allen & Unwin, 1991

Crofts, Stephen 'Cross-cultural reception studies: culturally variant readings of *Crocodile Dundee'*, *Literature/Film Quarterly*, 21:2, 1993

Cunningham, Stuart *Framing Culture: Criticism and Policy in Australia*, Sydney, Allen & Unwin, 1992

Dermody, Susan and Elizabeth Jacka *The Screening of Australia*, Vols 1 and 2, Sydney, Currency Press, 1987 and 1988

Docker, John 'The feminist legend: A new historicism?', in Susan Magarey *et al* (eds) *Debutante Nation: Feminism contests the 1890s*, Sydney, Allen & Unwin, 1993

Elton, Ben *Stark*, London, Sphere, 1989

Emmison, Mike ' "The economy": its emergence in popular discourse', in Howard Davis and Paul Walton (eds) *Language, Image, Media*, London, Basil Blackwell, 1983

Ferguson, Marjorie 'Globalisation of cultural industries: myths and realities', in Marcus Breen (ed.) *Cultural Industries: National Policies and Global Markets*, Proceedings of the CIRCIT Conference, December, 1992

Frankel, Boris *From Prophets the Deserts Come*, Melbourne, Arena, 1993

Frow, John 'Response to Michael Denning', in David Bennett (ed.) *Cultural Studies: Pluralism and Theory*, Melbourne, University of Melbourne Department of English, 1993

Frow, John and Meaghan Morris *Australian Cultural Studies: A Reader*, Sydney, Allen & Unwin, 1993

Fry, Tony and Anne-Marie Willis 'Expo 88: Backwoods into the future', *Cultural Studies*, 2:1, 1988

Giddens, Anthony *The Consequences of Modernity*, Stanford, Stanford University Press, 1993

Grace, Helen 'Business, pleasure, narrative: the folktale in our times', in Roslyn Diprose and Robyn Ferrell (eds) *Cartographies: poststructuralism and the mapping of bodies and spaces*, Sydney, Allen & Unwin, 1991

——'A house of games: serious business and the aesthetics of logic', in John Frow and Meaghan Morris (eds) *Australian Cultural Studies: A Reader*, Sydney, Allen & Unwin, 1993

Grossberg, Lawrence, Cary Nelson and Paula Treichler (eds) *Cultural Studies*, New York, Routledge, 1992

Gunew, Sneja 'Denaturalizing cultural nationalisms: multicultural readings of "Australia"', in Homi Bhabha (ed.) *Nation and Narration*, London, Routledge, 1990

Hall, Stuart 'Culture, community, nation', *Cultural Studies*, 7:3, 1993

Hamilton, Peter and Sue Matthews *American Dreams: Australian Movies*, Sydney, Currency, 1986

Hartley, John *The Politics of Pictures: The Creation of the Public in the Age of Popular Media*, London, Routledge, 1992

Hayward, Philip (ed.) *From Pop to Punk to Postmodernism: Popular Music and Australian Culture from the 1960s to the 1990s*, Sydney, Allen & Unwin, 1992

——'Safe, exotic and somewhere else: Yothu Yindi, *Treaty* and the mediation of Aboriginality', *Perfect Beat*, 1:2, 1993

Hebdige, Dick 'Towards a cartography of taste 1935–62', in *Hiding in the Light*, London, Comedia, 1988

Henningham, John 'Journalism's Threat to the Freedom of the Press', University of Queensland Inaugural Lecture, St Lucia, University of Queensland Press, 1992

Jacka, Elizabeth 'Australian cinema: an anachronism in the 1980s?', in Graeme Turner (ed.) *Nation, Culture, Text: Australian cultural and media studies*, London, Routledge, 1993

Lake, Marilyn 'The politics of respectability: identifying the masculinist context', in Susan Magarey *et al* (eds) *The Debutante Nation: Feminism Contests the 1890s*, Sydney, Allen & Unwin, 1993

Lawe Davies, Chris 'Black rock and Broome: musical and cultural specificities', *Perfect Beat*, 1:2, 1993

——'Relations with the media', in John Wanna (ed.) *Goss and the Labour Government: Promise and Performance in Queensland*, Brisbane, Centre for Australian Public Sector Management, 1993

Lawrence, Neil and Steve Bunk *The Stump Jumpers: A new breed of Australians*, Melbourne, Hale & Iremonger, 1985

McClelland, James *Stirring the Possum: A Political Autobiography*, Melbourne, Viking/Penguin, 1988

McKay, Jim *No Pain, No Gain?: Sport and Australian Culture*, Sydney, Prentice Hall, 1991

McManamy, John *Crash! Corporate Australia Fights For Its Life*, Sydney, Pan, 1988

Magarey, Susan, Susan Sheridan and Sue Rowley (eds) *Debutante Nation: Feminism Contests the 1890s*, Sydney, Allen & Unwin, 1993

Michaels, Eric 'Aboriginal content: Who's got it, who needs it?', *Art and Text*, 24, 1986

Miller, Toby 'Splitting the citizen', *Continuum*, 4:2, 1991

Milliken, Robert *No Conceivable Injury*, Melbourne, Penguin, 1986

Mitchell, Tony 'World music, indigenous music and music television in Australia', *Perfect Beat*, 1:2, 1993

Morley, David and Roger Silverstone 'Where the global meets the local: notes from the sitting room', in David Morley, *Television Audiences and Cultural Studies*, London, Routledge, 1992

Morris, Meaghan *Ecstasy and Economics: American Essays for John Forbes*, Sydney, EmPress, 1992

——'Panorama: the live, the dead and the living', in Graeme Turner (ed.) *Nation, Culture, Text*, London, Routledge, 1993

——'Tooth and Claw: Tales of Survival and *Crocodile Dundee*' , in *The Pirate's Fiancee: Feminism, Reading, Postmodernism*, London, Verso, 1988

Nairn, Tom 'Demonising nationalism', *London Review of Books*, 25 February, 1993

Neuenfeldt, Karl 'The didjeridu and the overdub: technologising and transposing aural images of Aboriginality', *Perfect Beat*, 1:2, 1993

Nicol, Lisa 'Culture, custom and collaboration: the production of Yothu Yindi's *Treaty* videos', *Perfect Beat*, 1:2, 1993

O'Regan, Tom 'Fair Dinkum Fillums: The *Crocodile Dundee* phenomenon', in Susan Dermody and Elizabeth Jacka (eds) *The Imaginary Industry: Australian Film in the Late '80s*, Sydney, AFTRS, 1988

——'The rise and fall of entrepreneurial TV: Australian TV 1986–1990', in Graeme Turner (ed.) *Nation, Culture, Text*, London, Routledge, 1993

O'Ryan, Gabrielle and Brian Shoesmith 'Speculation, promise and performance: businessmen as stars', *Australian Journal of Cultural Studies*, 4:2, 1987

Palmer, Kingsley 'Dealing with the legacy of the past: Aborigines and atomic testing in South Australia', *Aboriginal History*, 14:1, 1990

Perera, Suvendrini 'Representation wars: Malaysia, *Embassy*, and Australia's *Corps Diplomatique*', in John Frow and Meaghan Morris (eds) *Australian Cultural Studies: A Reader*, Sydney, Allen & Unwin, 1993

Pusey, Michael *Economic Rationalism in Canberra: A nation building state changes its mind*, Sydney, Cambridge University Press, 1991

Sanders, Noel 'Hot Rock in the Cold War: Uranium in the 1950s', in Ann Curthoys and John Merritt (eds) *Better Dead than Red*, Sydney, Allen & Unwin, 1986

Schaffer, Kay *Women and the Bush: Forces of Desire in the Australian Cultural Tradition*, Melbourne, Cambridge University Press, 1988

Schlesinger, Philip *Media, State and Nation: Political violence and collective identities*, London, Sage, 1991

Schultz, Julianne 'Failing the public: the media marketplace', in Helen Wilson (ed.) *Australian Communications and the Public Sphere*, Melbourne, Macmillan, 1989

Spearritt, Peter 'Australia Day, Australia Wide: A *Sydney* spectacle', *Australian Society*, December 1987/January 1988

Stratton, Jon 'Deconstructing the territory' *Cultural Studies*, 3:1, 1989

Tame, A. and F.J.P. Rowbotham *Maralinga: British A-bomb, Australian legacy*, Melbourne, Fontana/Collins, 1984

Tiffen, Rodney *News and Power*, Sydney, Allen & Unwin, 1989

Trotter, Robin 'Pioneering the past: the Stockman's Hall of Fame', in Tony Bennett *et al* (eds) *Celebrating the Nation*, Sydney, Allen & Unwin, 1992

Turnbull, Malcolm *The Spycatcher Trial*, Melbourne, Heinemann, 1988

Turner, Graeme 'American dreaming: The fiction of Peter Carey', *Australian Literary Studies*, 12:4, 1986

——'Australian popular music and its contexts', in Philip Hayward (ed.) *From Pop to Punk to Postmodernism*, Sydney, Allen & Unwin, 1992

——'*Crocodile Dundee*, 10BA, and the future of the Australian film industry', *Australian Studies*, 2, 1989

——(ed.) *Nation, Culture, Text: Australian cultural and media studies*, London, Routledge, 1993

——'Nationalising the author: The celebrity of Peter Carey', *Australian Literary Studies*, 16:2, 1993

——'Suburbia Verite', *Australian Left Review*, 144, October 1992

Walter, James 'The Failure of Political Imagination: reflections prompted by the 1993 federal election', *Australian Quarterly*, Autumn, 1993

Ward, Russel *The Australian Legend*, Melbourne, Oxford University Press, 1958

White, Richard *Inventing Australia*, Sydney, Allen & Unwin, 1981

Young, Peter 'The Ascendancy of the Military over the Media in the Gulf', *Australian Studies in Journalism*, 1, 1992

Index

Aboriginals
  the Bicentenary, 66–7, 73, 80–7;
  the Commonwealth Games
  (1982), 143; the Maralinga
  weapons tests, 61–2, 63;
  March for Freedom, Justice
  and Hope, 81–7;
  'Aboriginality' and popular
  music, 133–8
Adams, Phillip, 77
Advertiser, 54
Age, 26, 31, 33, 63, 75, 86, 148
Alomes, Stephen, 63, 65
'American Dreams', 93–5
America's Cup, 3, 4, 26–33, 140
Anderson, Benedict, 12, 120, 123,
  145, 167
Armstrong, Sir Robert, 45, 48–9
Auld, Robert, 58–9
Australia All Over, 9–10
Australia Day, 1988, 71–88
Australia Daze, 69, 75, 77–82
Australia Live, 70–1, 75–6, 79, 89,
  91, 92
Australia II, 11, 30, 32, 33, 140
Australian, 30, 31, 32, 36, 44, 75,
  85, 139, 149, 150, 177
Australian Bicentenary Authority,
  66, 69, 70, 74, 76, 168

Australian Broadcasting
  Corporation, 99–100
Australian Broadcasting Tribunal,
  29, 36
Australian Business, 20, 99
Australian Financial Review, 20,
  33
Australian Investment, 20
Australian Left Review, 28, 146
Australian legend, 5, 49
Australian Quarterly, 156
Australian Radiation Laboratory, 64
Australian Society, 146
Australian Tourism Commission,
  108

Bacon, Wendy, 140–1, 144
Barnes, Jimmy, 133
Barry, Paul, 35, 36
Beale, Howard, 54
Beazley, Kim, 63
Bedevil, 126
Bell, Phillip and Roger, 96–7
Bennett, Tony, 73, 88, 113–14
Berry, Chris, 126
Bhabha, Homi, 76, 120–1
BHP, 151
Bicentenary, 4, 5, 8, 66–92, 123,
  143

Big Steal, The, 8, 126, 127
Bishop, Bronwyn, 2
Bjelke-Petersen, Sir Joh, 35, 149
Blackfellas, 126
Blainey, Geoffrey, 2, 73
Bliss, 94
Blood Oath, 101
Bodyline, 48
Bond, Alan, 4, 5, 11, 16, 17, 19,
  25–37, 41, 45, 51, 138, 143,
  149, 160
Bond, Eileen, 164–5
Bond University, 47
Bonney, Bill, 163
Bornhorst, Pamela, 176
Bosch, Henry, 27
Brass, Ken, 86
Breaker Morant, 8, 48, 115
Brett, Judith, 157
Brown, Bryan, 127
Buckridge, Patrick, 67, 71–2
Bulletin, The, 15, 37, 83, 142
business
  and the law, 41–7; and the
    national interest, 13–14,
    15–16, 40; and the media,
    16–23, 28–9, 40; journalism,
    20–1
Business Daily, 20
Business Review Weekly, 19, 27,
  35, 36, 46, 149

Caddie, 115
Campion, Jane, 106
Canberra Times, 56, 57, 147
Canby, Vincent, 115–6
Carey, Peter, 4, 93–4, 108, 109, 154
Castan, Con, 123–4
Castles, John, 135, 136, 137
Castles, Stephen *et al*, 49–51, 91
Caughie, John, 103–5, 116, 156
Cawley, Evonne Goolagong, 154
Celebrating the Nation, 88–91
'Celebration of a Nation', 67–9
Chaney, David, 90–1
Channel 9, 36, 141, 145, 149

Clarke, Warren, 148
CNN, 99, 150
Cochrane, Peter and David
  Goodman, 7, 73, 80, 89
Cockburn, Robert, 64–5
Commonwealth Games, 1982, 143
Connell, Laurie, 38, 41
Consolidated Press, 141
Cops, 153
Couchman, Peter, 153
Courier-Mail, 151, 152
Coustas, Mary, 8
Cox, Paul, 128
Craik, Jennifer, 88–9, 109, 110, 111
Crocodile Dundee, 4, 108, 110,
  113, 114–17
Crofts, Stephen, 115–16
Crowe, Russell, 127
Cruise, Tom, 154
Current Affair, A, 152, 153, 154,
  176, 177
Cuthbert, Betty, 142

Dateline, 64
Dayan, D, and E. Katz, 90
Death in Brunswick, 8, 126,
  127–8, 131
Debutante Nation, 5–7
De Laurentis, Dino, 100–1
Delinquents, The, 101, 106
Department of Primary Industries
  and Energy, 64
Dermody, Susan and Elizabeth
  Jacka, 106
Devine, Frank, 176
Dimitriades, Alex, 127, 130
Dingo, Ernie, 25
Donaher, Noelene, 154
Done, Ken, 75
Doogue, Geraldine, 143
Downer, Alexander, 62
Dreamworld, 113

economic rationalism, 16
'the economy', 21–2
Electoral and Administrative

Review Commission (EARC), 146–51
Elkin, A.P., 62
Elliott, John, 4, 16, 17, 25, 42
Elton, Ben, 24–5, 38
Emmison, Mike, 21–2
Expo 88, 88–9, 113, 169

Fagan, David, 152
Far Eastern Economic Review, 27
Farnham, John, 5
Fast Forward, 25
Fatal Shore, The, 101
Filthy Lucre, 132–3
Fiske, Pat, 69, 77–82
Fitzpatrick, Kate, 47
Flirting, 127
Fortress, 101
Four Corners, 35, 36, 141
Frankel, Boris, 163
Frith, Bryan, 151
Frow, John, 170

GATT, 106
Gallipoli, 8, 48
Gibson, Mel, 4
Giddens, Anthony, 121–2
Good Morning Australia, 71, 74,
Gore, Mike, 39
Goss, Wayne, 97–8
Gottliebsen, Robert, 25
Goward, Prue, 141
Grace, Helen, 18,
Greiner, Nick, 2, 140
Gross Misconduct, 105–6
Gulf War, 97, 99–100

Hall, Stuart, 96, 119, 122, 124–5
Hamilton, Peter and Sue
    Matthews, 115
Hanging Rock seige, 153, 176
Hard Copy, 150, 153
Harris, Rolf, 143
Hartley, John, 88, 90, 91, 145,
    149, 150
Hartwell, Max, 27

Hawke, Bob, 5, 49, 64, 71, 92, 97,
    99, 140
Hayden, Bill, 2, 152, 159
Hayward, Phil, 132, 133, 137
Heartbreak Kid, The, 8, 126, 127,
    129–31
Hebdige, Dick, 98
Herald (Melbourne), 74
Hewson, John, 1, 3
Hiding in the Light, 98
Hinch, 55, 64, 150–1
Hinch, Derryn, 150–1
Hogan, Paul, 4, 75, 108, 114–15,
    154
Holmes a Court, Robert, 16, 17
Holt, Harold, 97·
Home and Away, 149
Horne, Donald, 30, 71
Howard, John, 3
Hughes, Lucy, 45
Hughes, Robert, 4, 101
Humphries, Barry, 4
Hunter, Holly, 106
hybridity, 124–5

Illywhacker, 94, 109
Implicated, 96
International Olympic Committee
    (IOC), 139–41
Investment Planning, 20
INXS, 133
Jackson, Michael, 99
James, Paul, 28
Jenkins, Michael, 129

Keating, Paul, 1, 2, 3, 4, 23, 49,
    56–7, 140, 152, 175
Keitel, Harvey, 106
Kennedy, Jim, 110
Kennerley, Kerri-Anne, 74
Kidman, Nicole, 154
Kostas, 128

Lake, Marilyn, 6–7
larrikin capitalism, 24–9, 42–3
Lateline, 98

Laurence, Peter, 110
Lawe Davies, Chris, 133, 149, 153
Lawson, Henry, 5, 9
Lawson, Sylvia, 71, 83–4, 85, 87
Lexcen, Ben, 32
Life Matters, 141
Lipski, Sam, 153
Little, Jimmy, 133
Littlemore, Stuart, 176
Lipstick Traces, 95
Lloyd, Clem, 152
Loosely, Stephen, 99

Mabo, 13, 85, 87, 144, 151–2
McAvaney, Bruce, 140
McClelland, Jim, 5, 47, 57–8, 60, 61, 64, 65
MacKay, Hugh, 173
McKay, Jim, 34, 164
McManamy, John, 19, 26, 39
McNamara, Ian, 10
McPherson, Elle, 4, 154
McQueen, Humphrey, 141
Magarey, Susan
Mail on Sunday, 49
Maralinga atomic tests, 52–65
Maralinga Royal Commission, 57–65, 143
Marcus, Greil, 95
Martin, Ray, 140
Matthews, Marlene, 142
May, Norman, 143
Media Report, 150–1
MediaWatch, 176
Mendelsohn, Ben, 127
Menzies, Sir Robert, 59–60, 62, 157
Mercer, Colin, 145
Mercurio, Paul, 127
Methold, Ken, 67
Midnight Oil, 108
Miller, George (*Snowy River*), 106
Milliken, Robert, 59, 166
Mistaken Identity, 49–51, 91, 119
Mitchell, Tony, 136
Mixed Relations, 132
Modern Times, 146

Morgan, Hugh, 163
Morley, David and Roger Silverstone, 90–1, 145
Morris, Meaghan, 15, 18, 22, 71, 75, 87, 111, 116, 162, 165
Morton-Evans, Michael, 75, 89
Movie Show, 105–6
Mulholland, Stephen
Munro, Mike, 175, 176, 177
Murdoch, Rupert, 4, 19, 25, 160
My Brilliant Career, 115

Nairn, Tom, 120
Nation, 146
National Times, 59
Nation Review, 146
nationalism in Australia

and the Bicentenary, 67–74;
critiques of, 6–8, 74, 119–22;
'demise of', 49–53, 120–2; and
globalisation, 120–2; and
hybridity, 122–38; in the 1980s,
4–5, 8–10, 65, 155–7, 159–60;
uses of, 10–14, 138
Nature, 64
Neighbours, 4, 149
Nelson, H.G. and Roy Slaven, 78
News Ltd, 5, 177
Newton-John, Olivia, 154
New York Times, 147
New York Yacht Club, 30, 32
1980s, 3–10
No Conceivable Injury, 59
No Pain, No Gain, 164
Northern Territory, 111, 113

O'Brien, Kerry, 98
Old Sydney Town, 113
Oliphant, 54
Olympic Games, 139–42, 44
O'Regan, Tom, 34, 110

Packer, Kerry, 4, 25, 36, 46, 141, 161
Palmer, Kingsley, 61–2

Paradise Beach, 101
Parkes, Colin, 152
Perera, Suvendrini, 122
Perfect Beat, 132
Piano, The, 106, 127
Picnic at Hanging Rock, 115
Pincher, Chapman, 54
Pomerantz, Margaret, 105–6
popular music, 107, 125–6
Powell, Mr Jusice, 44
Prescott, John, 151
Prince Charles, 74
Princess Diana (Lady Di) 74, 80
Pusey, Michael, 16, 40, 156–7,
    162–3

Quadrant, 62
Queensland film industry, 97–8,
    104–5
Queensland Travel and Tourism
    Commission, 109–10

Republican Advisory Committee,
    47
republican movement, 1–3, 5–6,
    51,
Resorting to Tourism, 111
Rise and Fall of Alan Bond, The,
    36, 37
*Robert Menzies: The forgotten
    people*, 157
Robins, Kevin, 77
Robson, Frank, 37
Romper Stomper, 126, 127
Rowe, Sue, 6
Ruane, John, 127
Rubbery Figures, 25
Rushdie, Salman, 125, 137
Rydges, 26

Sanders, Noel, 54–5
Sanctuary Cove, 38–9
SBS, 105, 125
Schlesinger, Philip, 10, 120
7.30 Report, 141, 176
Sheridan, Greg, 67

Sheridan, Susan, 6
Simper, Errol, 152
Sixty Minutes, 37, 60, 176
Skase, Christopher, 4, 22, 25, 160
Smits, Jimmy, 105
Sorrenti, Vince, 8
Sovereign Hill, 113
Spalvins, John, 16
Spearritt, Peter, 68, 71, 74–5
Springborg, Robert, 99
Spycatcher, 41–8
Spycatcher Trial, The, 44
Stannard, Bruce, 34, 36
Stark, 24–5
Stockmen's Hall of Fame, 9, 89
Stratton, David, 105–6
Stratton, Jon, 111, 113
Strickland, Shirley, 142
Strictly Ballroom, 8, 126, 127,
    128–9
Sun-Herald, 55, 85
Sylvania Waters, 12, 154
Sydney Morning Herald, 26, 31,
    36, 44, 46, 60, 62, 73, 83, 84,
    85, 86, 139, 140, 141

Tame, A. and F. Rowbotham, 54
Taylor, Noah, 127
Telecom, 100
Telegraph-Mirror, 141
Tiffen, Rodney, 20
Timbertown, 113
Time magazine, 27
Times on Sunday, 36, 146
Titterton, Sir Ernest, 55, 56
Thompson, Jack, 127
tourism, 108, 109–18
Travelling Exhibition, 89
'Treaty', 132–3
Trotter, Robin, 89
Tribal Voice, 132, 138
Turnbull, Malcolm, 2, 5, 41–8, 51,
    60, 143

Uren, David, 28

Valder, John, 141
Vietnam, 97, 98
Village Roadshow, 100

WA Inc (Royal Commission), 37, 43
Walsh, Max, 25, 141
Walter, James, 156–8
Ward, Russel, 5, 49, 108
Warner Bros, 100–4
Washington Post, 147
Waterford, Jack
Watson, Don, 1, 2
Weekend Australian, 37, 45
Wendt, Jana, 35, 153, 154

Wentworth, W.C., 55
White, Patrick, 71, 73, 154
White, Richard, 95–6
Whitlam, Gough, 48
Whitlam, Nicholas, 47
Whitton, Evan, 58–9, 65
Willessee, Michael, 151–2, 177
Willoughby, Bart, 132
Wright, Peter, 41, 43

Yothu Yindi, 83, 126, 132–8, 174
Young Einstein, 101
Young Presidents Organisation, 81, 169
Yunupingu, Mandaway, 132, 138